African Names and Naming

Jonathan Musere

Shirley C. Byakutaga
Institute of Languages, Makerere University, Kampala, Uganda

Ariko Publications
Los Angeles

Publisher's Cataloging-in-Publication

Musere, Jonathan.
     African names and naming / Jonathan Musere. -- 3rd ed.
     p. cm.
     Includes bibliographical references.
     LCCN: 98-93629
     ISBN: 09645969-0-3

     1. Names, Personal--African--Dictionaries--English.
     2. Names, Personal--Africa--Dictionaries--English. 3. African
languages--Etymology--Names.   I. Byakutaga, Shirley C. II.
Title.

CS3080.A35M87 1998   929.4'096

Ariko Publications
12335 Santa Monica Blvd., PMB 155
Los Angeles, CA 90025
United States of America

Printed in the USA by

MORRIS PUBLISHING

3212 East Highway 30 • Kearney, NE 68847 • 1-800-650-7888

Acknowledgments

Several players were involved in helping compile this volume. They include Edward Callary (American Name Society/ Northern Illinois University), Peter J. Ibembe, Adrian Koopman (University of Natal, South Africa), and Willy van Langendonck (International Council of Onomastic Sciences, Belgium). Thanks is indeed due. Both the *Luganda-English Dictionary* by John D. Murphy and *Luganda Proverbs* by Ferdinand Walser provide a wealth of relevant instruction in detail. Thanks to the Catholic University of America Press and Dietrich Reimer Verlag respectively for permission to use these sources.

Jonathan Musere
Culver City, California
August 1998

Contents

Introduction

Personal names function to individualize and distinguish people from others. Naming in the central, eastern, and southern regions of Africa dealt with in this compilation (see table below) that contains approximately 2500 names, is closely linked to culture. African personal names have several functions. They may identify one with an occupation or implements used in this occupation, and establish one as an associate (or relation) of a group or a person involved in an occupation. They may infer one as an inhabitant (or a descendent of an inhabitant) of a locality. Names may identify one with phenomena that are prevalent in one's area of habitation. Names may also depict the past and present modes of production and living in an area. African names often reflect negative or positive opinions of the name givers towards the child or other people (usually kin, neighbors, or friends). The child's name can commemorate significant events or circumstances at the time of birth.

Since there is a dearth of written works in African languages, the best sources of names literature is oral exchanges with native language speakers, as well as translation and interpretation by those with reading and speaking knowledge of African languages. The best written literature on African names is found in journals. They are more readily available in the academic circles than to the general public, but a lot of journal extractions are included in this book. Many journal articles are come across with difficulty, and many that date back decades ago are invaluable. Journal articles are for the most part written by scholars who have expertise in the fields of African linguistics and onomastics, and who have carried out field studies and surveys on the names subject. Because a large volume of African names is based on circumstances surrounding the birth of the child, proper interpretation of them involves philosophical insight and application. The subject of names related to proverbs is little written about, though it is an intriguing and important aspect of African names. There is the difficulty of the little attention given to subjecting African proverbs to translated interpretation. It is hoped that journal articles (Musere 1998: 73-79; Musere 1997: 89-97) will stimulate exploration into this vastly neglected field. Worthy lengthy books on African names interpreted in the English language are limited. Most of such books define the names in simplistic and peripheral ways, the names defined in one or a few words. Most involve little or limited field work, most are poorly referenced and do not make adequate use of the academically wealthy journal world.

The data gathered in this book involved both literary and field research. The study involved examining most of the names from many perspectives and points of view. Edwin Lawson's *More Names and Naming: An Annotated Bibliography* (1995) and *Personal Names and Naming: An Annotated Bibliography* (1987) pointed to several onomastic sources. These sister volumes are lengthy compilations of magazine, journal, and book bibliographies from all over the world. The two point to numerous articles and books used to construct this volume. One with a strong interest in the subject of names is advised to consult the two. Some of the entries are on names in general, while others are on specific regions or groups. Regarding Africa, there are bibliographies on the region in general, on a mix of African groups, and specific African groups and regions that are greatly written about. The later includes groups such as the *Bini*, the *Igbo*, the *Zulu*, and the *Swahili*; and regions like Ghana, South Africa, and Zimbabwe. There are also bibliographies on African American names. Among the numerous journals that contain personal names articles are *Journal of African Languages, Journal of Anthropological Research, Language and Society, Man, Names, Nomina Africana, South African Journal of African Languages, African Studies, Uganda Journal, NADA,* and *Onoma.* However, the sources are infinite, and many manuscripts on African anthropology, culture, folklore, linguistics, proverbs, sociology have information on African names and naming that is not necessarily mentioned in any published annotated bibliography work. African naming is intimately associated with culture so we perused numerous African works written in both the past and the present to compile this work. Many of them are on specific African groups since the writers of such tend to go deep into the social dynamics. Works written in the distant past tend to offer more significance to the name meanings, as well as offer a larger variety of names than works written in the current era. This is in part because a lot of Africans have adapted to the western custom of taking after the parental name. In the past, naming had a lot to do with such factors as circumstances at birth, mode of birth, place of birth, clan membership, and sequence of birth in the family. Such issues are exemplified in the main name listing.

Many of the names compiled are based on the authors' personal knowledge of some of the native languages and names used in the African Great Lakes Region that generally includes Burundi, Congo (Zaire), Kenya, Rwanda, Sudan, Tanzania, Uganda which are part of eastern and central Africa. Most of the native languages of central, eastern, southern Africa are of Bantu ethnolinguistic structure, so there is a lot that is common in the cultures and names of this area addressed in this book. Nilotic, Semitic, and other ethnolinguistic influences are also significant in the naming culture of the region. It cannot be forgotten that the presence of Asians and Europeans on the African continent over the past several centuries has impacted African naming. Names associated with immigrant influence are common on coastal eastern Africa where Asian/ Arab influence contributed to the emergence of the Swahili language and names, and in South Africa where there is European culture and language from which some African names are adapted.

In addition to the names the compilers had known by virtue of long time residence on the continent, lengthy name listings were gathered from such agencies as schools, factories and hospitals. Literature in the native languages is an infinite source of personal names. Large lists of names were also obtained from published court and clan records and histories. Works by Apolo Kaggwa (1954; 1934), by Michael Nsimbi (1980; 1956), and by John Roscoe (1911) contain thousands of names used by the *Baganda* of Uganda. The names that could be interpreted were treated, sometimes with the assistance of translation dictionaries and the interviewing of native language speakers. Any native African is bound to know an infinite number of names that have never been interpreted on paper. Some of the names in the listings could not be interpreted since some of the languages in the region are not known to the compilers, and there was not an interpreter at hand. There are also names that cannot be interpreted because their meanings are either not apparent, or have been lost over time. Names adapted from a foreign group can be "meaningless." Name meaning loss can also result from a linguistic change in a name that originally had meaning. When tone or pronunciation changes in the name, the meaning can change or become lost. The change or loss can also result from letter substitutions in the name.

Some books on African names are worth mentioning. Chuks-Orji's *Names from Africa* (1972), I. Madubuike's *A Handbook of African Names* (revised, 1994), H. McKinzie and Issy Tindimwebwa's *Names from East Africa* (1980) and Bekitemba Sanyika's *Know and Claim Your African Name* (1975) represent some of the major pioneering book efforts on African personal names. *Names from East Africa* is only a few pages long and, as the title suggests, mostly deals with names used in the African Great Lakes Region. There are quite lengthy explanations on just some of the names. The other three books examine name examples from all the regions of Africa. Among all the four, it is Madubuike's *A Handbook of African Names* that has best stood out and maintained circulation. It offers more explanation and it has been referred to for a long time. Unlike most books on African names, this volume has been revised, this including additional names added. Chuks-Orji's *Names from Africa* and Sanyika's *Know and Claim Your African Name* contain a generalized overview, but though the names in both books are many, the meanings attached to them are brief.

Molefi Asante's *The Book of African Names* (1991) places the names in regional context other than with reference to the specific ethnic groups that use the names. Asante refers to this as a "Pan-Africanist" approach and an "Afrocentric orientation." The book does not go into detail, and does not address pronunciation. The book would hence tend to be welcomed by the general other than sophisticated reader on Africa. The meanings alloted are brief, the names numbering about 1200. Asante admits that he has avoided listing names with negative connotations. Yet, as will be shown in this book, a thorough understanding of African names requires the treatment of names of all kinds. African names that have negative connotations, are actually intended for the good of children born during adverse circumstances, and the study of these is part and parcel of African onomastics. Nevertheless, the book serves as a neat introduction for the African descendants of the diaspora. Molefi Kete Asante himself took the giant step of replacing his original names with African names.

In *What is in a Name?=Unaitwaje?: A Swahili Book of African Names* (1993), Sharifa Zawawi presents several names common in the Swahili culture of coastal eastern Africa. The introduction provides valuable information on the subject. Swahili culture developed over centuries, based mostly on

Arab-Islam and trade influence on the eastern African coast that extended into central Africa. Logically there are parallels between Swahili, Arabic, and Islamic names. Arabic-Islamic names have been written about for centuries, *Kiswahili* (language) remains one of the best developed lingua francas in Africa, and affiliated names are widely used by those of African descent. However, one who seeks to venture deep into indigenous African name dynamics is advised to seek, in addition, resources that deal with a lot more of the regions and cultures of Africa.

Alec Pongweni's *What is in a Name?: A Study of Shona Nomenclature* (1983) is an excellent literary work laden with varied and thorough explanatory detail on the names treated. Pongweni combines literature, linguistics, culture, history, and politics in defining the personal names. However, the book is small, the few names contained mainly relate to one African ethnic group--the Shona of South Africa. Further, the book does not seem to be that well marketed despite its immense value, another shortcoming being that it is published in Africa and not by a major publisher. Otherwise Pongweni is a splendidly dedicated writer, a translator of immense expertise, a master at both the African and the Shakespearean languages, and to whom is owed tremendous gratitude. Pongweni tells so much in a small and compact volume.

Alexandre Kimenyi in *Kinyarwanda and Kirundi Names: A Semiolinguistic Analysis of Bantu Onomastics* (1989) uses academic application to prove his point that onomastics is a crucial aspect of understanding African social dynamics. Thorough explanations are accorded the names of the *Tutsi, Hutu,* and *Twa* of eastern and central Africa. Kimenyi ventures deeply into the linguistic dynamics. This to some extent, renders the book very academic. He illustrates how African names get to be structured, including the prefixes used to form gender specific names. The relationship of names to such aspects as war, clanship, proverbs, poetry, praises, royalty, and social class is examined. At the same time the reader gets to absorb so much about the much highlighted issue of friction versus harmony amongst the groups. The main shortcoming of this master volume is the poor editing as illustrated by the many typographical errors, and the unnecessary repetition. Further, this hardback book is library and research oriented, therefore not readily exposed to the general public. The book deserves to be rewritten or re-edited, given the magnitude of information provided. A too specialized and ethnically loaded poor choice of title has likely limited the market for this book. The words *Kinyarwanda* and *Kirundi* are references to the languages of the people of Rwanda and Burundi respectfully, but this may not be easily apparent to one who is not a specialist in the field or one is not from the African Great Lakes area.

The approach by L. Crane in *African Names: People and Places* (University of Illinois, 1982) is dedicatedly academic.Yet the book is so well organized that it allows for both the average and the sophisticated reader to appreciate the dynamics of African naming. Among the issues Crane examines are naming ceremonies, foreign influences on African naming, categories and choices of African people names, and names of famous Africans. She examines the cultures of some of the west African groups in reasonable detail, as she relates their name practices. She touches on the issue of pronunciation. As the title suggests, Crane also delves into place naming. The ambitious reader would likely criticize the book for not having an adequate number of name examples. They are altogether only a few hundred in the book. And despite the wealth of information in this book, it does not appear to have been well marketed to the general public. This is likely because it is written as a step-by-step teaching and training manual on the subject of African names. The book is written on ordinary, letter length paper that is cheaply bound, so it would not be surprising if the book is out of print. The book deserves to be rewritten and published for the wide public audience.

Michael Nsimbi's *Amannya Amaganda n'Ennono zaago* (1956) is written for both the general readers and those in academia. He examines several aspects of the names of the *Baganda* including histories, proverbs, clan affiliation, war, royalty, and servitude. The major shortcoming of this book is that it has never been translated into an international language, though the book has stood out for a long time as a major work. The title of Nsimbi's book translates to "Kiganda Names and Name Traditions."

Mwizenge Tembo in *What does your African Name Mean?: the Meanings of Indigenous Names among the Tonga of Southern Zambia* (University of Zambia, 1989) combines field survey with theoretical translating of a good variety of names of the Tonga. There are numerous other African groups that ought to be subjected to such onomastic research. And this, as the Tembo's book exemplifies, yields excellent results when done at the local level, whereby the interviewers and researchers are of the indigenous population.

In *African Names* (1993), Stewart relates African names to famous African personalities that have used such names, and in the process falls short of giving the names or the personalities a thorough examination. In addition she mentions items like African Presidential reigns, African Independence days, and she also touches on some histories and on geography, making the book an excellent reference book for the average reader and one who simply wants to take a peripheral and generalized glance at Africa and African names. The book more so involves brief but symbolizing excerpts about Africa and African names, other than specialized and academic content. Stewart, however, displays a lot of commendable creativity in presenting to the Africa uninformed, through the avenue of names, the historical and cultural wealth of Africa. She suggests considerations and ways by which the African descended can take on African names. She suggests how some of the long ones can be shortened or likened to American names. The suggested bibliography on Africa in general is quite extensive. The sister volume *1001 African Names* (1996), involves a lot more academic research, including an additional array of African names and lots of other information on Africa. Stewart employs more resources specific to onomastics than she did in her earlier volume. But with both volumes, one would beg to differ on a lot of the pronunciations she links to the names, perhaps a consequence of her limited expertise in African linguistics. The two books still function as good handbooks and resource guides on personal names, and on Africa in general. Jonathan Musere is author of the lengthy books *Traditional African Names, African Ethnics and Personal Names,* and *African Proverbs and Proverbial Names,* all published in 1999.

African names employed in the traditionally cattle passionate, cattle keeping, and semi-nomadic economies such as those of the *Tutsi* and the *Karamojong* have tended to be related to raiding activity, war, captives, hunting, mobility, mobilization, bravery, and cowardice. The names also relate to cattle phenomena such as cattle names, cattle complexions, cattle classifications, and cattle ownership. Names in such cattle keeping societies also relate to pastures and rains, seasons, and other weather and vegetation conditions. They also relate to royalty and to the demeaning of those of cultivating (other than cattle owning) category. In the much larger, more settled, and more inclusive societies such as *Buganda* (in Uganda) which was a domineering, assimilating, and conquering kingdom-state more so prior to the twentieth century, the naming has tended to take on an even more sophisticated aura, containing virtually all elements mentioned above and much more.

Names can commemorate major occurrences or traditions at the time of the birth of the child. Among the *Nandi* of Kenya, some of the common names are (Hollis 1969: 67) *Kaptich* (one born in a cattle kraal), *Kimaiyo* (one born at a time of a beer drinking gathering), *Kimngeny* (one born during a time the oxen have been taken to lick salt rock), *Kimuike* (one born shortly after a relation is killed), *Kipet* (one born in the morning), *Kipkarai* (one born around the time a hornless cow is purchased or looted), *Kipkemboi* (one born in the evening), *Kipor* (one born by the roadside), *Kipruiot* (one born during the night), *Kiprukut* (one born during a period there is a food scarcity in the land), *Kipruto* and *Chepruto* (one born during a journey), and *Kipyator* (one born very early in the morning i.e. at the time the door is opened). Many of the modes of birth were more common in the past before the introduction of foreign maternity facilities, whereby women gave birth in a wide variety of settings usually with the help of local midwives. Such names as associated with giving birth in a kraal, a bush, and while traveling had more significance then. Names often describe physical, physiological, or behavioral characteristics of a newborn. Children are also given names that refer to characteristics or the occupation of one of their parents. The names *Muchemi* 'crybaby,' *Juru* 'brown termite' (implying a very brown complexioned child or "brownie"), *Gondo* 'eagle' (implying a child whose head resembles that of an eagle), *Dimba* 'little blue tit' (implying a tiny child), and *Bodo* 'black pot' (implying a very black complexioned child or "blackie") are used by the *Shona* of southern Africa (Jackson 1957: 120). The names *Mukankusi* (f) 'the spouse associated with the roarer of a war cry' (Kimenyi 1989: 135), *Matabaro* (m) 'defense, military expeditions' (Kimenyi 1989: 33, 93, 94, 107,

167), and *Mukamiheto* (f) 'the spouse associated with bows' are usually given to children whose parents are engaged in the occupation identified in the name, or to children born during an era of war, or to children born when their parents were on the war front line. The names are used by the *Hutu*, *Tutsi*, and *Twa* of eastern and central Africa.

African twins (or multiple birth children in general), according to their gender composition, are given specific names. In many cases, the siblings that preceded the twins, as well as the siblings that follow them are also given specific names. The traditional reactions to the birth of twins vary from culture to culture. However, a commonalty is the subjecting of twin births to ritual cleansing some of which may or may not involve wild partying. In general, such births are either treated as bad omens, or as mysterious extraordinary occurrences, or as symbols of goodwill from God or the ancestors that require proper ritual cleansing for the benefits to be realized. The mother is in most cases also subjected to ritual cleansing. Improper treatment of twins would cause the spirits to vent their anger on the family or community. The twins are indeed treated with extra care if not suspicion. The following is in a piece that Jan Daeleman devotes exclusively to the exploration of multiple birth naming traditions in Sub-Saharan Africa (1977: 189).

The birth of twins has a very particular meaning in many Sub-Saharan tribes, as the twins are considered to bring along a message from the ancestors to their living descendants. Their birth is accompanied by very specific rites and a carefully patterned name-giving. ...in the Ngwi language the twins are called *Nker*, "grave", which makes their relationship with the ancestor world very explicit: they are indeed considered to be mediators between the world of the living and the world of the dead. ...they are also designated as..."numinous children"...and compared with the bird...sent by God to guide all other birds (birds being believed to be of supernatural origin)....Twins are given names that refer not only to mysterious natural phenomena as "thunder" and "lightning", but also to mysterious aweinspiring [sic] animals such as the "snake"...or felines...such as the lion, the leopard, the serval...African tiger-cat...the "kingly" and "lordly" animals....The...Koongo interpret them to be..."sacred children"...pre-existent spirits...being incarnated in the family of their choice....Welcoming-rites...aim at making them realize that they are acknowledged as spirits.

Paulus Mohome writes on the *Basotho* of southern Africa (1972: 178).

...the birth of twins always is a cause of joy and anxiety. ...a great deal of excitement as well as concern surrounds the birth of twins, more so if they happen to be identical twins. They are regarded as a special gift from the ancestors. The birth of twins is said to indicate that the ancestral spirits are happy and proud about such parents. The cause for concern always stems from the belief that twins are delicate and thus frail. There exists a strong belief among the Basotho that twins rarely grow to be adults without dying. To insure the survival of twins, great precautionary and protective measures are taken. ...the mother receives special care by being given plenty of food so as to maximize her lactic capability. Rituals and taboos are elaborate. The joy of the parents is shown by organizing lavish food and beer parties to celebrate the occasion. Two sheep or goats are slaughtered to welcome the twins. Custom dictates that everything must be done twofold, for it is believed that if this is not done, one of the twins may die.

The *Nandi* have their side of the story (Hollis 1969: 68).

The birth of twins is looked upon as an inauspicious event, and the mother is considered unclean for the rest of her life. She is given her own cow and may not touch the milk or blood of any other animal. She may enter nobody's house until she has sprinkled a calabash full of water on the ground, and she may never cross the threshold of a cattle kraal again. One of the twins is always called *Simatua* (*Ficus sp.*) whilst the other receives an animal's name such as *Chep-tiony, Chep-sepet, Che-maket, Che-makut,* etc.

The *Luhya* of Kenya and Uganda have a lengthy traditional ritual (Wako 1985: 37-38).

If a woman gave birth to two children, they were called "Amakhwana." The mother of twins was nicknamed Nabakhwana or Balongo. ...But on giving birth to twins, the husband and herself shut in their hut for one month or more [sic]. A sheep would be slaughtered for her and neighbours would come and stage dances in the home. On the day of exposing the twins [to the public], the mother would cover her waist with special leaves called "amaatikhani." ...He [the father] would...choose the day for releasing the twins and their mother from staying indoors. ...the man would take a long three-pronged stick and a young cockerel while his wife would take a small hoe called "Akhasiri," a small pot of "busaa" and some water. Then they would set off for the ceremony, accompanied with a large crowd of men, women and children. ...On arrival at the home where the ceremony was to be held, there was no formal welcome as the home was full of people dancing and rejoicing. The new arrivals had therefore to force their way in. Often fighting erupted with those who attempted to prevent them from going in. The man specifically invited to perform the ceremony would proceed to the house in which the twins were, followed by his wife and using his three pronged stick, he would push the door open. The two pairs would meet at the entrance, where upon [sic] the door opener and his wife would spit some liquor in the twins' faces. This would be the climax of the ceremony and would be followed by drinking and dancing. ...Twins...the first [born]...was called Opiyo if a boy and Apiyo if a girl. The second [born]...was called Odongo if a boy and Adongo if a girl. If one of the twins died, it had to be buried behind the mother's house. There was no moaning for a dead twin. The living twin was referred to as *Abanji*. A woman who gave birth to twins was forbidden to enter any house at her original [parental] home until her husband had given her parents a heifer and the door opening ceremony had been performed. ...In other areas, the first twin...whether a girl or a boy was called Mukhwana. The second twin was called Mulongo. the child that followed twins was called Shisia whether a boy or a girl. The follower of Shisia was called Khamala. If one twin died, the surviving one was called Walekhwa.

Among multiple birth related names used in central Africa are *Ishemboyo* and *Boika* (for a father of twins), *Tangbo* and *Inababiri* (for a mother of twins), *Inabushuri* (for mother of triplets). *Manata* i.e. "carrier of the twins" and *Kibika* i.e. "the one who calls the twins" (for a sibling whose birth preceded that of twins), *Mputu* (for a first born sibling after twins), *Tingbo* i.e. "twin's arm" (for a second born sibling after twins), *Gerengbo* i.e. "twin's foot" (for a third born sibling after twins), *Tsiimba* i.e. wild cat and *Nzusi* i.e. serval tiger-cat (for female twins), *Khosi* i.e. lion and *Makaanzu* i.e. "the one who holds the lion by his feet" (for male twins), and (for triplets) *Omba*, *Shako*, and *Mbucu* (Daeleman 1977: 191-194). Among the *Baganda*, the twin that is given birth to first is commonly named *Wasswa* (m) or *Singoma* (m) or *Babirye* (f) or *Nangoma* (f), while the younger one is named *Kato* (m) or *Teenywa* (m) or *Nakato* (f) or *Wuuja* (f). The names *Wasswa*, *Babirye*, *Teenywa*, and *Wuuja* are adapted from ones used by the neighboring *Basoga*, while *Singoma* and *Nangoma* are adapted from names used by the neighboring *Banyoro*. According to Whitehead (1947: 46), the *Nuer* of Sudan name the first born after twins *Bol* (m) or *Nyabol* (f); the second born after twins is named *Geng* (m) or *Kaat* (m) or *Nyageng* (f) or *Nyacwiil* (f); and the third born after twins is named *Tot* (m) or *Nyatoot* (f). According to Evans-Pritchard (1948: 108), the first born after twins is called *Bol* (m) or *Bicok* (m) or *Nyibuol* (f), while the second born after twins is named *Tot* (m) or *Cuil* (m) or *Nyatot* (f).

In some African societies infants born with defects or atypical features, or those born in a way considered very strange, including albinos and cripples, are treated as sacred and are even given names that relate to supernaturalism. However, most of such infants were traditionally not given a pleasant welcome. The *Nandi* situation (Hollis 1969: 68) is largely in reference to the distant past.

Children are buried alive in cow-dung if they cry in their mother's womb, or if at birth they present their legs first, or are born with teeth, as these events are considered unlucky. Rich people, however, often pay a medicine man a large sum to avert the misfortune and save their children's lives. Children who are blind or badly deformed, and illegitimate children, i.e. the offspring of unmarried girls, are likewise made away with at birth.

The Baganda give the name *Nnambi* (f) or *Mukasa* (m) to one born with two umbilical cords. *Nnambi* is also the name of the traditional first woman, and *Mukasa* is the name of a highly esteemed God. One who is born alongside a premature and stillborn twin (called *mulongo* by the royals) is called *Nnakimu* 'that of one.' In the past, there was superstitious consternation at the birth of such a child who was greatly feared. The name *Nnakimu* is also given to one born with a harelip, and to one who turns out to be the last born. The names *Kiwanuka* (m) 'that which comes down' and *Nnaabawanuka* (f) 'the one of those that come down' are traditionally given to children with noticeable birthmarks said to have been effected, by *Kiwanuka* the God of lightning and thunder, while the child was still in the womb. The names are also given to ones born when the mother still often carries the preceding sibling. The names *Bitalo* (m), *Nabitalo* (f), and *Magero* (m) signify amazement. They tend to be given to children born with anomalous features such as visible teeth, and more or less than the normal number of fingers. Such names are also given to one born to a woman whose age is considered advanced for child bearing.

There are names that reflect composition of the family (such as disapproval of gender imbalances among the family offspring), and those that reflect the extension of the family. Children are named after their forefathers so as to appease the ancestral spirits and as a display of reverence. Ancestral spirits have the function of protecting their living descendants, so care is taken to please them through carrying out the proper observances and referring to them with respect. Among many of the societies of the *Bantu* mega group, a first born male is named after his paternal grandfather, the second born named after his father, while those that follow are named after greatgrandparents and great-great-grandparents and brothers of forefathers. This allows for the forefathers to be mentioned in everyday speech, and it is believed that the spirits of the forefathers watch over their namesakes. Names that have become associated with particular clans are usually descendent from ancestors of good reputation or status. Many of the children of the same family line are given names of such ancestors.

Among the *Nuba* of southern *Kordofan* in Sudan, a first born son is called *Kuku*, the second *Kafi*, the third *Tia*, the fourth son is given the female name *Tutu* in case a daughter has not yet been born, and the fifth boy is named *Nalu*. With girls, if a daughter is born first she is called *Kaka*, the second *Toto*, the third *Koshe*, the fourth *Kiki* (or *Ngori*, or *Kikingori*), and the fifth *Nalu* regardless of gender (Seligman 1932: 386-387). Giving a boy a female name, and vice versa, is a display of the gender preference. Thus a first born child that is female can be given a male name, though she will be given a proper female name upon the birth of a male sibling. Names can therefore exhibit the quantity of births in the family, and the progeny sequence of birth.

Names are originally derived from several sources. Many began as nicknames and as proverbial names. Many are derived from occupations and their implements, many are adapted from neighbors' and foreigners' names, and many are derived from natural phenomena. It is also common for a child to be given the name of a renowned person that is not related to the family. It was common in the past for people to take on names of their neighbors through a variety of assimilation processes. These included conquest and capture, blood-brotherhood rituals, mergence of clans into one, marriage, and long term residence in a clan village.

Names can corroborate the spiritual or religious backdrop of the child. A name can therefore reflect gratitude towards the Supernatural for the birth of the child. Among the Baganda, despite the extensive conversions to Christianity and Islam from the late nineteenth century, the names of the native deities and are still honored and still serve as popular personal names. Among the names of the Goddesses of the *Baganda* are *Nakayaga*, *Nalwoga*, *Nagaddya* (*Nagajja*), *Nanziri*, and *Namirembe*. The Gods include *Sserwanga*

(*Lwanga*) *Mukasa, Kyobe Kibuuka, Kiwanuka, Musisi, Musoke, Muwanga,* and *Kitinda*. Names that express gratitude to supernatural agencies for the birth of the child given the name, are common. The *Zulu* use the names *Bonginkosi* 'thank the Lord,' *Sipho* 'gift (from God),' *Thembinkosi* 'trust the Lord,' *Sibongile* 'we are grateful,' and *Bongani* 'be ye grateful' (Koopman 1987: 148-149).

Names can also promulgate an opinion of negative or positive bearing that may be directed by the namer to neighbors, family and kin, enemies, the newborn itself, and even to ancestral spirits and Gods. The *Shona* of central and southern Africa have such names as *Ruvengo* 'hatred,' *Hamundidi* 'you do not love me,' *Vengwa* 'the hated one,' *Masemani* 'you despised me,' *Ibvai* 'get away,' *Mativengerei* 'why have you been hating us?' and *Chomunorwa* 'what is all the fighting about?' (Jackson 1957: 116-117).

A name that embodies the expectations the parents have for a child is intended to serve as inspiration for the youngster as it grows up. The *Xhosa* of southern Africa employ such names as *Khokela* 'guide,' *Mxolisi* 'peacemaker,' *Malusi* 'shepherd,' *Solomzi* 'eye of the home,' *Thembeka* 'be faithful,' *Thozama* 'be meek,' *Mcebisi* 'counselor' and *Monde* 'perseverance' (Thipa 1987: 114).

Though the issue is not adequately explored, many African names are related to proverbs. Such names convey words of wisdom with respect to such issues as intelligence, friendship, cooperation, trust and mistrust, thankfulness and unappreciation, humility, giving, ignorance, showiness, boastfulness, jealousy, allegiance, alertness, warning, defense, laziness, speed, hastiness, bravery, cowardice, and patience. The *Baganda* have a generous array of proverbial names and though there are slight variations in the message the namer conveys, there exists standard interpretations for the proverb and the associated name. But there can be more than one interpretation of the proverb, and a proverbial name is not necessarily associated with just one proverb.

The name *Tamusuza* "the one not housing the person" is commonly associated with the proverb *"Atamusuza y'amutenda eggonjebwa"* 'The one not housing the person, praises this person for being meek, kind, and polite.' It implies that observations are often not as praiseworthy as they seem to be, as synonymous with "all that glitters is not gold." In the proverb *"Ebigambo tebyaasa (=tibyaasa) mutwe, nga tebabyoogera ku ggwe"* 'Words will not shatter your head, just as long as they are not spoken of you,' it is implied that actions and words which may appear trivial to the one they are not directed to, can be quite hurtful and have different connotations for the one they are directed to. Names associated with this proverb are *Bigambo* 'words, sayings, matters, affairs;' *Tebyasa (Tebyaasa)/ Tibyasa (Tibyaasa)* 'they (i.e. words) do not shatter' and *Mutwe* 'head.'

In the proverb *"Enkoko eteefe, etuusa mugenyi"* 'The chicken that will not die, would bring forth (or welcomes) a visitor,' the "chicken" represents the would-be victim. The aphorism is subject to several interpretations. In the instance of expecting or getting visitors, the host refrains from killing the chicken for his own meal, hence giving the chicken the opportunity to live longer. And the arrival of a visitor can be beneficial insofar as the hosts can then turn their attention to the visitor instead of continuing with a household argument that was going to be wrought with deadly ramifications. In addition a child that was about to be severely punished may be spared upon the arrival of a visitor as a result of the joy that follows the visitor's arrival and because the host about to mete out the punishment does not want to form a bad impression on the visitor. And similar to the foregone interpretation, a wife beating or spousal conflict that was about to take place or is going to be deadly, is often refrained from or dissolved upon the arrival of a visitor. Associated names are *Nkoko* 'chicken, hen,' *Teefe* 'that (i.e. the chicken) will not die' and *Mugenyi* 'visitor.' The name *Tebujjadda* '(lameness) does not come later in life' is commonly associated with the proverbial saying *"Obulema tebujja dda"* 'Lameness does not come later in life.' It is implied herewith that the virtues and vices of a person are displayed early in the person's life and do not just show up later in life from nowhere. The proverb also conveys the message that the youth should always be careful, not thinking of themselves as invincibly invulnerable to defects and mishaps that are usually associated with old age.

As more proverbial examples display in this and in earlier work (Musere 1998: 73-79; Musere 1997: 89-97), one may have to use a large volume of words to translate the meaning of a proverb into another language. This is partly because language is intimately linked to culture. Types of tensions, emphases and phenomena vary from society to society. African language communication when compared to the European mode of communication is highly metaphorical in content. There is a salient element of discreteness, circuitousness, allusion and secrecy in African language. This is in contrast to the western agency that is rather direct and confrontationist. Africans traditionally consider it disrespectful and even risky to directly confront those of a higher age or status rung, and those they are not adequately familiar with or related to. As a symbol of reverence, those who have children are commonly referred to by one of their children's name (i.e. 'mother of/ father of so-and-so') other than by their true name. Everyday African speech involves a lot of proverbial language. A proverbial name given to a child may symbolize a milestone achievement or happening in the family at the time of the birth. Such names may also connote disapproval of kin or neighbors, disappointment, gratitude to God and ancestral spirits, poverty, suffering, exuberance, and so forth. But though a proverbial name is often a circuitous message, the one (such as a haughty neighbor) to whom it is directed almost always knows that he or she is the intended recipient. The proverbial name is then a public communication that entails the targeted recipient to mend his or her ways.

Many African names that contain such messages are not always proverbial. Noleen Turner (1992: 42) assembles an impressive field survey collection of names of the *Zulu* of southern Africa as she:

...seeks to expound on the psychological functions of names that express tension, discontent and censure within the framework of the society and domestic setting in which they operate, and to examine their social function in working out stress situations, minimizing friction and providing a means of acceptance of indirect comment in a situation where direct confrontation or even accusation is unacceptable.

It is to be recalled that black African society is still rural and communal based. Alongside kin, neighbors living in close proximity therefore remain an important aspect of one's life that includes the process of naming one's child. "Within a community based society...'lack of communication' is tantamount to being cut off from the people around you, the thought of which is regarded as being totally abhorrent as well as unnatural..." (Turner 1992: 44). Again Turner goes on to state in a summary note (1992: 55-56).

...important to note...the message insinuated...as with all orally inclined communities, thrives only in its 'native' climate embedded in its own specific social logic. If one is unfamiliar with the background which motivated the name being given, then the implication recorded in the name, too is lost. The reflection of conflict in naming children may be seen...to occur for the following reasons:
a) It serves to *express dissatisfaction* or *vent frustration.*
b) A name of this sort can be used to *cast suspicion* or *level accusation* at a certain individual/s.
c) It may *ridicule, mock or warn* against an unacceptable mode of behaviour.
d) Such a name may be used to *challenge* a person who by virtue of his or her position, precludes normal channels of criticism and censure.
e) It may *dispute allegations* made, or *inform* the person/s who has made the allegations, that the namer is well aware of the situation.

Though by and large, one of or both the parents have precedence in the naming, in many societies the extended family has tremendous influence in this process that can involve a lot of discussion. There are cases for example where the combination of the mother, the traditional midwife (during and after the pregnancy and delivery of the child) and the child's paternal grand-mother has exclusive powers in the naming. So one can imagine why in many African societies, there is a wealth of names that openly involve negative and even derogatory remarks about one or both of the parents. African naming ceremonies vary from society to society.

Primary National Residences of the Ethnics Mentioned

Angola: *Kongo (Koongo).*
Botswana: *Tswana.*
Burundi: *Hutu, Tutsi, Twa.*
Central African Republic: *Kongo.*
Congo (Zaire): *Bashi (Shi), Bembe, Hutu, Koongo (Kongo), Luba, Rega, Tutsi, Twa.*
Congo Republic: *Koongo (Kongo).*
Kenya: *Nandi, Luhya (Luyia), Swahili.*
Lesotho: *Basotho (Sotho), Zulu.*
Rwanda: *Hutu, Kiga, Tutsi, Twa.*
South Africa: *Afrikaans, Basotho (Sotho), Lamba (Lambas), Ndebele, Nguni, Tswana, Xhosa, Zulu.*
Sudan: *Anuak, Bari, Jur, Nuba, Nuer.*
Tanzania: *Bashi (Shi), Chaga, Fipa, Hutu, Pare, Swahili, Tutsi.*
Uganda: *Baganda (Ganda), Banyoro (Nyoro), Basoga (Soga), Hutu, Karamojong (Karimojong), Kiga, Luhya (Luyia), Nyankore, Toro, Tutsi, Twa.*
Zambia: *Lamba (Lambas), Tonga.*
Zimbabwe: *Lamba (Lambas), Ndebele, Shona.*

Abaine (f/m) *[ah-bahy-neh]* "He/ she has (or is blessed with) them (i.e. relatives or friends)"; "he/ she has (or is blessed with) him (i.e. God)" [*Kiga, Nyankore*].

Abaire (f/m) *[ah-bahy-reh]* "He/ she was about to" [*Kiga, Nyankore*].

Abenawe (f/m) *[ah-beh-nah-weh]* "May he (i.e. God) be with you" [*Kiga, Nyankore*].

Abeniitwe (f/m) *[ah-beh-niih-tweh]* "May he (i.e. God) be with us" [*Kiga, Nyankore*].

Abiba (f) *[ah-bih-bah]* The beloved [*Bembe*].

Abigaba (f/m) *[ah-bih-gah-bah]* "He (i.e. God) gives them (i.e. things) away"; "he (i.e. God) provides (i.e. things)" [*Kiga, Nyankore*].

Abigamba (f/m) *[ah-bih-gahm-bah]* "He/ she says them (i.e. the words or things)" [*Kiga, Nyankore*].

Abigonza (f/m) *[ah-bih-gohn-zah]* "He/ she loves them (i.e. the things)" [The *Kiga, Nyankore*].

Abimanya (f/m) *[ah-bih-mah-ndjh-ah]* "He/ she knows them (i.e. the things)"; "he/ she would know them (i.e. the things)" [*Kiga, Nyankore*].

Abonga (f) *[ah-boh-ndgh-ah]* A name given to a third born [The *Anuak*] (Whitehead 1947: 46).

Acureera (f/m) *[ah-tch-uuh-reh-eh-rah]* "He/ she humbles himself/ herself"; the one who is quiet [*Kiga, Nyankore*].

Afuna (f/m) *[ah-fuh-nah]* "He/ she procures"; the one who obtains; the one who profits (or gains) [*Kiga, Nyankore*].

Agaba (f/m) *[ah-gah-bah]* "He (i.e. God) gives away"; "he (i.e. God) provides" [*Kiga, Nyankore, Nyoro, Toro*].

Agasa (f/m) *[ah-gah-sah]* "He/ she is of use" [*Kiga, Nyankore, Nyoro, Toro*].

Agasha (f/m) *[ah-gah-tsh-ah]* "He (i.e. God) is of use" [*Kiga, Nyankore*].

Agirembabazi (f/m) *[ah-gih-rehm-bah-bah-zih]* "He (i.e. God) displays mercy"; "he (i.e. God) is merciful" [*Kiga, Nyankore, Nyoro, Toro*].

Agondeze (f/m) *[ah-gohn-deh-zeh]* "He (i.e. God) has loved me" [The *Kiga, Nyankore, Nyoro, Toro*].

Agonza (f/m) *[ah-gohn-zah]* "He (i.e. God) loves" [*Kiga, Nyankore, Nyoro, Toro*].

Agubanshongolera (f/m) *[ah-guh-bahn-tsh-ohn-goh-leh-rah]* "That (such as spears) which they have sharpened for me" [*Kiga, Nyankore*].

Aguma (f/m) *[ah-guh-mah]* "He/ she is (always) firm" [*Kiga, Nyankore*].

Agwine (f/m) *[ah-guhy-neh]* "He/ she has it" implying that the person has a heart, or that the person has the willingness, or that the person is well behaved; this name is sometimes associated with the proverb "You would only give advice to the one who is willing to regard the advice" [The *Kiga, Nyankore*].

Ahabwe (f/m) *[ah-hah-bweh]* "On his (i.e. God's) behalf"; "for him (i.e. God)"; "for his (i.e. God's) sake" [*Kiga, Nyankore*].

Aheebwa (f/m) *[ah-heh-eh-bwah]* "He/ she is (or would be) given"; this name is sometimes associated with the (biblical) saying "The one who asks will be given" [*Kiga, Nyankore, Nyoro, Toro*].

Aheirwe (f/m) *[ah-hehy-rweh]* "He/ she has been given (i.e. by God)" [*Kiga, Nyankore*].

Ahumure (f/m) *[ah-huh-muh-reh]* "May he/ she rest"; "may he/ she feel free" [*Kiga, Nyankore*].

Ahumuza (f/m) *[ah-huh-muh-zah]* "He/ she causes to rest"; "he/ she causes to be at ease" [*Kiga, Nyankore*].

Ahurra (f/m) *[ah-hoo-rh-rah]* "He/ she listens"; "he/ she is obedient"; "he/ she hears" [*Kiga, Nyankore*].

Ainebyona (f/m) *[ahy-neh-bjoh-oh-nah]* "He/ she is endowed with everything" [*Kiga, Nyankore, Nyoro, Toro*].

Ainomucunguzi (f/m) *[ahy-noh-muh-tchs-oohn-guh-zih]* "He/ she has the Savior on his/ her side" [*Kiga, Nyankore, Nyoro, Toro*].

Ainomuhangi (f/m) *[ahy-noh-muh-hahn-gih]* "He/ she has the God on his/ her side" [*Kiga, Nyankore, Nyoro, Toro*].

Ainomujuni (f) *[ahy-noh-moo-djoo-nih]* "He/ she has the Savior on his/ her side" [*Kiga, Nyankore, Nyoro, Toro*].

Ajulo (f) *[ah-djuh-loh]* A name given to a second born [*Anuak*] (Whitehead 1947: 46).

Ajuna (f/m) *[ah-dzuh-nah]* "He (i.e. God) saves" [*Kiga, Nyankore, Nyoro, Toro*].

Akampa (f/m) *[ah-kahm-pah]* "He (i.e. God) gave to me"; "he (i.e. God) still gives to me" [*Kiga, Nyankore, Nyoro, Toro*].

Akampurira (f/m) *[ah-kahm-puh-rih-rah]* "He (i.e. God) listened to me"; "he (i.e. God) heard me"; "he (i.e. God) still listens to me" [*Kiga, Nyankore*].

Akankwasa (f/m) *[ah-kahn-kwah-sah]* "He (i.e. God) gave to me"; "he (i.e. God) participated with me"; "he (i.e. God) still gives to me" [The *Kiga, Nyankore, Nyoro, Toro*].

Akugiziibwe (f/m) *[ah-kuh-gih-ziih-bweh]* "May he (i.e. God) be praised" [*Nyoro, Toro*].

Akweitereho (f/m) *[ah-kweh-tehy-reh-hoh]* "He (i.e. God) has placed (or set) himself on you" implying that "God is with you" [*Nyoro, Toro*].

Alifaijo (f/m) *[ah-liih-fah-ih-joh]* "He/ she will die tomorrow" [*Nyoro, Toro*].

Aliganyirwa (f/m) *[ah-lih-gah-ndjh-ih-rwah]* "He/ she will be forgiven" [The *Nyoro, Toro*].

Aliigiza (f/m) *[ah-liih-gih-zah]* "He/ she will cause (to feel sympathy)" [The *Nyoro, Toro*].

Aliijaijo (f/m) *[ah-liih-dzahy-dzoh]* "He/ she will be forgiven" [*Nyoro, Toro*].

Aliikiriza (f/m) *[ah-liih-kih-rih-zah]* "He/ she will believe"; "he/ she will accept" [*Nyoro, Toro*].

Aliimanya (f/m) *[ah-liih-mah-ndjh-ah]* "He/ she will get to know" [*Toro*].

Amanya (f/m) *[ah-mah-ndjh-ah]* "He/ she knows (God)" [*Kiga, Nyankore, Nyoro, Toro*].

Amot (f) *[ah-moht]* A name given to a first born [*Anuak*] (Whitehead 1947: 46).

Ampa (f/m) *[ahm-pah]* "He (i.e. God) gives to me" [*Kiga, Nyankore*].

Ampiirwe (f/m) *[ahm-piih-rueh]* "He/ she has been given to me" [*Kiga, Nyankore*].

Ampire/ Ampiire (f/m) *[ahm-piih-reh]* "He (i.e. God) has given to me" [*Kiga, Nyankore*].

Amuhoogwe (f/m) *[ah-muh-hoh-oh-gueh]* "He (i.e. God) endows each one with particular qualities (or luck)" [*Kiga, Nyankore*].

Amwine (f/m) *[ah-muh-iih-neh]* "He (i.e. God) is with him/ her" [The *Kiga, Nyankore, Nyoro, Toro*].

Angwese (m) *[ahn-gweh-eh-seh]* Judo [*Rega*].

Araali (m) *[ah-raah-lih]* A special/ pet name (*empaako*) associated with strength or thunder [*Nyoro, Toro*].

Aribariho (f/m) *[ah-rih-bah-rih-hoh]* "The one who will be present"; "whoever will be there"; this name is sometimes associated with the saying "The one who will be there, will be the one to tell the story" [*Kiga, Nyankore, Nyoro, Toro*].

Ariikiriza (f/m) *[ah-riih-kiih-riih-zah]* "The one who will believe"; "whoever will believe" [*Kiga, Nyankore*].

Arimpa (f/m) *[ah-rihm-pah]* "He (i.e. God) will give to me" [The *Kiga, Nyankore*].

Arinda (f/m) *[ah-rihn-dah]* "He (i.e. God) protects"; "he (i.e. God) cares" [*Kiga, Nyankore*].

Aryaija (f/m) *[ah-rih-yahy-dzah]* "He (i.e. God) will come" [The *Kiga, Nyankore*].

Aryatuha (f/m) *[ah-rih-yah-too-hah]* "He (i.e. God) will give to us" [*Kiga, Nyankore*].

Aryatuzoora (f/m) *[ah-rih-yah-too-zoh-rah]* "He (i.e. God) will cause us to resurrect"; "he (i.e. God) will find us" [*Kiga, Nyankore*].

Asaasira (f/m) *[ah-saah-siih-rah]* "He (i.e. God) forgives" [*Kiga, Nyankore, Nyoro, Toro*].

Asaba (f/m) *[ah-sah-bah]* "He/ she asks for" [*Nyoro, Toro*].

Ashaba (f/m) *[ah-tsh-ah-bah]* "He/ she asks for" [*Kiga, Nyankore*].

Ashibu (m) *[ah-tsh-ih-buh]* "The father associated with the rainbow" [*Rega*].

Asiimwe (f/m) *[ah-siih-mueh]* "Thanks be to him (i.e. God)" [The *Kiga, Nyankore, Nyoro, Toro*].

Atagwirweho (f/m) *[ah-tah-guih-rueh-hoh]* "The one who is not found"; "the one who is not come upon"; "the who is not befallen (by problems)" [*Nyoro, Toro*].

Atalyeba (f/m) *[ah-tah-lieh-bah]* "The one who will never be forgotten" [The *Nyoro, Toro*].

Ataragaboine (f/m) *[ah-tah-rah-gah-bohy-neh]* "The one who did not find them" [*Nyoro, Toro*].

Ataryeba (f/m) *[ah-tah-rieh-bah]* "The one who will never be forgotten" [The *Kiga, Nyankore*].

Atuganyira (f/m) *[ah-tuh-gah-ndjh-ih-rah]* "He (i.e. God) forgives us" [The

Nyoro, Toro].

Atugonza (f/m) *[ah-tuh-gohn-dzah]* "He (i.e. God) loves us" [*Nyoro, Toro*].

Atuhaire (f/m) *[ah-tuh-hahy-reh]* "He (i.e. God) has given us" [*Nyoro, Toro*].

Atuhairwe (f/m) *[ah-tuh-hahy-rueh]* "He (i.e. God) has been given to us" [*Nyoro, Toro*].

Atuhurra (f/m) *[ah-tuh-hurh-rah]* "He (i.e. God) listens to us" [*Nyoro, Toro*].

Atukunda (f/m) *[ah-tuh-kuhn-dah]* "He (i.e. God) loves us" [The *Kiga, Nyankore*].

Atumanyire (f/m) *[ah-tuh-mah-ndjh-ih-reh]* "He (i.e. God) knows us" [The *Nyoro, Toro*].

Atuzaariirwe (f/m) *[ah-tuh-zaah-riih-rueh]* "He/ she has been given birth to for us (or for our sake)" [*Kiga, Nyankore*].

Atwine (f/m) *[ah-tuih-neh]* "He (i.e. God) is with us" [The *Kiga, Nyankore, Nyoro, Toro*].

Atwoki (f/m) *[ah-tuoh-kih]* A special/ pet name (*empaako*) [*Nyoro, Toro*].

Atwongiirwe (f/m) *[ah-tuoh-ngiih-rueh]* "He/ she has been added on to us" [*Kiga, Nyankore, Nyoro, Toro*].

Ayamba (f/m) *[ah-yah-mbah]* "He (i.e. God) helps/ aids" [*Kiga, Nyankore*].

Ayebare (f/m) *[ah-yeh-bah-reh]* "Thanks be to him (i.e. God)" [The *Kiga, Nyankore*].

Ayesiga (f/m) *[ah-yeh-sih-gah]* "He/ she trusts" [*Nyoro, Toro*].

Ayeza (f/m) *[ah-yeh-zah]* "He/ she cleanses" [*Kiga, Nyankore, Nyoro, Toro*].

Ayine (f/m) *[ahy-neh]* "He/ she has (i.e. God)" [*Kiga, Nyankore*].

Azaahuura (f/m) *[ah-zaah-hoo-rah]* "He (i.e. God) prevents one from going astray"; "he (i.e. God) liberates" [*Nyoro, Toro*].

Azaarirabusha (f/m) *[ah-zaah-rih-rah-buh-tsh-ah]* "He/ she gives birth (or produces) for nothing" [*Kiga, Nyankore*].

Azimio (m) *[ah-zih-mjoh]* (Political) declaration; (political) program [*Pare, Swahili* and several other ethnics of eastern and central Africa] (Herbert 1997: 10; Omari 1970: 66).

-B-

Baanaki (m) *[baah-nah-kih]* "What kind of children!?" [*Kiga, Nyankore, Nyoro, Toro*].

Babeiha (m) *[bah-behy-hah]* "They (i.e. children) tell lies"/ "they deceive": this name signifies despair in implying that children can apparently be so healthy and beautiful when they are born and as they grow, yet they are deceptive in that they are still fragile and vulnerable to sickness and death, and can die when still beautiful--the name can then be appropriate for a newborn whose older siblings died [*Kiga, Nyankore*].

Babhekile (f/m) *[bah-beh-kih-leh]* "They (i.e. the in-laws) are looking for it (i.e. the dowry items)": a name such as given to a newborn by it's mother's mother-in-law who is expressing that the in-laws are still awaiting the customary dowry (*umambo*) such as sleeping mats, blankets, calabashes, and brooms that she did not bring with her into the marriage [*Zulu*] (Turner 1992: 49-50).

Babihuga (m) *[bah-bih-hoo-gah]* "They (i.e. people) go astray" [The *Kiga*, *Nyankore*].

Babiiha (m) *[bah-biih-hah]* "They (i.e. children) tell lies"/ "they deceive": this name signifies despair in implying that children can apparently be so healthy and beautiful when they are born and as they grow, yet they are deceptive in that they are still fragile and vulnerable to sickness and death, and can die when still beautiful--the name can then be appropriate for a newborn whose older siblings died [*Nyoro, Toro*].

Babinyaga (m) *[bah-bih-ndjh-ah-gah]* "They confiscate them" [The *Nyoro*, *Toro*].

Babiri (f) *[bah-bih-rih]* Two people; "they are two people"; this name is sometimes associated with the proverb "two masters (or elders) of the same village, that are jealous of each other, will not guarantee peace in the village" [*Ganda*].

Babishiisha (m) *[bah-bih-tsh-iih-tsh-ah]* "They destroy them (i.e. the things)"; "they spoil them (i.e. the things)"; "they waste them (i.e. the things)" [*Kiga, Nyankore*].

Babona (f) *[bah-boh-nah]* "They (i.e. people) see (a lot)" [*Nyoro, Toro*].

Babumba (m) *[bah-boo-mbah]* "They mould" [*Nyoro, Toro*].

Babunga (m) *[bah-buhn-gah]* "They seek refuge"; refugees [*Rega*].

Babushereka (m) *[bah-boo-tsh-eh-reh-kah]* "They hide (or conceal) it/ them (i.e. such as their virtues, vices, or ugliness)" [*Kiga, Nyankore*].

Badogwa (f/m) *[bah-doh-gwah]* A name given to a first born [The *Jur*] (Whitehead 1947: 46).

Bafaki (f/m) *[bah-fah-kih]* "What do they fight (or die) for?" [The *Kiga*, *Nyankore, Nyoro, Toro*].

Bafokworora (f/m) *[bah-foh-kuoh-roh-rah]* "You just bring them (i.e. the children) up"; "you just care for them": this name signifies despair in implying that one just has to work hard at bringing up children though they are fragile and vulnerable to sickness and death [*Kiga, Nyankore*].

Bagaba (f/m) *[bah-gah-bah]* "They give away"; "they provide" [The *Kiga*, *Nyankore, Nyoro, Toro*].

Bagada (f/m) *[bah-gah-dah]* "They (i.e. parents or mothers) toil" [*Nyoro*, *Toro*].

Bagambaki (m) *[bah-gah-mbah-kih]* "What do they (i.e. the people, or neighbors) say?" [*Nyoro, Toro*].

Bagambe (m) *[bah-gah-mbeh]* "Let them (i.e. the people, or neighbors) talk" [*Nyoro, Toro*].

Bagarukayo (m) *[bah-gah-ruh-kah-yoh]* "They go back (i.e. such as to a place they had deserted)" [*Kiga, Nyankore, Nyoro, Toro*].

Bagenda (m) *[bah-gehn-dah]* "They (i.e. the people, or neighbors) go/ move" [*Nyoro, Toro*].

Bagire (m) *[bah-gih-reh]* "Let them (i.e. the people, or neighbors) do"; "let them say" [*Kiga, Nyankore, Nyoro, Toro*].

Bagirwa (m) *[bah-gih-ruah]* "They (i.e. the people, or neighbors) are owned" [*Kiga, Nyankore, Nyoro, Toro*].

Bagonza (m) *[bah-goh-nzah]* "They (i.e. the people, or neighbors) love" [The *Nyoro, Toro*].

Bagumire (m) *[bah-guh-mih-reh]* "They (i.e. the people, or neighbors) are firm"; "they are patient"; "they are okay" [*Kiga, Nyankore, Nyoro, Toro*].

Bagunda (m) *[bah-guh-ndah]* "They (i.e. the people, or neighbors) grow very old" [*Kiga, Nyankore, Nyoro, Toro*].

Bagutaatira (m) *[bah-guh-taah-tih-rah]* "They (i.e. the people, or neighbors) placate (or please) it (i.e. the heart)" [*Kiga, Nyankore, Nyoro, Toro*].

Bagwa (m) *[bah-guah]* "They (i.e. the people, or neighbors) fall" [*Kiga, Nyankore, Nyoro, Toro*].

Bahaburwa (m) *[bah-hah-buh-ruah]* "They (i.e. the people, or neighbors) are advised (i.e. when they are still young enough to be receptive to advice)" [*Kiga, Nyankore, Nyoro, Toro*].

Bahangire (m) *[bah-hahn-gih-reh]* "They (i.e. the people, or neighbors) are popular": this can be a sarcastic remark directed to neighbors [The *Kiga, Nyankore, Nyoro, Toro*].

Baharagate (m) *[bah-hah-rah-gah-teh]* "Let them (i.e. the people, or neighbors) scrape" [*Kiga, Nyankore, Nyoro, Toro*].

Bahemuka (m) *[bah-heh-muh-kah]* "They become ashamed": a name such as implying that the father doubted during the pregnancy that this child was his, but the child at birth turned out to so much resemble him--hence the father became ashamed of himself [*Kiga, Nyankore, Nyoro, Toro*].

Bahemurwaki (m) *[bah-heh-muh-ruah-kih]* "What are they to be ashamed of?"; "what (on earth) do they get ashamed of?": this name can be a statement directed to shameless neighbors [*Kiga, Nyankore, Nyoro, Toro*].

Bahindura (m) *[bah-hih-ndoo-rah]* "They (i.e. the people, or neighbors) rehabilitate" [*Kiga, Nyankore, Nyoro, Toro*].

Baigarakanwa (m) *[bahy-gah-rah-kah-nuah]* "They (i.e. the people, or neighbors) close their mouth" [*Kiga, Nyankore, Nyoro, Toro*].

Baihehoki (m) *[bahy-heh-hoh-kih]* "What should they (i.e. the people, or neighbors) pick/ get?" [*Kiga, Nyankore, Nyoro, Toro*].

Baijanibeera (m) *[bahy-dzah-nih-beh-eh-rah]* "They (i.e. the people, or neighbors) come in while clean (but after some time their appearance is in contrast)"; "they are becoming clean" [*Kiga, Nyankore, Nyoro, Toro*].

Bainakanwa (m) *[bahy-nah-kah-nuah]* "They (i.e. the people, or neighbors) have a mouth (so let them go ahead and talk)" [The *Kiga, Nyankore, Nyoro, Toro*].

Baingana (m) *[bahy-ndgh-ah-nah]* "They (i.e. the people) are equal" [*Kiga, Nyankore, Nyoro, Toro*].

Bainobwengye (m) *[bahy-noh-bueh-ndzeh]* "They (i.e. the people, or neighbors) are intelligent/ wise" [*Kiga, Nyankore, Nyoro, Toro*].

Bainomujinya (f/m) *[bahy-noh-moo-zih-ndjh-ah]* "They are ambitious" [The

Kiga, Nyankore, Nyoro, Toro].

Bairuka (f/m) *[bahy-ruh-kah]* "They (i.e. the people) run" [*Kiga, Nyankore, Nyoro, Toro*].

Bairukanga (m) *[bahy-ruh-kah-ahn-gah]* "They (i.e. the people) run" [*Kiga, Nyankore, Nyoro, Toro*].

Baitwaki (m) *[bahy-tuah-kih]* "What would they (i.e. the people, or neighbors) be fighting (or dying) for?"; "what (on earth) would kill them?" [*Kiga, Nyankore, Nyoro, Toro*].

Baitwenda (f/m) *[bahy-tueh-ndah]* "They (i.e. the people, or neighbors) are killed by way of the stomach": this can be a statement directed to neighbors, implying that they are greedy [*Kiga, Nyankore, Nyoro, Toro*].

Baizire (m) *[bahy-zih-reh]* "They (i.e. the people) came" [*Kiga, Nyankore, Nyoro, Toro*].

Bajabhisile (f/m) *[bah-jah-bih-sih-leh]* "They are disappointed": a name such as given to a newborn by the mother who had consistently maintained that she would eventually bear a child, despite the criticism directed to her by her in-laws--the name symbolizes vindicating herself against her now disproved and disappointed in-laws who had for years caused her suffering and indignity as they denounced her for being childless [The *Zulu*] (Turner 1992: 49).

Bakaihwahenki (m) *[bah-kahy-huah-heh-ntsih]* "What would take them (i.e. the people, or neighbors) away?" [*Kiga, Nyankore, Nyoro, Toro*].

Bakainyaga (m) *[bah-kahy-ndjh-ah-gah]* "They raided them (i.e. the cattle)" [*Kiga, Nyankore, Nyoro, Toro*].

Bakairoha (m) *[bah-kahy-roh-hah]* "They wasted them (i.e. such as cattle)"; "they dropped them/ it (i.e. in the water, lake, or river)" [*Kiga, Nyankore, Nyoro, Toro*].

Bakajwaha (m) *[bah-kah-dzuah-hah]* "They (i.e. the people) got tired" [The *Kiga, Nyankore, Nyoro, Toro*].

Bakamuturaki (m) *[bah-kah-moo-too-rah-kih]* "For what reason did they (i.e. the people) turn against him/ her?" [*Kiga, Nyankore, Nyoro, Toro*].

Bakanga (m) *[bah-kah-ngah]* "They (i.e. the people, or neighbors) threaten"; "they refused" [*Kiga, Nyankore, Nyoro, Toro*].

Bakangaga (m) *[bah-kah-ngah-gah]* "They (i.e. the people, or neighbors) always threaten"; "they always refused"; "they used to reject the little one" [*Kiga, Nyankore, Nyoro, Toro*].

Bakaremwa (m) *[bah-kah-reh-muah]* "They (i.e. the people, or neighbors) fail"; "they experience difficulty in dealing with" [*Kiga, Nyankore, Nyoro, Toro*].

Bakatara (m) *[bah-kah-tah-rah]* "They (i.e. the people, or neighbors) have wandered all over" [*Kiga, Nyankore, Nyoro, Toro*].

Bakeehena (m) *[bah-keh-eh-heh-nah]* "They punished themselves" [*Kiga, Nyankore, Nyoro, Toro*].

Bakeesigaki (m) *[bah-keh-eh-sih-gah-kih]* "What did they trust?"; "what gave them the courage?" [*Kiga, Nyankore, Nyoro, Toro*].

Bakeesisira (m) *[bah-keh-eh-sih-sih-rah]* "They spoilt for themselves"; "they misused their chance" [*Kiga, Nyankore, Nyoro, Toro*].

Bakyenga (m) *[bah-tseh-ngah]* "They understand" [*Kiga, Nyankore, Nyoro, Toro*].

Balelwa (f) *[bah-leh-lwah]* "They are nursed/ carried": name given to a child that always likes to be nursed and carried [*Rega*].

Bambeiha (m) *[bahm-behy-hah]* "They (i.e. children) tell me lies"/ "they deceive me": this name signifies despair in implying that children can apparently be so healthy and beautiful when they are born and as they grow, yet they are deceptive in that they are still fragile and vulnerable to sickness and death, and can die when still beautiful--the name can then be appropriate for a newborn whose older siblings died [*Kiga, Nyankore, Nyoro, Toro*].

Bambaija (m) *[bah-mbahy-zah]* "They (i.e. neighbors) cut me up"; "they harass me"; "they eat me up raw" [*Kiga, Nyankore, Nyoro, Toro*].

Bamuhiiga (m) *[bah-moo-hiih-gah]* "They (i.e. the people, or neighbors) hunt him down" [*Kiga, Nyankore, Nyoro, Toro*].

Bamuke (m) *[bah-moo-keh]* "Be small"; "humble yourself" [*Kiga, Nyankore, Nyoro, Toro*].

Bamuloho (m) *[bah-moo-loh-hoh]* "They (i.e. the people, or neighbors) are upon him" implying for example that they are involved in talking about him, or involved in hunting him down [*Kiga, Nyankore, Nyoro, Toro*].

Bamuturaki (m) *[bah-moo-too-rah-kih]* "Why are they (i.e. the people, or neighbors) always against him?" [*Kiga, Nyankore, Nyoro, Toro*].

Bamuturenda (m) *[bah-muh-tuh-reh-ndah]* "They (i.e. the people, or neighbors) are against his stomach (i.e. womb, or progeny)" implying that they are not in favor of his being blessed with a bountiful of children [*Kiga, Nyankore, Nyoro, Toro*].

Bamuziire (m) *[bah-muh-ziih-reh]* "They gave birth to him" [The *Kiga, Nyankore, Nyoro, Toro*].

Bananuka (m) *[bah-nah-noo-kah]* "They (i.e. the people) feel free"; "they feel relaxed" which can imply that they know the truth [*Kiga, Nyankore, Nyoro, Toro*].

Bandoobesa (m) *[bah-ndoh-oh-beh-sah]* "They (i.e. the people, or neighbors) cause me to be poor" [*Kiga, Nyankore, Nyoro, Toro*].

Banduho (m) *[bah-nduh-hoh]* "They (i.e. the people, or neighbors) are upon me" implying for example that "they are involved in talking about me," or "they are involved in hunting me down" [*Kiga, Nyankore, Nyoro, Toro*].

Bangana (m) *[bah-ngah-nah]* "They (i.e. the people, or neighbors) hate each other" [*Kiga, Nyankore, Nyoro, Toro*].

Bangelizwe (m) *[bahn-geh-lih-zweh]* Creator of a nation [The *Xhosa*] (Wainwright 1986: 297).

Bangi (f/m) *[bahn-jih]* "Many people"; this name is sometimes associated with the proverb "a beautiful woman is the sister of many" which implies that many are eager to claim relationship to one that is good looking, and is synonymous with "a fair face is half a portion, a pretty face is a good recommendation" [*Ganda*].

Bangihlebile (f/m) *[bahn-gih-leh-bih-leh]* "They whispered against me": a name such as given to a newborn by its mother who had taken an unexpectedly long period to give birth, and during which period she was rumored to be barren [*Zulu*] (Koopman 1987: 152).

Bangirana (m) *[bah-ngih-rah-nah]* "They envy one other" [*Kiga, Nyankore, Nyoro, Toro*].

Banoba (m) *[bah-noh-bah]* "They (i.e. the people, or neighbors) hate/ dislike" [*Kiga, Nyankore, Nyoro, Toro*].

Banobere (f/m) *[bah-noh-bah]* "They (i.e. the people, or neighbors) hate/ dislike me (or him, or her)" [*Kiga, Nyankore, Nyoro, Toro*].

Banserurra (m) *[bah-nseh-ruhr-rah]* "They search for on my behalf" [*Kiga, Nyankore, Nyoro, Toro*].

Bantebya (m) *[bah-nteh-biah]* "They talk (ill) about me" [*Kiga, Nyankore, Nyoro, Toro*].

Bantu (m) *[bah-ntuh]* "They are people"; people [*Kiga, Nyankore, Nyoro, Toro*].

Banturebyangye (m) *[bah-ntuh-reh-biah-njyeh]* "They hate me because of my possessions" [*Kiga, Nyankore, Nyoro, Toro*].

Banugire (m) *[bah-nuh-gih-reh/ bah-nuh-zih-reh]* "They despise me/ it" [*Kiga, Nyankore, Nyoro, Toro*].

Banura (m) *[bah-nuh-rah]* "They (i.e. children) are sweet" [*Kiga, Nyankore, Nyoro, Toro*].

Banyanga (m) *[bah-ndjh-ah-ngah]* "They hate me"; "they dislike me" [*Kiga, Nyankore, Nyoro, Toro*].

Banyoya (m) *[bah-ndjh-oh-yah]* "They harass me"; "they crave for me" [The *Kiga, Nyankore, Nyoro, Toro*].

Barabara (f/m) *[bah-rah-bah-rah]* "Road" (from the *Kiswahili* language) [*Fipa*] (Willis 1982: 229).

Barahuka (m) *[bah-rah-huh-kah]* "They (i.e. the people/ neighbors) hurry" [*Kiga, Nyankore, Nyoro, Toro*].

Barahukire (m) *[bah-rah-huh-kih-reh]* "They (i.e. the people, or neighbors) have hurried" [*Kiga, Nyankore, Nyoro, Toro*].

Barhasima (f/m) *[bahr-hah-sih-mah]* "They are never happy/ pleased" [The *Bashi*].

Baribona (m) *[bah-rih-boh-nah]* "They (i.e. the people, or neighbors) will (eventually) see/ realize/ experience" [*Kiga, Nyankore, Nyoro, Toro*].

Baribonwoha (m) *[bah-rih-boh-nuoh-hah]* "Who will find them?" [*Kiga, Nyankore, Nyoro, Toro*].

Barigye (m) *[bah-rih-dzeh]* "They (i.e. the people) are okay"; "they are doing fine" [*Kiga, Nyankore, Nyoro, Toro*].

Barikurungi (m) *[bah-rih-kuh-ruh-ngih]* "They (i.e. the people, or neighbors) are okay"; "they are experiencing good times"; "they are doing fine"; this name is sometimes associated with the proverb "Those that are well off would not understand the plight of those that are badly off" [The *Kiga, Nyankore, Nyoro, Toro*].

Barinda (m) *[bah-rih-ndah]* "They (i.e. the people) wait"; "they guard against" [*Kiga, Nyankore, Nyoro, Toro*].

Barindeeba (m) *[bah-rih-ndeh-eh-bah]* "They (i.e. the people, or neighbors) will see me" which can also mean that "they will eventually experience my wrath (or my negative side) as a consequence of what they did to me" [*Kiga, Nyankore, Nyoro, Toro*].

Barindonda (m) *[bah-rih-ndoh-ndah]* "They (i.e. the people, or neighbors) will look for me" [*Kiga, Nyankore, Nyoro, Toro*].

Barireeta (m) *[bah-rih-reh-eh-tah]* "They (i.e. the people) will bring" [*Kiga, Nyankore, Nyoro, Toro*].

Barongo (m) *[bah-roh-ngoh]* "They are twins" [The *Kiga, Nyankore, Nyoro, Toro*].

Barozi (m) *[bah-roh-zih]* "They (i.e. the people, or neighbors) are perceivers"; "they are seers" [*Kiga, Nyankore, Nyoro, Toro*].

Barugahare (m) *[bah-ruh-gah-hah-reh]* "They (i.e. the people, or neighbors) come from there afar"; "they have come from far away" [*Kiga, Nyankore, Nyoro, Toro*].

Baruhirabusha (m) *[bah-ruh-hih-rah-buh-tsh-ah]* "They (i.e. the people) get worn out for nothing"; "they do not gain anything from their tiring" [*Kiga, Nyankore, Nyoro, Toro*].

Barungi (f/m) *[bah-roo-ngih]* "They (i.e. the people, or neighbors) are good" [*Kiga, Nyankore, Nyoro, Toro*].

Barungindoho (f/m) *[bah-ruh-ngih-ndoh-hoh]* "They (i.e. the people, or neighbors) are good (or nice) when I am in their presence" [The *Kiga, Nyankore, Nyoro, Toro*].

Barusigira (f/m) *[bah-ruh-sih-gih-rah]* "They (i.e. the people, or the parents) leave something for it (i.e. death)": a name commonly given to a child who is alarmingly sick, or to a child that has lost some previously born siblings to death [*Kiga, Nyankore, Nyoro, Toro*].

Baruti (m) *[bah-ruh-tih]* "Gunpowder" (from the *Kiswahili* language) [*Fipa*] (Willis 1982: 229).

Baruzaliire (f/m) *[bah-ruh-zah-liih-reh]* "They (i.e. the people, or the parents) have given birth for it (i.e. death)": name commonly given to a child who is alarmingly sick, or to a child that has lost some previously born siblings to death [*Kiga, Nyankore, Nyoro, Toro*].

Baryasigarwaki (f/m) *[bah-riah-sih-gah-ruah-kih]* "What will they (i.e. the people) gain from the energies they have expended?" [*Kiga, Nyankore, Nyoro, Toro*].

Baryanengwe (m) *[bah-riah-neh-ngueh]* "They (i.e. the people, or neighbors) eat with leopards" [*Kiga, Nyankore, Nyoro, Toro*].

Baryaruha (m) *[bah-riah-ruh-hah]* "They (i.e. the people, or neighbors) will tire" [*Kiga, Nyankore, Nyoro, Toro*].

Baryayanga (m) *[bah-riah-yah-ngah]* "They will refuse" [*Kiga, Nyankore*,

Nyoro, Toro].

Basemera (f) *[bah-seh-meh-rah]* "They (i.e. children) are nice/ lovely" [The *Kiga, Nyankore, Nyoro, Toro*].

Basigirenda (f) *[bah-sih-gih-reh-ndah]* "They (i.e. the people, or neighbors) leave exclusively for the stomach (or the inside)" implying that "they disclose (or let out) very little" [*Kiga, Nyankore, Nyoro, Toro*].

Basigirwa (f/m) *[bah-sih-gih-ruah]* Those for whom things are put aside exclusively for [*Kiga, Nyankore, Nyoro, Toro*].

Basoberwa (f/m) *[bah-soh-beh-ruah]* "They become confused (or baffled)" [*Kiga, Nyankore, Nyoro, Toro*].

Bataringaya (m) *[bah-tah-rih-ngah-yah]* "They should never despise me" [*Kiga, Nyankore, Nyoro, Toro*].

Bateemanya (f/m) *[bah-teh-eh-mah-ndjh-ah]* "They (i.e. people, or neighbors) do not know themselves" implying that "they do not reflect on themselves, so do not properly comprehend what their faults and weaknesses are" [*Kiga, Nyankore, Nyoro, Toro*].

Bath (m) *[bah-sth]* To be lost: a name such as given to one whose previously born siblings died [*Nuer*] (Evans-Pritchard 1948: 167).

Batho (m) *[bah-toh]* People [*Sotho*] (Thipa 1987: 116).

Bato (f/m) *[bah-toh]* Younger brothers; young persons; children; "they are young"; this name is sometimes associated with the proverb "friendship between children is broken up by laughter" implying that unlike adults who can more readily take jokes and ignore those laughing at them, children are very sensitive at their peers laughing at them (such as when one falls down) [*Ganda*].

Bazana (f/m) *[bah-zah-nah]* A name given to a third born [*Jur*] (Whitehead 1947: 46).

Beebwa (f/m) *[beh-eh-buah]* "They forget" [*Kiga, Nyankore, Nyoro, Toro*].

Beekunda (f/m) *[beh-eh-kuhn-dah]* "They (i.e. people, or neighbors) love themselves" implying that "they are so arrogant and selfish" [The *Kiga, Nyankore, Nyoro, Toro*].

Beeraheeru (f/m) *[beh-eh-rah-heh-eh-ruh]* "They (i.e. people, or neighbors) are pure (or white) on the outside" implying that "they are nice by outward appearance, but inside (their minds) they harbor thoughts of evil and hatred" [*Kiga, Nyankore, Nyoro, Toro*].

Beesanga (m) *[beh-eh-sah-ngah]* "They (i.e. people, or neighbors) kill themselves (before their time is up)"; "their own actions cut down on the time they will live"; "they hasten themselves to their deaths" [*Kiga, Nyankore, Nyoro, Toro*].

Beesigensi (f/m) *[beh-eh-sih-geh-nsih]* "They (i.e. people, or neighbors) are (overly) trusting of the world"; "they trust the world" [*Kiga, Nyankore, Nyoro, Toro*].

Beesisira (m) *[beh-eh-sih-sih-rah]* "They (i.e. people, or neighbors) spoil for themselves" [*Kiga, Nyankore, Nyoro, Toro*].

Beeyanga (m) *[beh-eh-yah-ngah]* "They (i.e. people, or neighbors) hate themselves" [*Kiga, Nyankore, Nyoro, Toro*].

Beeyeza (m) *[beh-eh-yeh-zah]* "They (i.e. people, or neighbors) make themselves (appear) clean" which can imply that "they pretend to be clean as they disguise their deeds and thoughts of evil" [The *Kiga, Nyankore, Nyoro, Toro*].

Beeyinika (f/m) *[beh-eh-yih-nih-kah]* "They (i.e. people, or neighbors) bend themselves" [*Kiga, Nyankore, Nyoro, Toro*].

Bekiita (m) *[beh-kiih-tah]* "They (i.e. people, or neighbors) rejoice" [*Kiga, Nyankore, Nyoro, Toro*].

Bendebule (m) *[beh-ndeh-buh-leh]* "They (i.e. people, or neighbors) want it to disappear": implying "in their thoughts of malice, they want all of mine such as property, children (or progeny), house, etc. to be harmed and to disappear" [*Kiga, Nyankore, Nyoro, Toro*].

Bendezayaabo (m) *[beh-ndeh-zah-yaah-boh]* "They (i.e. people, or neighbors) exclusively want it for their own (or their progeny, or their womb)": implying "in their greed and selfishness, they want all that is good or luxurious for themselves and their kin" [*Kiga, Nyankore, Nyoro, Toro*].

Beshunga (m) *[beh-tsh-uh-ngah]* "They (i.e. people, or neighbors) unduly count on" implying that they are stubborn, spoilt, or risk taking [The *Kiga, Nyankore, Nyoro, Toro*].

Bhasikidi (m) *[bah-sih-kih-dih]* "Basket" (as adapted from the European word): a name such as given to one who, when out to court girls, habitually utters the saying "even he without a basket can go to the market" meaning that even one without the cows to pay dowry for a wife can still go out to court [*Zulu*] (Koopman 1987: 160).

Bhavuma (f) *[bhah-vuh-mah]* "The one with a rough and growling voice" [*Xhosa*] (Neethling 1985: 89).

Bhekamandlovu (m) *[beh-kah-mahn-dloh-vuh]* "Look to the *Ndlovus* (i.e. those of the Elephant Clan)" [*Zulu*] (Koopman 1987: 149).

Bhekamuphi (m) *[beh-kah-muh-pih]* "Which one is to be watched out for?": a name such as given to a newborn by its father who is accusing the community of ill will and possibly witchcraft against his household, given that a good number of misfortunes have befallen the family [*Zulu*] (Turner 1992: 54).

Bhekisisa (m) *[beh-kih-sih-sah]* "Look carefully": a name such as given to a newborn by it's mother's mother-in-law who is expressing to her son that this child may not be his given the extramarital affairs the mother of the child has engaged in [*Zulu*] (Turner 1992: 50).

Bhekizinja (m) *[beh-kih-zihn-jah]* A nickname such as given to a newborn by persons in the community the father of this child's responds to by naming him *Bhekizitha* 'Watch out for the enemies' to point out that he is well aware of their enmity towards him--*Bhekizinja* becomes an insulting name directed at the father to imply that he is a coward who has to rely on his son to deal with issues with enemies [*Zulu*] (Turner 1992: 54).

Bhekizitha (m) *[beh-kih-zih-tah]* "Watch out for the enemies": a name such as given to a newborn by it's father to point out to certain persons in the community that he is aware of their enmity towards him [*Zulu*] (Turner 1992: 54).

Bhekokwahke (f/m) *[beh-koh-kwah-keh]* "The one who looks after his own": a name such as given to a newborn by it's paternal grandmother who is chastising her son, who snubs the advice and requirements of other family members regarding kindred issues, for his pigheadedness [*Zulu*] (Turner 1992: 53).

Bhekumuzi (f/m) *[beh-kuh-muh-zih]* "Look within the homestead": a name such as given to one born to a family accusing a neighbor of practicing witchcraft [*Zulu*] (Turner 1992: 54).

Bhekuzalo (f/m) *[beh-kuh-zah-loh]* "Look within the clan": a name such as given to one born to a family accusing a neighbor of practicing witchcraft [*Zulu*] (Turner 1992: 54).

Bicok (m) *[bih-tch-ohk]* A name given to one whose birth follows that of his twin siblings [*Nuer*] (Evans-Pritchard 1948: 168).

Biet (m) *[bih-yeht]* Silent [*Nuer*] (Evans-Pritchard 1948: 170).

Bifeeramunda (m) *[bih-feh-eh-rah-muh-ndah]* "They (i.e. words, or problems) perish inside (the body)": implied in this proverb (or proverbial name) is that one should always be cautious, therefore keep most of the thoughts and feelings to oneself, not liberally mentioning them [The *Kiga, Nyankore, Nyoro, Toro*].

Bikaitoha (m) *[bih-kahy-toh-hah]* "Whom have they (i.e. words, or issues) ever killed?" [*Kiga, Nyankore, Nyoro, Toro*].

Bikanyanga (m) *[bih-kah-ndjh-ah-ngah]* "They (i.e. possessions) have rejected me": this can imply that the parent that gives his child this name is poor, and is convinced (following his dedicated efforts) that there is little chance that he will ever become rich [*Kiga, Nyankore, Nyoro, Toro*].

Bikanyangira (m) *[bih-kah-ndjh-ah-ngih-rah]* "I have failed them" which can imply that "I have totally failed to profit from my ventures" [*Kiga, Nyankore, Nyoro, Toro*].

Bikanyanjweri (m) *[bih-kah-ndjh-ah-njueh-rih]* "They (i.e. possessions) are always in abundance at the other (i.e. neighbor's) house": this can imply that the parent that gives his child this name is poor, and is so perplexed that he has failed to become as well off as his neighbors [*Kiga, Nyankore, Nyoro, Toro*].

Bilieu (m) *[bih-ljehw]* "You will die": a name such as given to one whose previously born siblings died [*Nuer*] (Evans-Pritchard 1948: 167).

Bingi (m) *[bih-ngih]* "They (i.e. the issues) are many"/ "it is (too) much" which can imply that "it is too much to mention (or talk about)" [*Kiga, Nyankore, Nyoro, Toro*].

Bintu (m) *[bih-ntuh]* "They are things"; things [The *Kiga, Nyankore, Nyoro, Toro*].

Birakwate (m) *[bih-rah-kuah-teh]* "Those (i.e. things, or issues) that will catch on" [*Kiga, Nyankore, Nyoro, Toro*].

Bireke (m) *[bih-reh-keh]* "Leave them (i.e. issues, problems) alone"; "ignore those (i.e. issues)" [*Kiga, Nyankore, Nyoro, Toro*].

Biriibwabaali (m) *[bih-riih-buah-baah-lih]* "They (i.e. things) are consumed by eaters" which can translate to "those who are well off and are living and feeding luxuriously, are the ones that usurp and consume on top of what they are already indulging in" [*Kiga, Nyankore, Nyoro, Toro*].

Birungi (m) *[bih-ruh-ngih]* "Those (i.e. things, or issues) that are good (or desirable, or right)" [*Kiga, Nyankore, Nyoro, Toro*].

Biryabarema (m) *[bih-riah-bah-reh-mah]* "They (i.e. people, or neighbors) will not be able to manage them (i.e. the things, or issues)" [The *Kiga, Nyankore, Nyoro, Toro*].

Bisangwaengume (m) *[bih-sah-nguah-eh-nguh-meh]* "They (i.e. problems, or difficult issues) search out and find the ones who are strong and patient" which can also imply that "it is only those that are patient and strong that can stand problems" [*Kiga, Nyankore, Nyoro, Toro*].

Bisereka (m) *[bih-seh-reh-kah]* "They (i.e. things, or issues) hide" [*Kiga, Nyankore, Nyoro, Toro*].

Bisereko (m) *[bih-seh-reh-kah]* "They (i.e. things, or issues) are hidden" [*Kiga, Nyankore, Nyoro, Toro*].

Bishanga (m) *[bih-tsh-ah-ngah]* "They (i.e. problems, or difficult issues) search out and find (i.e. the ones who are strong and patient)" which can also imply that "it is only those that are patient and strong that can stand problems" [*Kiga, Nyankore, Nyoro, Toro*].

Bishekwa (f/m) *[bih-shweh-kah]* "Rubbish" [*Bashi*].

Bisimwa (m) *[bih-sih-mwah]* Things that are enjoyed; things that people are pleased with [*Bashi*].

Bisobere (m) *[bah-soh-beh-reh]* "They (i.e. things, or issues) that are per-plexing/ faulty" [*Kiga, Nyankore, Nyoro, Toro*].

Bitarisha (m) *[bih-tah-rih-tsh-ah]* "They (i.e. things, or issues) cause (peo-ple) to wander" [*Kiga, Nyankore, Nyoro, Toro*].

Bitature (m) *[bih-tah-tuh-reh]* "Those (i.e. things, or issues) that will not last long" [*Kiga, Nyankore, Nyoro, Toro*].

Bitondo (f) *[bih-toh-ndoh]* "Words" [*Rega*].

Bodogoma (f/m) *[boh-doh-goh-mah]* A name given to a second born [*Jur*] (Whitehead 1947: 46).

Boipar (m) *[bohy-parh]* An ox name [*Nuer*] (Evans-Pritchard 1948: 169).

Boitumelo (m) *[bohy-tuh-meh-loh]* "Happiness": a name such as given to a newborn by its mother to indicate that it is indeed a baby boy that she wished for and so she is so glad [*Tswana*] (Herbert 1997: 8; Herbert 1995: 3; Herbert 1990: 9).

Bojo (f) *[boh-joh]* "The one who despises her twin sibling": a name comm-only given to a first born of female twins, the second born named *Jore* [*Bari*] (Whitehead 1947: 45).

Bol (m) *[bohl]* A name given to one whose birth follows that of his twin sib-lings [*Nuer*] (Evans-Pritchard 1948: 168; Whitehead 1947: 46).

Bongani (m) *[bohn-gah-nih]* "Be ye grateful (i.e. to God for this child)" [The *Zulu*] (Koopman 1987: 149).

Bonginkosi (m) *[bohn-gihn-koh-sih]* "Thank the Lord (i.e. for this child)" [*Zulu*] (Koopman 1987: 148).

Bonginkosi (m) *[bohn-gihn-koh-sih]* "Thank the Lord" [The *Xhosa*, *Zulu*] (Herbert 1997: 8; Thipa 1987: 110, 111).

Bonokwahke (f/m) *[boh-noh-kwah-keh]* "The one who looks after his own": a name such as given to a newborn by it's paternal grandmother who is chastising her son, who snubs the advice and requirements of other family members regarding kindred issues, for his pigheadedness [*Zulu*] (Turner 1992: 53).

Boomera (m) *[bih-tah-tuh-reh]* "They (i.e. people, or neighbors) live long" [*Kiga, Nyankore, Nyoro, Toro*].

Both (m) *[boh-sth]* "The one that goes ahead of the other": a name given to the older twin [*Nuer*] (Evans-Pritchard 1948: 167).

Boyibo (f/m) *[boh-yih-boh]* A name given to a fourth born [*Jur*] (Whitehead 1947: 46).

Buchunde (f) *[buh-tch-uhn-deh]* Wealth [*Rega*].

Bukelwa (f) *[buh-keh-lwah]* To be admired [*Xhosa*] (Neethling 1994: 92).

Bulambo (m) *[buh-lahm-boh]* A name given to a child who survives, though his prior born sibling died [*Rega*].

Bulelani (m) *[buh-leh-lah-nih]* "Thank (him)" [*Xhosa*] (Thipa 1987: 110).

Buli (f) *[buh-lih]* A nickname-abbreviation for *Nombulelo*: "Gratitude" [*Xhosa*] (Neethling 1994: 92).

Bungilila (f) *[buhn-gih-lih-lah]* "Famous"; "popular" [*Rega*].

Busanga (f) *[buh-sah-ngah]* Pearls [*Rega*].

Busisiwe (f) *[buh-sih-sih-weh]* "Being blessed" [The *Zulu*] (Koopman 1987: 151).

Busisiwe (f/m) *[buh-sih-sih-weh]* "Blessed" [*Nguni, Sotho, Zulu*] (Herbert 1995: 2; Herbert 1990: 8).

Busungu (f) *[buh-suhn-guh]* Anger; ire, wrath; this name is sometimes ass-ociated with the proverb "a man of wrath is like the venomous viper" [The *Ganda*].

Butimbushi (m) *[buh-tihm-buh-tsh-ih]* Trader; seller [*Rega*].

Byemba (m) *[bjeh-ehm-bah]* That are fat [*Rega*].

-C-

Chilupulamatipa (m) *[tch-ih-luh-puh-lah-mah-tih-pah]* "Mud Treader" [The *Lamba*] (Doke 1931: 146).

Chinami (f/m) *[tch-ih-nah-mih]* "Bluffer" [*Lamba*] (Doke 1931: 146).

Chipeso (f/m) *[tch-ih-peh-soh]* "Sleeping Mat" [*Lamba*] (Doke 1931: 146).

Chirhabwira/ Cirhabwira (f/m) *[tch-ihr-hah-bwih-rah]* "That which destroys friendship" [*Bashi*].

Chishambo/ Cishambo (f/m) *[tch-ih-tsh-am-boh]* "Thief" [*Bashi*].

Chith'umuzi (m) *[tch-iht-uh-muh-zih]* "Destroy the household": a name such as given to a newborn by it's mother who is drawing attention to the issue of her husband who engaged in bewitching acts on his brothers because he did not wish to share his inheritance--the brothers consequently left the homestead as the family became disunited and discordant [*Zulu*] (Turner 1992: 51).

Chyendanawulwani (m) *[chjeh-ndah-nah-wuh-lwah-nih]* "Traveler with Ferocity" [*Lamba*] (Doke 1931: 146).

Chyowola (f/m) *[chjoh-woh-lah]* "Blasphemy" [*Lamba*] (Doke 1931: 146).

Cuil (m) *[tch-uhyl]* A name given to the second born following the birth of his twin siblings [*Nuer*] (Evans-Pritchard 1948: 168).

Cuol (m) *[tch-wohl]* To compensate: a name such as given to one whose previously born siblings died [*Nuer*] (Evans-Pritchard 1948: 167).

-D-

Dalingozi (m) *[dah-lih-ndgoh-zih]* "Creator of danger" [*Xhosa*] (Wainwright 1986: 297).

Deng (m) *[deh-ndgh]* The God of the sky; the name of a spirit: a name given to one born to a mother who because she had not conceived for so long, was subjected to a ritual and a prayer offered to enable her to conceive [*Nuer*] (Evans-Pritchard 1948: 167).

Dideka (m) *[dih-deh-kah]* "Be confused": a name such as given to one born out of wedlock or infidelity [*Xhosa*] (Thipa 1987: 112).

Dihlahleng (m) *[dih-lah-leh-ndgh]* "In the bush": a name such as given to one born out of wedlock or infidelity [*Sotho*] (Thipa 1987: 113).

Dit (m) *[diht]* Bird: a name given to a twin [*Nuer*] (Evans-Pritchard 1948: 167).

Dithwele (m) *[dih-tweh-leh]* Dust (especially of a room or house): a name such as given to one born out of wedlock or infidelity [*Sotho*] (Thipa 1987: 113).

Doggale (m) *[dohg-gah-leh]* A name commonly given to a fourth born male [*Bari*] (Whitehead 1947: 45).

Duduzile (f) *[duh-duh-zih-leh]* "She has comforted": a name such as given to one born during or following circumstances of discomfort, pain, or beravement [*Zulu*] (Koopman 1987: 152).

Dumazile (f/m) *[duh-mah-zih-leh]* "You have disappointed me": a name such as given to a newborn whose mother is lamenting her declining marital relationship with her husband which she wants rectified; or a name such as given to a child born out of wedlock and whose grandmother is expressing disappointment in her daughter who was the pride and joy of the family when she was acknowledged in the community as a chaste virgin [*Zulu*] (Turner 1992: 48).

Duob (m) *[duh-wohb]* Path: a name given to one born along a path or wayside [*Nuer*] (Evans-Pritchard 1948: 167).

Duoth (m) *[duh-woh-sth]* "The one who follows the other": a name given to the younger twin [*Nuer*] (Evans-Pritchard 1948: 167).

-F-

Fikanaye (f/m) *[fih-kah-nah-yeh]* "Arrive with him/ her": a name such as given to a newborn by the mother's mother-in-law who is airing the suspicion that the newborn is not her son's biological child since it was born only seven months after the marriage, and therefore the mother had likely come into the marriage after the conception of this child [The *Zulu*] (Turner 1992: 49).

Funani (f/m) *[fuh-nah-nih]* "What do you want now?": a name in reference to and given to one born at a time of friction between the parents, or friction between the parents and kin or neighbors [*Zulu*] (Koopman 1987: 150).

Funelinjani (f/m) *[fuh-neh-lihn-jah-nih]* "Which one (i.e. testicle) do you want?": a name such as directed by the father to his promiscuous wife who bears this child named so [*Zulu*] (Turner 1992: 48).

Funelinjani (f/m) *[fuh-neh-lihn-jah-nih]* "Which one (i.e.vagina) do you want?": a name such as directed by the mother to her promiscuous husband who is the father of this child named so [*Zulu*] (Turner 1992: 48).

Funimali (m) *[fuh-nih-mah-lih]* "Look for money" [*Zulu*] (Koopman 1987: 149).

Funokukhulu (f/m) *[fuh-noh-kuh-kuh-luh]* "Wanting a big share": a name such as given to a newborn by it's father who is the oldest of two brothers and who is chastising his greedy younger brother for going against custom by contesting the right of the eldest brother to receive a larger share of the inheritance--the child was born shortly after the dispute between the two brothers took place [*Zulu*] (Turner 1992: 52).

Funokwakhe (f/m) *[fuh-noh-kwah-keh]* "Wants his own possessions": a name such as given to a first born by it's father who is the youngest of three brothers and who is informing his older brothers that he is very much aware that they usurped part of his inheritance while he was too young to do anything about it [*Zulu*] (Turner 1992: 52-53).

Fuzuyise (m) *[fuh-zuh-yih-seh]* "Takes after his father"/ "looks like his father": a name such as given to a newborn whose mother is responding to her husband who is suspicious as to whether this child is biologically his [*Zulu*] (Turner 1992: 49).

-G-

Gaak (m) *[gaahk]* Quarrel: a name such as given to one born during a family dispute [*Nuer*] (Evans-Pritchard 1948: 167).

Gac (m) *[gah-tch]* To be dismayed: a name such as given to one whose previously born siblings died [*Nuer*] (Evans-Pritchard 1948: 167).

Ganephi (f/m) *[gah-neh-pih]* "Where did you marry?": a name such as given to a first born by its paternal grandmother who is drawing attention to her daughter-in-law that the paternal family of the child is displeased with her frequent visits to her parent's homestead [*Zulu*] (Turner 1992: 51).

Gcinikhaya (m) *[gtch-ih-nih-kah-yah]* "Look after the home" [*Xhosa*] (Thipa 1987: 114, 115).

Geng (m) *[geh-ndgh]* A name given to the second born following the birth of his twin siblings [*Nuer*] (Whitehead 1947: 46).

Ginyibunu (m) *[gih-ndjh-ih-buh-nuh]* "Swallow the (oppressive) Boer" [The *Zulu*] (Herbert 1997: 11).

Gugulethu (m) *[guh-guh-leh-tuh]* "Our treasure" [*Zulu*] (Herbert 1997: 8).

Gumba/ Ggumba (m) *[guhm-bah]* Bone; this name is sometimes associated with the proverb "an oarsman (has to concentrate so) does not gnaw at a bone" which advises against carelessness that involves engaging in distracting activity that would lead those with responsible duties to disaster [The *Ganda*].

Gumenya (f) *[guh-meh-ndjh-ah]* "It causes to break down"; "it causes to destroy"; "it causes to get fractured"; "it causes to get broken"; this name is also sometimes associated with the proverb "friendship breaks down even a person of strong will" which implies that creating friendship with people allows for many advantages, for even persons of strong character can be more easily acquired from and compromised with, and their opinions more easily swayed through negotiating with them in a friendly manner [*Ganda*].

Gune (m) *[guh-neh]* "The big-headed one": a name commonly given to one whose immediately preceding siblings are twins [*Bari*] (Whitehead 1947: 45).

Gwith (f/m) *[gwih-sth]* Pride [*Nuer*] (Evans-Pritchard 1948: 169).

Gwith-Mathda (f) *[gwih-sth-mah-sth-dah]* "Pride, my friend" [The *Nuer*] (Evans-Pritchard 1948: 169).

Gwong (m) *[gwoh-ndgh]* Guinea fowl: a name given to a twin [The *Nuer*] (Evans-Pritchard 1948: 167).

-H-

Hlalezwini (f/m) *[hlah-leh-zwih-nih]* "Stick to the word": a name such as given to a newborn by the father whose wife had consistently maintained that she would eventually bear a child, despite the criticism directed to her by her husband's parents--the name symbolizes the husband vindicating the wife against his own parents who had for years denounced her for being childless [*Zulu*] (Turner 1992: 49).

Hlamukiwe (f) *[huh-lah-muh-kih-weh]* "They all left me": a name such as given to a newborn by its father who is expressing unhappiness and puzzlement over the four families that had lived alongside his in the same kraal having gradually left over a period of three years--there remained only the man, his wife, and their two week old baby when the fourth family deserted the kraal for no good reason [*Zulu*] (Turner 1992: 51).

Hlebani (m) *[huh-leh-bah-nih]* "What are you gossiping about?": a name such as given to a newborn by its paternal aunt who is fed up with and is chastising the child's mother for her penchant for disseminating news which has caused trouble in numerous instances [*Zulu*] (Turner 1992: 53).

Hluphuyise (f/m) *[hluh-puh-yih-seh]* "Worry your father": a name such as given to a newborn by the father who is lamenting over the torment he endured during the pregnancy from an extremely irritable wife who is normally quiet and affable [*Zulu*] (Turner 1992: 48).

-I-

Itumeleng (f) *[ih-tuh-meh-leh-ndgh]* "Be happy": a name such as given to a newborn by its mother to indicate that she is overjoyed with the birth of this girl [*Sotho*] (Herbert 1990: 9).

Itumeleng (f) *[ih-tuh-meh-leh-ndgh]* "Rejoice": a name such as given to a newborn by its mother to indicate her hope that the birth of this child will cement and add happiness to the marriage [*Tswana*] (Herbert 1997: 8; Herbert 1995: 3; Herbert 1990: 9).

Iwaasakiya (f) *[ih-waah-sah-kih-yah]* A satirical name such as given by the family midwife to a newborn whose mother "has no respect for her husband who is meek and humble towards her" [*Fipa*] (Willis 1982: 230).

-J-

Jabhile (f/m) *[jah-bih-leh]* "They are disappointed": a name such as given to a newborn by the mother who had consistently maintained that she would eventually bear a child despite the criticism directed to her by her in-laws-- the name symbolizes vindicating herself against her now disproved and disappointed in-laws who had for years caused her suffering and indignity as they denounced her for being childless [*Zulu*] (Turner 1992: 49).

Jabu (f) *[jah-buh]* A pet form of the name *Jabulisiwe*: "Happiness" [*Zulu*] (Koopman 1987: 155).

Jabulani (m) *[jah-buh-lah-nih]* "Be happy" [*Zulu*] (Herbert 1997: 8).

Jabulani (m) *[jah-buh-lah-nih]* "Be ye happy (i.e. for the birth of this child)" [*Zulu*] (Koopman 1987: 150, 151).

Jabulisiwe (f) *[jah-buh-lih-sih-weh]* "Happiness" [*Zulu*] (Koopman 1987: 151, 155).

Jamhuri (m) *[jahm-huh-rih]* "Republic": a name associated with independence or the formation of a republic (of *Tanzania*) so is appropriate for one born on or associated with this day [*Pare, Swahili* and several other ethnics of eastern and central Africa] (Herbert 1997: 10; Omari 1970: 66).

Joklieth (m) *[johk-lih-yeh-sth]* An ox name [*Nuer*] (Evans-Pritchard 1948: 169).

Jongilanga (m) *[john-gih-lahn-gah]* "Starer at the sun" [*Xhosa*] (Wainwright 1986: 297).

Jore (f) *[joh-reh]* "Full": a name commonly given to a second born of female twins, the first born named *Bojo* [*Bari*] (Whitehead 1947: 45).

Jwan (f) *[jwahn]* A name commonly given to a third born amongst several
(at least four) female siblings that have fortunately survived death [*Bari*]
(Whitehead 1947: 45).

-K-

Kaabuto (m) *[kaah-buh-toh]* The little one that is associated with the young
[*Ganda*].

Kaagya (m) *[kaah-jah]* The little one that became fitting/ suitable/ appropriate [*Ganda*].

Kaakulira (m) *[kaah-kuh-lih-rah]* The little one that grew up/ or matured at
(or in); the little one that was in charge of (such as a department or organ-
ization) [*Ganda, Soga*].

Kaaluba (m) *[kaah-luh-bah]* The little one having a peculiarity of his jaws
[*Ganda, Soga*].

Kaamudda (m) *[kaah-muhd-dah]* The little one that is of a return; the little
one that is of a coming up (of crops) [*Ganda*].

Kaamunvi (m) *[kaah-muhn-vih]* That is in/ or has to do with gray hair (of
the head) [*Ganda*].

Kaasabbanda (m) *[kaah-sahb-bahn-dah]* "The little one splits the hollow-
stemmed perennial mountain bamboo" [*Ganda*].

Kaasandege (m) *[kaah-sahn-deh-geh]* "The little one splits the small bell-
like ornament" [*Ganda*].

Kaat (m) *[kaaht]* A name given to the second born following the birth of his
twin siblings [*Nuer*] (Whitehead 1947: 46).

Kaatatta (m) *[kaah-taht-tah]* "That which he (or she) does not kill" [*Ganda*].

Kaawannaku (m) *[kaah-wahn-nah-kuh]* The little one that is of an environment of trouble (or sorrow, or sadness) [*Ganda*].

Kaaweeru (m) *[kaah-weh-eh-ruh]* The little one that is in (or of) lightness/ or
brightness/ or clearness/ or a white environment (or place) [*Ganda*].

Kaayabula (m) *[kaah-yah-buh-lah]* The little one that departed (or left, or
lived through, or went through, or traversed); the little one that dismissed
(such as a meeting) [*Ganda*].

Kaayi (m) *[kaah-yih]* Little marauder (or plunderer, or pillager); little
forager; small dried plantain fiber [*Ganda, Soga*].

Kabaalekasu (m) *[kah-baah-leh-kah-suh]* "A small stone that is hot" [*Soga*].

Kabaalu (m) *[kah-baah-luh]* The little one that is screeching (or raucous, or
wild, or uncontrollable); a small uproar [*Ganda*].

Kabaazi (m) *[kah-baah-zih]* Little butcher (or flayer, or surgeon) [*Ganda*].

Kababembe (m) *[kah-bah-behm-beh]* The little one that is of the *Bembe*
ethnics; that of those with crusts (on burnt food); that of those with burnt
portions adhering to the pans; that of those with (formations of) crusts or
scabs; that of those with coagulations; that of those with a swarming; that of

those with an abundance [*Ganda*].

Kababi/ Kaababi (m) *[kaah-bah-bih]* The little one of those that are bad (or evil, or dangerous, or in poor condition, or dirty, or ugly) [*Ganda, Soga*].

Kabagaane (f) *[kaah-bah-gaah-neh]* The little one that is of (or belongs to) those that are refused (or forbidden, or prevented, or denied, or withheld) [*Ganda*].

Kabagane (f) *[kaah-bah-gah-neh]* The little one that is of (or belongs to) those told (tales) of; the little one that is of (or belongs to) those that are allowed (or permitted, or given approval of, or authorized) [*Ganda*].

Kabagenzi (f/m) *[kaah-bah-gehn-zih]* The little one belonging to (or associated with) departed ones (or travelers) [*Ganda*].

Kabaggya (m) *[kaah-bahj-jah]* The little one that is of those who are new-comers (or recruits); the little one that is of those who are concubines (or second wives, or new wives in the household) [*Ganda*].

Kabagombe (m) *[kah-bah-gohm-beh]* The little one that is of (or is associated with) those that are complicated (or entangled) [*Ganda*].

Kabagyo (m) *[kah-bahj-joh]* That is fitting/ suitable/ appropriate; chip of wood; piece of carpentry work [*Ganda*].

Kabahima (f) *[kaah-bah-hih-mah]* Belonging to (or associated with) the *Hima* people [*Kiga, Nyankore, Nyoro, Toro*].

Kabahutu (f/m) *[kaah-bah-huh-tuh]* Belonging to (or associated with) the *Hutu* ethnics [*Kiga, Nyankore, Nyoro, Toro*].

Kabala (f) *[kah-bah-lah]* "Young" [*Rega*].

Kabalaba (m) *[kaah-bah-lah-bah]* The little one that is of (or belongs to) those that see (or perceive, or get, or are conscious, or are alert, or are awake, or are perceptive) [*Ganda*].

Kabali (m) *[kah-bah-lih]* One associated with small gluttons (or small eaters) [*Ganda*].

Kabambwe (m) *[kah-bahm-bweh]* That has been stretched out/ or pegged out (such as in the case of a skin to dry) [*Ganda*].

Kabandagala (m) *[kah-bahn-dah-gah-lah]* That takes a short time to cook; that is slightly cooked; that acts or does quickly; that is done quickly; that stays for a short time [*Ganda*].

Kabarundi (f) *[kah-bah-ruhn-dih]* Of (or associated with) the *Rundi* ethnics [*Kiga, Nyankore, Nyoro, Toro*].

Kabaseke (f) *[kah-bah-seh-keh]/* ***Kabasheke*** (f) *[kah-bah-tsh-eh-keh]* "Let them laugh (or smile) (at me)" [*Kiga, Nyankore, Nyoro, Toro*].

Kabashi (f/m) *[kah-bah-tsh-ih]* Of (or associated with) the *Bashi* ethnics [*Kiga, Nyankore, Nyoro, Toro*].

Kabasumba (m) *[kaah-bah-suhm-bah]* The little one affiliated with herds-men (or shepherds, or religious service) [*Ganda*].

Kabatanya (f) *[kaah-bah-tah-ndjh-ah]* The little one associated with (or belonging to) those that cause to deteriorate (or make worse, or cause to become infected, or cause to fester) [*Ganda*].

Kabattanya (f) *[kaah-baht-tah-ndjh-ah]* The little one of those that damage (or ruin, or spoil) [*Ganda*].

Kabatwa (f) *[kaah-bah-twah]* Of (or associated with) the *Twa* ethnics [*Kiga, Nyankore, Nyoro, Toro*].

Kabayonga (f/m) *[kaah-bah-yohn-gah]* The little one of (or belonging to) the Large Black Ant (*Kinyomo*) clan; the little one of (or belonging to) those that char (or burn) food; the little one of (or belonging to) those that produce sparks from a fire; the little one of (or belonging to) those that tailor fucus cloth [*Ganda*].

Kabemba (m) *[kah-behm-bah]* Small crust (on burnt food); burnt portion adhering to the pan; (small formation of) a crust or scab; a coagulation; a swarming; an abundance [*Ganda*].

Kabengaano (f) *[kah-beh-ndgh-aah-noh]* The little one that is of (or associated with) those with wheat [*Ganda*].

Kabennano (f) *[kah-behn-nah-noh]* Attractive; fitting; appropriate; suitable [*Ganda*].

Kabereega (m) *[kah-beh-eh-reh-eh-gah]* That of those who quarrel (or are insolent, or make a fuss); that of those who become stretched (or taut, or tightened) [*Ganda*].

Kabibi (f/m) *[kah-bih-bih]* Fat and beautiful child; (small) mound of earth (more so that on which sweet potatoes are planted) [*Ganda*].

Kabigya (f) *[kah-bih-jah]* One who puts on a surly face [*Ganda*].

Kabiriko (f) *[kah-bih-rih-koh]* "Your small body"; "the little one is on (or upon) it" [*Ganda*].

Kabiswa (m) *[kaah-bih-swah]* That is genuine (or pure); that is of (or is associated with) termite hills/ termites [*Ganda*].

Kabona (m) *[kah-boh-nah]* Priest [*Kiga, Nyankore, Nyoro, Toro*].

Kabuka/ Kabuuka (m) *[kah-buuh-kah]* The little one that jumps [*Ganda*].

Kabulidde (f) *[kah-buh-lihd-deh]* "The little one has eaten (or consumed) them"; "the little one has taken up high office"; "the little one has disappeared / become lost/ gone astray in (or at)" [*Ganda*].

Kabungo (f) *[kah-buhn-goh]* A species of forest tree that is well liked [The *Rega*].

Kabungulu (f) *[kah-buh-nguh-luh]* An esteemed wild animal [*Rega*].

Kabuye (m) *[kah-buh-yeh]* The little one abducted (by the spirit); small stone [*Ganda*].

Kabwire/ Kabwiire (m) *[kaah-bwiih-reh]* That of the night [*Soga*].

Kabyuuma (m) *[kah-bjuuh-mah]* The little one that is associated with machines (or metals) [*Ganda, Soga*].

Kadama/ Kadaama (f/m) *[kah-daah-mah]* That takes refuge (or takes shelter, or dwells) [*Soga*].

Kaddugala (f/m) *[kahd-duh-gah-lah]* The little one that is black (or becomes darkened); the little one of negroid pigmentation [*Ganda*].

Kadhuli (m) *[kah-tdh-uuh-lih]* One that reprimands [*Soga*].

Kadhumbula (m) *[kah-tdh-uhm-buh-lah]* That takes great interest in; that is diligent in; that is zealous about; that causes to be zealous about; that causes to quarrel (or to become furious, or to become vexed) [*Soga*].

Kadoli (f/m) *[kah-doh-lih]* Small bed pan; that talks on and on [The *Ganda*, *Soga*].

Kaduuli (m) *[kah-duuh-lih]* Hemp seed [*Soga*].

Kaduumya (m) *[kah-duuh-mjah]* That grows rapidly; that springs up rapidly; that commands/ orders (e.g. the police and the military) [*Ganda*, *Soga*].

Kadyeebo (m) *[kah-djeh-eh-boh]* A deception; a lie [*Ganda*].

Kafi (m) *[kah-fih]* A name given to a second born [*Nuba*] (Seligman 1932: 386).

Kafudde (f/m) *[kah-fuhd-deh]* The little one that has become useless (or become spoilt, or become sour); the little one that has been destroyed (or has died, or has been killed); the little one that has got into trouble (or is in a jam, or has got out of order) [*Ganda*].

Kafuko (f/m) *[kah-fuh-koh]* Case for carrying arrows; bag; purse [*Soga*].

Kafunvu (m) *[kah-fuhn-vuh]* Persevering; persistent; the little one that is self exerting; the little one that is insistent [*Ganda*].

Kagaata (m) *[kah-gaah-tah]* That sits in a sprawled out legged manner [The *Soga*].

Kagali (m) *[kah-gah-lih]* Monetary gift offered to a God; basket in which the sacrificial gift money is placed; (small) camel foot tree from which both dye and a substitute for soap are obtained; (small) flat tray that is made from the fibers of papyrus or other plants, and is often used for winnowing [*Ganda*].

Kagayo (m) *[kah-gah-yoh]* That involves scorn (or despising, or having contempt for) [*Ganda*, *Soga*].

Kagombe (m) *[kah-gohm-beh]* That is tied crosswise (or plaited with reeds); (small) place of the dead; grave [*Ganda*, *Soga*].

Kagwa (f/m) *[kah-gwah]* Small rope; string; tape [*Ganda*].

Kagya (f/m) *[kah-jah]* That is fitting/ suitable/ appropriate [*Ganda*].

Kahaya (f/m) *[kah-hah-yah]* Of (or associated with) the *Haya* ethnics [*Kiga*, *Nyankore*, *Nyoro*, *Toro*].

Kahiji (m) *[kah-hih-jih]* Name of a deity [*Kiga*, *Nyankore*, *Nyoro*, *Toro*].

Kahlifah (m) *[kah-lih-fah]* Holy child; successor; viceroy [*Swahili*].

Kahutu (f/m) *[kah-huh-tuh]* One of (or one associated with) the *Hutu* ethnics [*Kiga*, *Nyankore*, *Nyoro*, *Toro*].

Kaihuzi (m) *[kahy-huh-zih]* Name of a spirit medium [The *Kiga*, *Nyankore*, *Nyoro*, *Toro*].

Kaijabahoire (f/m) *[kahy-jah-bah-hoy-reh]* That is born (or comes) when most of the family is dead (i.e. "finished") [*Kiga*, *Nyankore*, *Nyoro*, *Toro*].

Kaijamurubi (m) *[kahy-jah-muh-ruh-bih]* That is born during/ or comes during times of trouble [*Kiga*, *Nyankore*, *Nyoro*, *Toro*].

Kaima/ Kayima (m) *[kah-yih-mah]* One that stands up (or comes forth) on behalf of another; sponsor; patron; member of (or relative of, or one associated with) the aristocratic cattle keeping ethnics called the *Hima*; name-title of a chief (of *Mawokota*) [*Ganda*, *Soga*].

Kairu (m) *[kahy-ruuh]* Servant; member of the cultivator social class as opposed to the aristocratic cattle keeping class; captive [The *Kiga, Nyankore, Nyoro, Soga, Toro*].

Kaiterebye (m) *[kahy-teh-reh-bjeh]* "Your property is destroyed by your own people" [*Kiga, Nyankore, Nyoro, Toro*].

Kajjumbula (m) *[kahj-juhm-buh-lah]* That takes great interest in; that is diligent in; that is zealous about; that causes to be zealous about [*Ganda*].

Kajumbula (m) *[kah-juhm-buh-lah]* That takes great interest in; that is diligent in; that is zealous about; that causes to be zealous about; that causes to quarrel (or to become furious, or to become vexed) [*Ganda*].

Kaka (f) *[kah-kah]* A name given to a first born [*Nuba*] (Seligman 1932: 387).

Kakakungu (m) *[kah-kah-kuhn-guh]* That of (or belonging to) a high ranking chief, official, or dignitary [*Ganda*].

Kakale (m) *[kah-kah-leh]* That is a small cloud; that is all right; that is thick and dense; that is public (or communal); that has become dry (or dried up); that has withered; that has stiffened (or grown rigid); that has become well established; that has become firm (or resolute); that stands up for oneself; that has died [*Ganda*].

Kakembo (m) *[kah-kehm-boh]* (Small) monkey; a strut about in a proud and pompous manner; doubling one's effort [*Ganda, Soga*].

Kakiwe (f/m) *[kah-kih-weh]* "Surrounded": a name such as given to a newborn to serve as a reminder that a family dispute that took place several months ago has not as yet been resolved, hence the family is still immersed and surrounded in dispute [*Zulu*] (Turner 1992: 52).

Kako (f) *[kah-koh]/* **Kako-Diong** (f) *[kah-koh-dih-yoh-ndgh]* A name denoting misfortune that is commonly given to one who lost one older sibling (usually sister) to death [*Bari*] (Whitehead 1947: 45).

Kakuma (m) *[kah-kuh-mah]* Corner or angle; that makes a fire; that blows on a fire to keep it going; that gathers together; that piles together; that heaps up [*Ganda, Soga*].

Kakumbwa (m) *[kah-kuhm-bwah]* One who is often blamed for others' misdeeds [*Rega*].

Kalekezi (f/m) *[kah-leh-keh-eh-zih]* Little elite defender of the country [*Kiga, Nyankore, Nyoro, Toro*].

Kalemeera/ Kalemeera (f/m) *[kah-leh-meh-eh-rah]* "The one that is heavy"; that remains stalled; that remains at a standstill; that refuses to budge; that gets stuck; that refuses to go [*Ganda, Kiga, Nyankore, Nyoro, Toro*].

Kalibakate (f) *[kah-lih-bah-kah-teh]* Skin hide of a small cow (or calf); that will turn out to be a strong and healthy calf [*Ganda*].

Kalibakya (f) *[kah-lih-bah-tch-ah]* "It will dawn (upon you)"; "(the rain) will let up"; "(the famine) will end" [*Ganda*].

Kalibata (m) *[kah-lih-bah-tah]* A walk; a tread; a step on [*Ganda*].

Kalibbala (m) *[kah-lihb-bah-lah]* Bearing (ripe) fruit; having spots (on the skin) [*Ganda*].

Kalibu (m) *[kah-lih-buh]* Small gap/ breach (such as of the teeth); "come in!"

[*Ganda, Soga*].

Kaliga (m) *[kah-lih-gah]* Lamb; small sheep [*Ganda, Soga*].

Kaligijjo (m) *[kah-lih-gihj-joh]* Playing; romping; frolicking [*Ganda*].

Kaligya (m) *[kah-lih-jah]* That will be fitting/ suitable/ appropriate [*Ganda*].

Kaliibwa (f/m) *[kah-liih-bwah]* Edible; that is fit for consumption; that is eaten (or consumed) [*Ganda, Soga*].

Kaliibwane (f/m) *[kah-liih-bwah-neh]* "It is eaten with"; "it is eaten in spite of"; with a long piece of cloth worn as underwear clothing [*Ganda*].

Kaliika (f/m) *[kah-liih-kah]* Edible; fit for consumption [*Ganda, Soga*].

Kaliimi (m) *[kah-liih-mih]* A lookout; a spying policeman; that lies in wait for [*Ganda*].

Kaliisa (m) *[kah-liih-sah]* Lark; pipit; yellow wagtail [*Ganda*].

Kaliiti (m) *[kah-liih-tih]* Snare for trapping antelopes and warthogs [*Ganda*].

Kalikuwona (m) *[kah-lih-kuh-woh-nah]* "The little one is getting healed (or cured)"; "the little one is getting saved"; "the little one is escaping from" [*Ganda, Soga*].

Kalikuwoona (m) *[kah-lih-kuh-woh-oh-nah]* "The little one is pursuing"; "the little one is claiming"; "the little one is seeking" [*Ganda*].

Kalimanama (m) *[kah-lih-mah-nah-mah]* "Cultivator of Animals" [*Lamba*] (Doke 1931: 146).

Kalubaale (m) *[kah-luh-baah-leh]* Little native God/ deity; of God/ a deity [*Ganda, Soga*].

Kalugendo/ Kaalugendo (m) *[kaah-luh-gehn-doh]* The little one of (or associated with) a trip/ or voyage/ or journey [*Ganda*].

Kalugye (m) *[kah-luh-jeh]* "Let it (or may it) be fitting/ suitable/ appropriate"; "may it correspond (or fit, or be equivalent)" [*Ganda*].

Kalule (m) *[kah-luh-leh]* That is associated with light clouds (or scattered clouds, or rain); that is caused to develop an appetite; that is caused to have a lucky escape [*Ganda*].

Kalundi (m) *[kah-luhn-dih]* Tended; herded; kept in view; small *Rundi* ethnic [*Ganda*].

Kalutte (m) *[kah-luht-teh]* "May it (or let it) ruin (or kill, or cancel, or destroy)"; "it goes on ruining (or killing, or destroying)" [*Ganda*].

Kaluuma (m) *[kah-luuh-mah]* Small metal wire [*Ganda*].

Kalwana (m) *[kah-lwaah-nah]* The little one belonging to fighting; the little one that fights [*Kiga, Nyankore, Nyoro, Toro*].

Kalwanyi/ Kalwaanyi (m) *[kah-lwaah-ndjh-ih]* Little fighter; the little one that fights or struggles towards a goal [*Ganda*].

Kalwe/ Kkalwe (m) *[kkah-lweh]* Iron; steel [*Ganda*].

Kamaanyiro (m) *[kah-maah-ndjh-ih-roh]* Where there is plucking off/ or out (of feathers, or hair) [*Ganda*].

Kamabati (f) *[kah-mah-baah-tih]* The little one of (or born under) corrugated iron roofing [*Kiga, Nyankore, Nyoro, Toro*].

Kamakya (m) *[kah-mah-tch-ah]* That of dawn; that of the time of (the rain) letting up; that of the end (of famine) [*Ganda*].

Kamalebo (m) *[kah-mah-leh-boh]* One who cherishes being young and youthful *[Rega]*.

Kamamba/ Kammamba (m) *[kahm-mahm-bah]* The little one associated with lung fish; plantain used for making beer *[Ganda]*.

Kamanga (m) *[kah-mahn-gah]* Fish *[Rega]*.

Kambayaaya (m) *[kahm-bah-yaah-yah]* Insolence; impudence *[Ganda]*.

Kambe (m) *[kahm-beh]* Locally made knife normally used for peeling and cutting food crops; this name is sometimes associated with the proverb "the stone anvil that is instrumental in forging the needle, also helps forge the knife" implying that a mother's position in the world is paramount, as synonymous with "the hand that rocks the cradle, rules the world"; this name is also sometimes associated with the proverb "a man whose occupation is cutting salt and extracting salt from it, depends on his knife for his livelihood" implying that every income earner fundamentally has a device on which his earnings depend *[Ganda]*.

Kambuya (m) *[kaahm-buh-yah]* Silliness *[Ganda, Soga]*.

Kamihanda (f) *[kah-mih-haahn-dah]* One associated with roads: name of one born while parent was traveling (or on the way to the hospital to deliver) *[Kiga, Nyankore, Nyoro, Toro]*.

Kamira (m) *[kah-mih-rah]* To milk for (or in); "the little one that swallows" *[Soga]*.

Kamirante (m) *[kah-mih-rahn-teh]* "Milk for the cow(s)"; "that swallows cows" *[Ganda, Soga]*.

Kammanje (m) *[kahm-mahn-jeh]* (One that is associated with) that which is demanded of payment of a debt *[Ganda]*.

Kamr (m) *[kah-mrh]* This name of part of a scaffolding of a building is associated with wrestling, so can be appropriate for one who is skilled in the sport *[Nuba]* (Seligman 1932: 387).

Kamulali/ Kaamulali (m) *[kaah-muh-lah-lih]* (Hot) pepper *[Ganda, Soga]*.

Kamuntu/ Kaamuntu (f/m) *[kaah-muhn-tuh]* Beloved; sweetheart; darling *[Kiga, Nyankore, Nyoro, Toro]*.

Kamunya (m) *[kah-muh-ndjh-ah]* The little one of (or attributed to) the lizard *[Ganda]*.

Kamurasi (m) *[kah-muh-rah-sih]* That of shooting (or the archer, or the rifleman) *[Kiga, Nyankore, Nyoro, Toro]*.

Kanaaba (m) *[kah-naah-bah]* "That will be"; that washes oneself; that cleans up; that gets easy money *[Ganda, Soga]*.

Kanaabi (m) *[kah-naah-bih]* That washes oneself; that cleans up; that gets easy money *[Ganda, Soga]*.

Kanaggye (m) *[kahn-nahj-jeh]* The little one that is of the army (or ground forces) *[Ganda]*.

Kanamakampanga (f/m) *[kah-nah-mah-kahm-pahn-gah]* "Little Buck of the Veldt" *[Lamba]* (Doke 1931: 146).

Kanamalesanja (m) *[kah-naah-mah-lehs-sahn-jah]* "That which will finish off (or be adequate for) the dry (or withered) plantain leaves" *[Ganda]*.

Kanene (m) *[kah-neh-neh]* The little one that is big (or large) [*Ganda, Soga*].

Kangaawo (m) *[kahn-gaah-woh]* Name-title of a chief of *Bulemeezi*; "frighten/ scare/ startle/ threaten there (or then, or thereupon)" [*Ganda*].

Kanhago (m) *[kah-ndh-ah-goh]/* *Kanyago* (m) *[kah-ndjh-ah-goh]* The shaft of a spear [*Soga*].

Kanjuki/ Kanjuchi (m) *[kahn-juh-tch-ih]* Of (or attributed to) the bee [The *Ganda*].

Kannamuwangi (m) *[kahn-nah-muh-wahn-jih]* That is associated with one that is in many places [*Ganda, Soga*].

Kannanda (m) *[kahn-nahn-dah]* That is associated with a wife (or a woman); that looks attractive; that is well dressed; that is spruced up; that is well done [*Ganda*].

Kannyanjwa (m) *[kahn-ndjh-ahn-jwah]* Associated with a spread out (or an unfolding, or a beginning); that associated with presenting (such as a proposal); that associated with the bringing up (of a matter) [*Ganda*].

Kansigaire (m) *[kaahn-sih-gaahy-reh]/* *Kansigairemu* (m) *[kaahn-sih-gahy-reh-muh]* "I am still doubtful (despite the prevailing circumstances)"; "the bit of doubting remains in me" [*Kiga, Nyankore, Nyoro, Toro*].

Kansiime (m) *[kaahn-siih-meh]* "Let me acknowledge (God) with gratitude" [*Kiga, Nyankore, Nyoro, Toro*].

Kansiime-Ruhanga (m) *[kaahn-siih-meh-ruh-hahn-gah]* "Let me (or may I) acknowledge God with gratitude" [*Kiga, Nyankore, Nyoro, Toro*].

Kansolya (m) *[kahn-soh-ljah]* The little one that is associated with the roofs of houses; the little one that is associated with heads of clans [*Ganda, Soga*].

Kantinti (m) *[kahn-tihn-tih]* That of abundance; that of a large amount; the little one that flourishes/ prospers; that of a proliferation (of plants) [The *Ganda*].

Kanya (m) *[kah-ndjh-aah]* An abundance; an increase; (small) lizard [The *Ganda*].

Kanyakula (m) *[kah-ndjh-ah-kuh-lah]* "Killer at One Shot" [*Lamba*] (Doke 1931: 146).

Kanyanya (f) *[kah-ndjh-ah-ndjh-ah]* Little sister [*Ganda*].

Kanyeenye (m) *[kah-ndjh-eh-eh-ndjh-eh]* The little one that is shaken (or moved, or moved to and fro) [*Ganda*].

Kanyeenyenkule (m) *[kah-ndjh-eh-eh-ndjh-ehn-kuh-leh]* Small cricket [The *Ganda*].

Kanyenye (m) *[kah-ndjh-eh-ndjh-eh]* The little one that is set on edge; the little one that experiences a sharp sensation (in the teeth) [*Ganda*].

Kanyerezi/ Kanyeerezi (m) *[kah-ndjh-eh-eh-reh-zih]* Soft to touch; shiny; oily [*Ganda*].

Kanyiga (m) *[kah-ndjh-ih-gah]* The little one that presses (or jostles, or pushes together); the little one that oppresses [*Ganda*].

Kanyiikuuli (f) *[kah-ndjh-iih-kuuh-lih]* Trifle; that is tiny; that is insignificant [*Ganda*].

Kanyike (m) *[kah-ndjh-ih-keh]* That is sad (or sorrowful); sadness; sorrow [*Ganda*].

Kanyolo (m) *[kah-ndjh-oh-loh]* Small drumstick; door handle [*Ganda*].

Kanyonyi (f/m) *[kah-ndjh-oh-ndjh-ih]* Chief collector of market dues; caretaker of a rest camp; small bird [*Ganda*].

Kanyoro (f) *[kah-ndjh-oh-roh]* One of/ or one associated with the *Nyoro* ethnics [*Ganda*].

Kanywamugule (m) *[kah-ndjh-wah-muh-guh-leh]* "One that drinks (or absorbs) that which has been bought" [*Ganda*].

Kanywamusaayi (m) *[kah-ndjh-wah-muh-saah-yih]* "That drinks (or absorbs) blood" [*Ganda*].

Kanywanyi (m) *[kah-ndjh-wah-ndjh-ih]* Little close friend [*Ganda*].

Kanzige (m) *[kahn-zih-geh]* That is of the locusts [*Ganda, Soga*].

Kapaacha/ Kapaaca (f) *[kah-paah-tch-ah]* One who moves about excitedly; a small slap (or smack) [*Ganda*].

Kapuki (f) *[kah-puh-kih]* A name commonly given to a first born amongst several (at least four) female siblings that have fortunately survived death [*Bari*] (Whitehead 1947: 45).

Karabo (m) *[kah-rah-boh]* Response: a name such as given to a newborn by its father to indicate that this child is a response to what he has longed for-- a child, especially a boy who will carry on the family name [The *Tswana*] (Herbert 1995: 3; Herbert 1990: 10).

Karibara (m) *[kah-riih-bah-rah]* Bearing (ripe) fruit; having spots (on the skin) [*Kiga, Nyankore, Nyoro, Toro*].

Karugyendo (f/m) *[kah-ruh-jeh-ehn-doh]* The little one of (or associated with) a trip (or voyage, or journey) [*Kiga, Nyankore, Nyoro, Toro*].

Karuhanga (m) *[kaah-ruh-haahn-gah]* Belonging to God; intelligent [*Kiga, Nyankore, Nyoro, Toro*].

Karukiko (f/m) *[kah-rug-tch-iih-koh]* Of the council (which traditionally meets on Monday, so can imply one born on Monday) [The *Kiga, Nyankore, Nyoro, Toro*].

Karundi (f/m) *[kah-ruhn-dih]* Of/ or associated with the *Rundi* ethnics; "little *Rundi*" [*Kiga, Nyankore, Nyoro, Toro*].

Kasaabanda (m) *[kah-saah-bahn-dah]* "It causes the death of the one who attempts to cut across (or make one's way)" [*Ganda*].

Kasaaga/ Kasaga (m) *[kah-saah-gah]* That jokes (or jesters) [*Ganda*].

Kasaanya (m) *[kah-saah-ndjh-ah]* That makes suitable (or fitting); that merits [*Ganda*].

Kasangwira (m) *[kah-sahn-gwih-rah]* A force (such as a storm or strong wind) that fells or knocks down bunches of bananas from their trees [The *Ganda*].

Kasedde (m) *[kah-sehd-deh]* That has milled (or ground) [*Ganda*].

Kaseegu (m) *[kah-seh-eh-guh]* Dissolute (or wasteful, or shameless) person; that is wild in behavior [*Ganda*].

Kaseekende (m) *[kah-seh-eh-kehn-deh]* That is accused (or denounced) [The

Ganda].

Kaserula (f/m) *[kah-seh-ruh-lah]* One who pushes forward bit by bit (imperceptibly) [*Ganda*].

Kasese (m) *[kah-seh-seh]* Red tailed finch [*Ganda*].

Kaseyeeye (m) *[kah-seh-yeh-eh-yeh]* That drifts (or floats, or glides, or soars, or cruises along) [*Ganda*].

Kashibondo (f) *[kah-shiih-bohn-doh]* "Nice girl" [*Rega*].

Kashumba (m) *[kah-tsh-uhm-bah]* "Little cattle herder" [*Kiga, Nyankore, Nyoro, Toro*].

Kasi (m) *[kah-sih]* Small country (or land) [*Ganda, Soga*].

Kasiba (f) *[kah-sih-bah]* Moderator [*Rega*].

Kasibante (m) *[kah-sih-bahn-teh]* Cattle keeper [*Ganda*].

Kasibbali (m) *[kah-sihb-bah-lih]* "The small land (or country) aside" [The *Ganda*].

Kasiga (m) *[kah-sih-gah]* Small cooking stone; that sows (or plants seeds in); the little one of the planting season [*Ganda*].

Kasiira (m) *[kah-siih-rah]* Plaited reed work; reed fence that is upright and close together; that walks slowly or casually [*Ganda, Soga*].

Kasiiro (m) *[kah-siih-roh]* Plaited reed work; a slow or casual walk [*Ganda, Soga*].

Kasiiswa (m) *[kah-siih-swah]* That is caused to walk slowly (or to stroll) [*Ganda*].

Kasiita (m) *[kah-siih-tah]* One who rolls around on the ground; one who plays a game involving red seeds [*Ganda*].

Kasiiwuukira (m) *[kah-siih-wuuh-kih-rah]* With a dry/ or pale skin (or one that lacks luster) [*Ganda*].

Kasimaggwa (m) *[kah-sih-mahg-gwah]* "Small land of thorns" [*Ganda*].

Kasimba (f/m) *[kah-sihm-bah]* Genet cat; small animal; small lion [*Ganda*].

Kasimbi (m) *[kah-sihm-bih]* Genet cat; the little one that erects foundations (or pillars, or poles) [*Ganda*].

Kasindi (m) *[kah-sihn-dih]* A child whose hand emerged first when being given birth to [*Rega*].

Kasindula (m) *[kah-sihn-duh-lah]* That uproots; that overturns; that overthrows [*Ganda*].

Kasinga (f/m) *[kah-sihn-gah]* One that is of the *Basinga* clan [*Ganda*].

Kasiriivu (m) *[kah-sih-riih-vuh]* One hundred thousand; that is burnt to smithereens; (food or meat) that is burned (or scorched); that is roasted; that is wasted [*Ganda*].

Kasirye (m) *[kah-sih-rjeh]* That is rubbed smooth [*Ganda*].

Kasisaki (f) *[kah-sih-sah-tch-ih]* One who pulls at or seizes by force; one who struggles [*Ganda*].

Kasobozi (m) *[kah-soh-boh-zih]* Enabler; commissioner; authorizer; one who empowers (to happen or for good results to be achieved) [*Ganda*].

Kasobya (m) *[kah-soh-bjah]* That makes a mistake; that errs; that causes to exceed (or go in excess of); that spoils (or injures); that rapes [*Ganda*].

Kasole (m) *[kah-soh-leh]* That which is dug up (or harvested); that which is dropped [*Ganda*].

Kasoma (m) *[kah-soh-mah]* The little studious one; religious practitioner; student; intellectual [*Ganda, Soga*].

Kasomba (m) *[kah-sohm-bah]* The little one that collects (or brings) together [*Ganda, Soga*].

Kasondeke (f) *[kah-sohn-deh-keh]* Contribution; gathered together, little by little [*Ganda*].

Kasongovu (m) *[kah-sohn-goh-vuh]* That is sharpened (or pointed); that comes to a point; that puts on airs; that is proud [*Ganda, Soga*].

Kasonseka (m) *[kah-sohn-seh-kah]* That inserts (or slips in, or puts in, or pushes in) [*Ganda*].

Kasookolindo (m) *[kah-soh-oh-koh-lihn-doh]* Excrement of fowls [*Ganda*].

Kasota (m) *[kah-soh-tah]* Little snake [*Ganda, Soga*].

Kasozi (m) *[kah-soh-zih]* Small hill [*Ganda*].

Kassammeeme (m) *[kahs-sahm-meh-eh-meh]* That relaxes (or cools down) the soul (or heart, or seat of emotions) [*Ganda*].

Kassesse (m) *[kahs-sehs-seh]* One associated with the red tailed finch; one associated with *Ssese* Islands in Lake Victoria [*Hutu, Tutsi, Twa*].

Kassezzooba (m) *[kahs-sehz-zoh-oh-bah]* The lunar month [*Ganda*].

Kasujja (m) *[kah-suhj-jah]* Small fever [*Ganda*].

Kasujju (m) *[kah-suhj-juh]* Small pumpkin; name-title of the chief entrusted to taking care of being guardian to the princes; name-title of a chief (of *Busujju*) [*Ganda*].

Kasulamunkanja (m) *[kah-suh-lah-muhn-kahn-jah]* Llittle one that dwells in the dregs (or sediment) of millet in beer [*Ganda*].

Kasule (m) *[kah-suh-leh]* That spent the night; that remained; that lived; that dwelled [*Ganda*].

Kasulumba (m)· *[kah-suh-luhm-bah]* The little one that acts spoilt (or unruly); the little one that distances oneself from; the little one that avoids [The *Ganda*].

Kasumba (m) *[kah-suhm-bah]* Little herdsman; little shepherd; little bishop; little servant [*Ganda, Soga*].

Kasumbi (m) *[kah-suhm-bih]* Small pitcher [*Ganda*].

Kasunsa (m) *[kah-suhn-sah]* Leaf of the pumpkin (or vine gourd) that is used as relish [*Ganda*].

Kasuuti (m) *[kah-suuh-tih]* That is associated with a dress suit (as adapted from the European word "suit" [*Ganda, Soga*].

Kaswakizi (m) *[kah-swah-kih-zih]* The little one that is furious [*Ganda*].

Kaswaswa (m) *[kah-swah-swah]* Little monitor lizard; itching; paining; hurting; burning [*Ganda*].

Kata (m) *[kah-tah]* That lets go (or releases, or frees) [*Ganda*].

Kataakala (m) *[kah-taah-kah-lah]* That did not become firm (or resolute, or well established); that did not wither (or dry up, or waste away, or grow rigid) [*Ganda*].

Kataale (m) *[kah-taah-leh]* That will not spread (or increase, or multiply, or become abundant) [*Ganda*].

Katabira (m) *[kah-tah-bih-rah]* Puzzled; mislead; baffling; confusing; sprinkling of water (on fire) [*Ganda*].

Katabu (m) *[kah-tah-buh]* That is mixed up; that is confused; that is in turmoil; that is disturbed [*Ganda*].

Katabula (m) *[kah-tah-buh-lah]* The little one that mixes up (or confuses, or causes turmoil, or sets people against each other); the little one that does not disappear (or become lost, or go astray, or become missing, or become lacking) [*Ganda*].

Kataggwa (m) *[kah-tahg-gwah]* That does not cease (or end) [*Ganda*].

Kataggya (f/m) *[kah-tahj-jah]* That does not get fully cooked; that does not give in; that does not get exhausted; that does not take up [*Ganda*].

Katagwa (m) *[kah-tah-gwah]* That does not fall (or collapse) [*Ganda, Soga*].

Katagya (f/m) *[kah-tah-jah]* That is not fitting (or suitable, or appropriate, or corresponding); that does not fit into [*Ganda*].

Katajjwa (m) *[kah-tahj-jwah]* That is not come by; that is not come upon [*Ganda*].

Kataka (m) *[kah-tah-kah]* Little head of a clan or clan subdivision; little notable or respected resident [*Ganda, Soga*].

Katalaga (m) *[kah-tah-lah-gah]* That does not indicate (such as intention to arrive or depart); that does not point out; small interval [*Ganda*].

Katalama (m) *[kah-tah-lah-mah]* Species of bush (or tree) that grows to about six feet; one who squats with the knees apart; the little one that does not survive (after an illness); the little one that does not flourish; that does not turn out to be well done; the little one that does not remain in good health [*Ganda, Soga*].

Katale (m) *[kah-tah-leh]* Market; this name is sometimes associated with the proverb "barkcloths (for sale) that are bad (or in poor condition) are despisingly unwanted at the market place" implying that one is expected to act or show one's best while in public [*Ganda*].

Katalo (m) *[kah-tah-loh]* Small battle (or war); a small hex (or spell, or enchantment) [*Ganda*].

Katama (m) *[kah-tah-mah]* Small cheek; the little one that is disgusting; the little one that you get fed up with [*Ganda, Soga*].

Katamba (m) *[kah-tahm-bah]* Sacrifice for ritual purposes; execution; slaughter [*Ganda*].

Katambaala (m) *[kah-tahm-baah-lah]* Small cloth; napkin; handkerchief; the little one that stands up to (or against); the little one that faces up to (or confronts); the little one that dares (to) [*Ganda*].

Katambala (m) *[kah-tahm-bah-lah]* "The little one that does not count me in"; "the little one that does not consider me"; "the little one that does not regard me"; name-title of a chief (of *Butambala*) [*Ganda*].

Katamiira (m) *[kah-tah-miih-rah]* The little one that gets intoxicated; little drunkard [*Ganda, Soga*].

Katana (f/m) *[kah-tah-nah]* An inadvertent source of an accident; that causes to be infected (or to fester, or to grow septic) *[Ganda]*.

Katanda (m) *[kah-tahn-dah]* Carrier on the top of a vehicle; a crib; small bed; small crack; the little one that advances by climbing (or clinging to) an object; the little one that spreads; the little one that strides along *[Ganda, Soga]*.

Katangaza (m) *[kah-tahn-gah-zah]* That is amazing; that is dumfounding *[Ganda]*.

Katantazi (m) *[kah-tahn-tah-zih]* Little adventurer; the little one that goes here and there *[Ganda, Soga]*.

Katanyooleka (m) *[kah-tah-ndjh-oh-oh-leh-kah]* The little one that cannot be twisted; the little one that is not easy to twist *[Ganda]*.

Katassi (f) *[kah-tahs-sih]* Little spy; little scout *[Ganda]*.

Kataswa/ Kataaswa (m) *[kah-taah-swah]* The little one that is protected; the little one that defended *[Ganda, Soga]*.

Katatta (m) *[kah-taht-tah]* The little one that does not kill *[Ganda]*.

Katazza (m) *[kah-tahz-zah]* One who does not bring back; busybody; one who moves about, to and fro; one who paces up and down; one who gets ready for battle *[Ganda]*.

Kate (m) *[kah-teh]* Small cow *[Soga]*.

Katebe (m) *[kah-teh-beh]* Small chair; small stool *[Ganda]*.

Katebere (m) *[kah-teh-beh-reh]* That is outwitted (or foiled, or baffled); that is related about in detail; that is given an account of *[Ganda]*.

Kateeba (m) *[kah-teh-eh-bah]* One who hits the bull's eye or mark; that aims (at); that shoots (at); that hits the mark; that guesses (or conjectures); that counts on (or reckons on) *[Ganda]*.

Kateebe (m) *[kah-teh-eh-beh]* Bull's eye shot; boggy field; a quagmire [The *Ganda*].

Kateega (m) *[kah-teh-eh-gah]* The little one that lies in wait for (or is on the watch out for); that ambushes; the little one that bewitches (or hexes) [The *Ganda, Soga*].

Kateeko (m) *[kah-teh-eh-koh]* Tranquil; quiet; well set or put *[Ganda]*.

Kateenyooleka (m) *[kah-teh-eh-ndjh-oh-oh-leh-kah]* The little one that cannot be twisted; the little one that is not easy to twist; the little one that cannot be twisted around; the little one that is not easy to twist around [The *Ganda*].

Kateesigwa (m) *[kah-teh-eh-sih-gwah]* The little one that is not trustworthy (or reliable, or faithful) *[Ganda]*.

Kateete (m) *[kah-teh-eh-teh]* The little one that pants (or breathes) with difficulty; sickly; a net trap made of grass *[Ganda]*.

Kateetemera (m) *[kah-teh-eh-teh-meh-rah]* The little one that does not cut for himself *[Ganda]*.

Kateeteru (m) *[kah-teh-eh-teh-ruh]* The little one that pants (or breathes) with difficulty; sickly *[Ganda]*.

Katekaluusi/ Katekalusi (f/m) *[kah-teh-kah-luuh-sih]* A small cow (or a small domestic bovine that is female) [*Ganda, Soga*].

Katenda (m) *[kah-tehn-dah]* The little one that speaks well of; the little one that praises; the little one that commends; glorification; honor [*Ganda*].

Katende (m) *[kah-tehn-deh]* The little one that is relaxed; the little one that is at peace [*Ganda*].

Katenga (m) *[kah-tehn-gah]* Little drum player; the little one that wags (the tail); the little one that shakes; the little one that beats (with a barkcloth mallet) [*Ganda, Soga*].

Katengwa (m) *[kah-tehn-gwah]* That is disobeyed; that is not complied with [*Ganda, Soga*].

Katente (m) *[kah-tehn-teh]* Path (or ridge of earth) in front of the doorway of a hut; small basket net for catching lake flies [*Ganda*].

Kateranduulu (m) *[kah-teh-rahn-duuh-luh]* The little one that habitually (or who usually, or who quickly) utters a warning sound; the little one that is always on the brink of uttering a warning sound [*Ganda, Soga*].

Kateregga (m) *[kah-teh-rehg-gah]* Little prince of high rank that is a potential candidate to the kingship; the little one that talks slowly or drawlingly; little king [*Ganda*].

Katereza/ Katereeza (m) *[kah-teh-reh-eh-zah]* The little one that makes level (or smooth); the little one that puts straight; the little one that straightens out (e.g. a situation); the little one that corrects; the little one that pacifies; the little one that settles; the little one that organizes; the little one that puts in good condition [*Ganda*].

Katete (m) *[kah-teh-teh]* That is burnt; that is associated with the chief charged with supervising older men who guarded the area in the rear of the palace and cared for the plantain gardens of the king's womenfolk [*Ganda*].

Katibita (m) *[kah-tih-bih-tah]* Runner [*Rega*].

Katiginya (m) *[kah-tih-gih-ndjh-ah]* That is small (or tiny) [*Ganda*].

Katiiti (f/m) *[kah-tiih-tih]* Small bead; timid; fearful; one who is pampered or treated overindulgently [*Ganda*].

Katikamu (f) *[kah-tih-kah-muh]* One small tree; one small stick [*Ganda*].

Katimbiri (f) *[kah-tihm-bih-rih]* Decorated; showoff; the little one that exhibits oneself [*Ganda*].

Katimbo (m) *[kah-tihm-boh]* A small decoration; that which is hang up (such as a picture or curtain); that which is bound (or lashed) [*Ganda, Soga*].

Katimpa (m) *[kah-tihm-pah]* Leaf of the arum lily used as vegetables; "now give me" [*Ganda*].

Katittuba (m) *[kah-tiht-tuh-bah]* Small ficus barkcloth tree [*Ganda*].

Katleho (m) *[kaht-leh-loh]* Success [*Sotho*] (Thipa 1987: 114).

Kato (m) *[kah-toh]* The younger; the young; a name commonly given to a boy who is the second born of twins [*Ganda*].

Katoloba (m) *[kah-toh-loh-bah]* The little one that has a showdown with somebody; the little one that moves at great speed; the little one that races [*Ganda*].

Katomera (m) *[kah-toh-meh-rah]* The little one that runs into (or bumps into, or knocks into) *[Ganda, Soga]*.

Katondaayawula (f) *[kah-tohn-daah-yah-wuh-lah]* "It is God who distinguishes and cleanses (souls)" *[Ganda]*.

Katondayaamanyi (f) *[kah-tohn-dah-yaah-mah-ndjh-ih]* "It is God who knows" *[Ganda]*.

Katonera (f/m) *[kah-toh-neh-rah]* Very tiny ant that bites *[Ganda]*.

Katonga (m) *[kah-tohn-gah]* The little one that makes official; the little one that becomes official (or officially recognized); the little one that gives official approval to; the little one that recognizes (such as a foreign government) *[Ganda]*.

Katongero (m) *[kah-toh-ohn-geh-roh]* "The little young one is representative of several stories (or sayings)"; "the little young one is of (precise) measurements" *[Ganda]*.

Katongolo (m) *[kah-tohn-goh-loh]* "The little one is a gorilla (or bogey, or monstrous imaginary figure)" *[Ganda]*.

Katonnya (m) *[kah-tohn-ndjh-ah]* A small episode of rain; a small leak; a small drip; a small come down; a small drop *[Ganda]*.

Katoogo (m) *[kah-toh-oh-goh]* Small ebony tree; small stalk of papyrus; a patch of papyrus *[Ganda]*.

Katoologo (m) *[kah-toh-oh-loh-goh]* (Animal) that is aborted; an abortion (of an animal) *[Ganda]*.

Katotto (m) *[kah-toht-toh]* That is hesitant and indecisive; that goes into unnecessary detail; that relates in detail; that clarifies; that divulges [The Ganda].

Katta (m) *[kaht-tah]* The little one that kills (or murders, or destroys, or ruins, or abolishes, or cancels) *[Ganda]*.

Kattabu (m) *[kaht-taah-buh]* The little one that is of trouble (or difficulty, or hardship) *[Ganda]*.

Kattaggye (m) *[kaht-tahj-jeh]* "That destroys (or ruins) an army" *[Ganda]*.

Kattante (m) *[kaht-tahn-teh]* Cattle killer (such as a parasite, flooding, a marsh, or a drought) *[Ganda]*.

Katudde (m) *[kah-tuhd-deh]* The little one that remains seated (or dwelling, or residing) *[Ganda]*.

Katugga (m) *[kah-tuhg-gah]* Small giraffe; small bracelet *[Ganda]*.

Katulikira (m) *[kah-tuh-lih-kih-rah]* The little one that bursts out; the little one that breaks out all over *[Ganda]*.

Katuluba (m) *[kah-tuh-luh-bah]* The little one that becomes livid with rage; the little one that becomes swollen *[Ganda]*.

Katulugu (m) *[kah-tuh-luh-guh]* The little one that is treated harshly (or handled roughly); that is pressed firmly (or bound, or twisted, or fastened) *[Ganda]*.

Katulume (m) *[kah-tuh-luh-meh]* The banded mongoose; the little one that becomes livid with rage; the little one that is enraged *[Ganda]*.

Katuluntu (m) *[kah-tuh-luhn-tuh]* The little one that rummages (or hunts); a hunt; foraging [*Ganda*].

Katumba (m) *[kah-tuhm-bah]* The month of March; a species of swamp inhabiting fish; small bundle (of cloth); small porter's load; small burden [*Ganda*].

Katumwa (m) *[kah-tuh-mwah]* Messenger; the little one that is sent (or assigned, or commissioned) [*Ganda*].

Katunda (m) *[kah-tuhn-dah]* The passion fruit; fruit of the passion flower [*Ganda, Soga*].

Katuntu (m) *[kah-tuhn-tuh]* Water grass [*Ganda*].

Katuulakujjengo (m) *[kah-tuuh-lah-kuhj-jehn-goh]* The little one that sits (or stays) on the water wave [*Ganda*].

Katwanga (m) *[kah-twahn-gah]* Intone (of a hymn or song) [*Ganda*].

Katwe (m) *[kah-tweh]* Small head; small leader; heading; small chief [The *Ganda*].

Katwere (m) *[kah-tweh-reh]* Beer during the fermentation process [*Ganda*].

Kavebukasa (f) *[kah-veh-eh-buh-kah-sah]* The little one that comes from (or is associated with) *Bukasa* [*Ganda*].

Kaviiri (m) *[kah-viih-rih]* Small hair of the head [*Ganda*]

Kavubu (m) *[kah-vuh-buh]* Small hippopotamus [*Ganda*].

Kavulu (m) *[kah-vuh-luh]* The little one that becomes smeared (or filthy); the little one that looks furiously at; the little one that rolls; the little one that fidgets; the little one that stammers; the little one that abounds [*Ganda*].

Kavuma (m) *[kah-vuh-mah]* Profit; booty; that insults (or slanders) [*Ganda*].

Kawa/ Kaawa (f) *[kaah-wah]* A name of the originating Eve [*Ganda*].

Kawaase (m) *[kah-waah-seh]* "The knife has peeled off (the plantains)" [*Ganda*].

Keat (m) *[keh-yaht]* A species of riverside shrub [*Nuer*] (Evans-Pritchard 1948: 169).

Keledi (f) *[keh-leh-dih]* Tear [*Sotho*] (Herbert 1990: 10).

Kembwa (m) *[kehm-bwah]* The beloved [*Rega*].

Keneilwe (f) *[keh-nehy-lweh]* "(The child) has been given to us" [*Sotho*] (Thipa 1987: 109).

Kenna (f) *[kehn-nah]* A nickname-abbreviation for *Bukelwa*: "To be admired" [*Xhosa*] (Neethling 1994: 92).

Kgotso (m) *[kgoh-tsoh]* The peacemaker [*Sotho*] (Thipa 1987: 114).

Khaya (m) *[khah-yah]* A nickname-abbreviation for *Khayalethu*: "Our home" [*Xhosa*] (Neethling 1994: 92).

Khayalethu (m) *[khah-yah-leh-sth-uh]* Our home [*Xhosa*] (Neethling 1994: 92).

Khensani (m) *[kehn-sah-nih]* "Thanks": a name such as expressing gratitude for the birth of this child which can be the firstborn [*Tswana*] (Herbert 1995: 6).

Khephu (m) *[keh-poo]* Snow: a name such as given to one born during snow conditions [*Xhosa*] (Thipa 1986: 289).

Khethani (m) *[keh-tah-nih]* "Choose ye": a name such as given by a father to a child born soon after he was accused of stealing a goat, and the magistrate after finding him guilty told him to choose between jail and a fine [*Zulu*] (Koopman 1987: 152).

Khokela (m) *[koh-keh-lah]* "Lead"; "guide" [*Xhosa*] (Thipa 1987: 114).

Khuduego (m) *[kuh-dweh-goh]* "Riots": a name such as given to one born on a day of a political disturbance [*Tswana*] (Herbert 1995: 2; Herbert 1990: 8).

Khululisizwe (m) *[kuh-luh-lih-sih-zweh]* "Release the nation" [*Zulu*] (Herbert 1997: 11).

Khuphuyithi (m) *[kuh-puh-yih-tih]* "Get off!": a name such as given to one born out of wedlock or infidelity [*Xhosa*] (Thipa 1987: 112).

Kibira (f/m) *[tch-ih-bih-rah]* Forest; this name is sometimes associated with the proverbs "the young trees make the forests firm" and "the young trees are the forest" implying that children are the foundation and hope for the future so they ought to be carefully and adequately nourished, nurtured, and trained [*Ganda*].

Kibukila (m) *[kih-buh-kih-lah]* "Cover up" [*Rega*].

Kibungo (m) *[kih-buhn-goh]* One that is falsely accused [*Rega*].

Kiden (f) *[kih-dehn]* A name commonly given to a first born daughter among several (at least three) older male siblings [*Bari*] (Whitehead 1947: 45).

Kika (f/m) *[tch-ih-kah]* Clan; family; type; kind; deserted kraal; this name is sometimes associated with the proverb "a serf who becomes a member of the clan becomes (i.e. gets to take on the honorary title of) the 'father of twins' (i.e. *Ssaalongo*)" whereby aside from family connection, an one can traditionally become a clan member through such means as adoption, assimilation, long term residence, capture, and blood ritual; this name is also sometimes associated with the proverb "just that one person that violates the clan and totemic taboo by eating mudfish, gives the entire clan a bad reputation" which implies that just one person can cause a family or a community to have a bad reputation [*Ganda*].

Kikere (m) *[tch-ih-keh-reh]* Frog; this name is sometimes associated with the proverb "a miser is (like) the frog which hides its young (i.e. the tadpoles) in the water" implying that the stingy hardly expose their treasures [The *Ganda*].

Kiki (f) *[kih-kih]/* **Kikingori** (f) *[kih-kih-ndgh-oh-rih]* A name given to a fourth born [*Nuba*] (Seligman 1932: 387).

Kikumbu (m) *[kih-kuhm-buh]* "The elders' hat" [*Rega*].

Kilayo (m) *[kih-lah-yoh]* Supper [*Chaga*] (Raum 1967: 340).

Kilungu (m) *[kih-luhn-guh]* "Other people's medicine" [*Rega*].

Kimu (m) *[tch-ih-muh]* One (thing); this name is sometimes associated with the proverb "an only child is like a single rain cloud" implying that just like a single rain cloud that is unreliable since it will likely empty itself quickly and be followed by a hot and dry spell, the traditional African family prefers to have many children since the infant mortality rate is high [*Ganda*].

Kinyong (f) *[kih-ndjh-oh-ndgh]* Crocodile: a name denoting misfortune that is commonly given to one who lost more than one older sibling (usually sister) to death [*Bari*] (Whitehead 1947: 45).

Kire (f) *[tch-ih-reh]* Cloud; this name is sometimes associated with the proverb "an only child is like a single rain cloud" implying that just like a single rain cloud that is unreliable since it will likely empty itself quickly and be followed by a hot and dry spell, the traditional African family prefers to have many children since the infant mortality rate is high [*Ganda*].

Kisero (f/m) *[tch-ih-seh-roh]* Basket; large plaited basket; this name is sometimes associated with the proverb "one coffee seed that falls from the basket causes the whole basketfull to be spilled" implying that as in this instance of one stooping down to pick up the one fallen seed, one individual can cause suffering to a whole community, concentrating on the trivial and losing sight of the great things is counterproductive, and the proverb is also synonymous with "penny wise, pound foolish" [*Ganda*].

Kishamba-Kyauruka (m) *[kih-tsh-ahm-bah-tch-ah-uh-ruh-kah]* "The great one of the country" [*Chaga*] (Raum 1967: 340).

Kisoka (m) *[kih-soh-kah]* "Crossed fingers" [*Rega*].

Kitambila (m) *[kih-tahm-bih-lah]* "The one that is good at shouting" [*Rega*].

Kito (f) *[kiih-toh]* A name given to the younger of twins [*Rega*].

Kitoga (m) *[kih-toh-gah]* The beloved child of the family [*Rega*].

Kitoko (f) *[kiih-toh-koh]* Beauty [*Kongo*].

Kitumba (m) *[kih-tuhm-bah]* Corpse [*Rega*].

Kiyirikiti (m) *[tch-ih-yih-rih-kih-tih]* A species of red-blossomed tree; this name is commonly associated with the proverb "do not despise the Red-hot Poker tree (which is unflowered and unsightly most of the time) in the burnt out bush--the time (of the sowing season) the savanna has not yet greened up is when the tree crowns itself with a bloom" i.e. the trees paradoxically bloom in the season when there are piles of ugly refuse and burnt out vegetation, including little greened stumps of savanna, the proverb implying that the unsightly can bloom into beauties so should not easily be dismissed [*Ganda*].

Kkubo (m) *[kkuh-boh]* Path; street; road; way; method; this name is sometimes associated with the proverb "kinship comes from meeting on the road" implying that oftentimes people get to know how and that they are related by bumping into each other while walking along, therefore it is important to be cordial to whomever one meets; this name is also sometimes associated with the proverb "that which burns the house, points the pied wagtail to take on to the roadway" i.e. the wagtail's dwelling in the thatched roof is destroyed upon the hut getting burnt down, such that it is forced to go and seek a habitation elsewhere--it is implied in the proverb that a calamity (such as death) that comes upon a house (or social unit), inevitably creates problems for members of the unit; this name is also sometimes associated with the proverb "one who has plenty of food at home is (paradoxically) still killed by famine starvation conditions while on the road traveling" implying that those who have much become blind to the fact that eonditions away from home can be far different from those at home [The *Ganda*].

Komombo (m) *[koh-mohm-boh]* "Nice bird" [*Rega*].

Konibwile (m) *[koh-nih-bwih-leh]* "Little Bird with Darkness Here" i.e. "I have no fear of night" [*Lamba*] (Doke 1931: 147).

Konyi (m) *[koh-ndjh-ih]* A name commonly given to a first born son among several (at least three) older female siblings [*Bari*] (Whitehead 1947: 45).

Koshe (f) *[koh-tsh-eh]* A name given to a third born [*Nuba*] (Seligman 1932 : 387).

Kuaar-Nyang (f) *[kuh-waahr-ndjh-ah-ndgh]* A cow name conventionally restricted to married women [*Nuer*] (Evans-Pritchard 1948: 170).

Kuku (m) *[kuh-kuh]* A name given to a first born [*Nuba*] (Seligman 1932: 386).

Kulya (f/m) *[kuh-ljah]* Consuming; eating; this name is sometimes associated with the proverb "kin relationships go along with eating--if a related person leaves your home while hungry, then this relative will not come back" implying that treats are an important aspect of cultivating relations not only with friends, but also with kin; this name is also sometimes associated with the proverb "the stomach ought to be fed" implying that good nourishment is a paramount aspect of good health, wellbeing, and resourcefulness; this name is also sometimes associated with the proverbs which dramatise that greed or passion blinds reasoning: "the need to eat leads the rat (blindingly) into the calabash" (i.e. to where it is easily caught and killed) and "the need to eat makes one lose the needle" (i.e. when busy with needlework, on notice that the food is ready, drops what he or she is doing) [*Ganda*].

Kungwa (f) *[kuhn-gwah]* A name given to the older of twins [*Rega*].

Kurjok (m) *[kurh-johk]* An ox name [*Nuer*] (Evans-Pritchard 1948: 169).

Kwagala (f) *[kwaah-gah-lah]* Liking; loving; searching for; to like; to love; this name is sometimes associated with the proverb "a chiefship (or a chief) that likes you, entices you to even build on hardy (or infertile) ground" implying that being a favorite of the rulers is so cherished that it would make anyone maintain that closeness even if it means forgoing some personal needs (which you would anyway be able to obtain when living close to a ruler who likes you); this name is also sometimes associated with the proverb "the place of a chief where you are so much liked, is worth more than hunters' traps put together" meaning that being in the good books of, or being a favorite of the rulers is a highly cherished asset given the numerous advantages [*Ganda*].

Kwaysko (f) *[kwahy-skoh]* A nickname-abbreviation for *Nokwayiyo*: "Also one--a girl" [*Xhosa*] (Neethling 1994: 92).

Kyalo (m) *[tch-aah-loh]* Village; large estate; this name is sometimes associated with the proverb "jealousy against jealousy does not make the village prosperous" implying that heated jealousy between two prominent leaders in the village will involve so much friction and disorder that the entire community will not likely settle down and thrive; this name is also sometimes associated with the proverb "a swarm of edible flying ants attracts every elder in the village" implying that there are things, such as the delicious flying ants, which will attract almost everybody; this name is also sometimes associated with the proverbs "the master (or father) that does not eat in his home village, causes his children to not get enough nourishment" and "the master (or father) that eats in his home village, allows for his children to get adequately fed" which imply that the presence of a father is essential to the growth and wellbeing of the children [*Ganda*].

Kyambikwa (m) *[kjah-mbih-kwah]* The beloved [*Rega*].

Kyanga (f) *[kjahn-gah]* Clothes worn in the courtyard [*Rega*].

Kyayi (m) *[tch-aah-yih]* Dry plantain fiber; this name is sometimes associated with the proverb "the cutting of the fiber from the plantain trunk renders scattered the tiny ants that had built in the trunk" implying that when the owner of a household dies, his dependents become disunited, or they stop gathering or living together [*Ganda*].

Kyose (m) *[kjoh-seh]* "All" [*Rega*].

Kyoto (m) *[tch-oh-toh]* Hearth; fireplace; this name is sometimes associated with the proverb "a thinned out dog is only despised when it is lying by the fireplace--when it gets into the wilds, it makes a remarkable transition from the weak and tired state" implying that just like a lazy looking dog that is actually a tireless hunter, nothing or nobody that is apparently insignificant or useless is to be easily dismissed, as synonymous with "appearances are deceiving"; this name is also sometimes associated with the proverb (similar to the above) "the jawbone of a dog is only despised when the dog is resting peacefully and quietly by the fireplace" implying that just like the dog which looks so docile when its jaws are closed as it rests quietly by the fireplace, a person may in threatening or other circumstances turn out to be one of fiery and aggressive character just like such a dog that is in actuality a tireless and fierce hunter that would make one wince upon the appearance of its teeth--therefore nothing or nobody that is apparently insignificant or useless is to be easily dismissed, as synonymous with "appearances are deceiving" [*Ganda*].

-L-

Lado (m) *[lah-doh]* A name commonly given to a second born amongst several (at least four) male siblings that have fortunately survived death; a name given to a second born of male twins, the first born named *Ulang* [*Bari*] (Whitehead 1947: 45).

Lako (m) *[lah-koh]/* ***Lako-Diong*** (m) *[lah-koh-dih-yoh-ngh]* A name denoting misfortune that is commonly given to one who lost one older sibling (usually brother) to death [*Bari*] (Whitehead 1947: 45).

Lako-Wurudiang (m) *[lah-koh-wuh-ruh-djah-ngh]* A name denoting misfortune that is commonly given to one who lost one older sibling (usually brother) to death [*Bari*] (Whitehead 1947: 45).

Langa (m) *[lahn-gah]* Sun: a name such as given to one born during a period of intense sunshine conditions [*Xhosa*] (Thipa 1986: 289).

Lebitso (m) *[leh-bih-tsoh]* Name [*Sotho*] (Thipa 1987: 116).

Lebohang (m) *[leh-boh-hah-ndgh]* "Be grateful": a name such as given to a newborn by its mother to imply that the family is so grateful to God for the gift of a baby boy, given that all the older children in the family are girls [*Sotho*] (Herbert 1990: 10).

Lebohang (m) *[leh-boh-hah-ndgh]* "Thank (him)" [The *Sotho*] (Thipa 1987: 110).

Lefa (m) *[leh-fah]* Inheritance [*Sotho*] (Thipa 1987: 116).

Legge (m) *[lehg-geh]* Stranger: a name denoting misfortune that is commonly given to one who lost more than one older sibling (usually brother) to death [*Bari*] (Whitehead 1947: 45).

Lehogang (m) *[leh-hoh-gah-ndgh]* "Be grateful": a name such as given to a newborn by its mother to point out to her in-laws that they ought to be thankful that she has managed to get her Senior Teacher's Diploma and a baby at the same time [*Tswana*] (Herbert 1997: 8; Herbert 1990: 9).

Lengsuk (f) *[leh-ndgh-suhk]* A name commonly given to a first born son who has one older female sibling [*Bari*] (Whitehead 1947: 45).

Lerato (m) *[leh-rah-toh]* Love [*Sotho*] (Thipa 1987: 116).

Lesedi (m) *[leh-seh-dih]* Light [*Sotho*] (Thipa 1987: 114).

Lind (m) *[lih-ndh]* A nickname-abbreviation for *Lindelo*: "Expectation" [The *Xhosa*] (Neethling 1994: 92).

Lindela (m) *[lihn-deh-lah]* To wait for [*Xhosa*] (Neethling 1994: 92).

Lindelo (m) *[lihn-deh-loh]* Expectation [*Xhosa*] (Neethling 1994: 92).

Lindie (f) *[lihn-dee]* A nickname-abbreviation for *Lindiwe*: "The one waited for" [*Xhosa*] (Neethling 1994: 92).

Lindipasi (m) *[lihn-dih-pah-sih]* Rinderpest (as adapted from the European word) [*Xho*sa] (Thipa 1986: 288).

Lindiwe (f) *[lihn-dih-weh]* "The awaited one": a name such as given either to one born into a family that already has a disproportionately large number of male children, or to one born to a mother that took a relatively long time to conceive [*Zulu*] (Koopman 1987: 150).

Lindiwe (f) *[lihn-dih-weh]* "The one waited for" [*Xhosa*] (Neethling 1994: 92).

Lindsie (f) *[lihnd-see]* A nickname-abbreviation for *Lindiwe*: "The one waited for" [*Xhosa*] (Neethling 1994: 92).

Lister (m) *[lihs-tah]* A nickname-abbreviation for *Lindela*: "To wait for" [*Xhosa*] (Neethling 1994: 92).

Litas (f) *[lih-tahs]* Nickname-abbreviation for *Nolita*: "Light" [The *Xhosa*] (Neethling 1994: 92).

Liziwe (f/m) *[lih-zih-weh]*/ ***Lizo*** (f) *[lih-zoh]* "The one who has consoled us"/ "the one who has made us cross": names given to ones who have lost two or more preceding siblings to death, the names implying that such newborns serve as solace, by the action of God or the ancestors, for the family of the deceased [*Xhosa*] (Thipa 1986: 290).

Lizo (f) *[lih-zoh]* A nickname-abbreviation for *Nomalizo*: "Comforter" [The *Xhosa*] (Neethling 1994: 92).

Loyiso (m) *[loh-yih-soh]* Victory [*Xhosa*] (Neethling 1994: 92).

Loys (m) *[lohys]* A nickname-abbreviation for *Loyiso*: "Victory" [The *Xhosa*] (Neethling 1994: 92).

Luaak (m) *[luh-waahk]* Cattle byre: a name given to one born in a cow barn [*Nuer*] (Evans-Pritchard 1948: 167).

Lubaale (m) *[luh-baah-leh]* A deity; a native God; the Heavens; the sky; a witchdoctor; this name is sometimes associated with the proverb "the concept of God is like hide wear--everyone that comes out is wearing it in his or her own way" implying that religious worshipping styles, and beliefs about God vary widely; this name is also sometimes associated with the proverb "the spirit medicine man profits either way" implying that he gets paid, whether the treated person turns out to die or to live [*Ganda*].

Lubusa (f) *[luh-buh-sah]* The one that questions [*Rega*].

Lubwa (m) *[luh-bwah]* Misfortune; sickly (or half starved, or miserable) dog; species of insect; this name is sometimes associated with the proverb "a thinned out dog is only despised when it is lying by the fireplace--when it gets into the wilds, it makes a remarkable transition from the weak and tired state" implying that just like a lazy looking dog that is actually a tireless hunter, nothing or nobody that is apparently insignificant or useless is to be easily dismissed as synonymous with "appearances are deceiving"; this name is also sometimes associated with the proverb "a skinny but freely strolling dog is better off than the one that is properly fed but is on a leash" implying that freedom is more essential and advantageous to wellbeing than material satisfaction devoid of liberty [*Ganda*].

Luganda (m) *[luh-gahn-dah]* Brotherhood; sisterhood; kinship; the language of the *Ganda* ethnics; this name is sometimes associated with the proverb "kin are (like) the scar/ mole--it never leaves the body (or it cannot be washed off)" implying that kinship goes much further than friendship which can come to an end; this name is also sometimes associated with the proverb "kin relationships improve further with friendship" implying that it is counterproductive to be genetically related without liking each other; this name is also sometimes associated with the proverb "kinship comes from meeting on the road" implying that oftentimes people get to know how and that they are related by bumping into each other while walking along, therefore it is important to be cordial to whomever one meets; this name is also sometimes associated with the proverb "kin relationships go along with eating--if a related person leaves your home while hungry, then this relative will not come back" implying that treats are an important aspect of cultivating relations not only with friends, but also with kin [*Ganda*].

Lugenda (m) *[luh-gehn-dah]* A going away; that goes away; this name is sometimes associated with the proverb "kin relationships go along with eating--if a related person leaves your home while hungry, then this relative

Luggya

will not come back" implying that treats are an important aspect of cultivating relations not only with friends, but also with kin [*Ganda*].

Luggya (m) *[luhj-jah]* That is new; this name is sometimes associated with the proverb "an old proverb is a devising precedent for a new one" implying that literary and academic works, laws, and societal values build on past works and stipulations as references [*Ganda*].

Lugo (m) *[luh-goh]* Leopard; enclosure; kraal; fence enclosing cattle; this name is sometimes associated with the proverb "the miserably hungry leopard prowling in new territory, neither knows nor respects which goat is destined for sacrifice to a deity" implying that the ravages involved in war and raiding naturally involve gross disrespect for the adversary's norms and territorial bounds, or that a newcomer would not be expected to immediately know and adhere to the rules of the place that is new [*Ganda*].

Lugoolugenyi (m) *[luh-goh-oh-luh-geh-ndjh-ih]* "The miserably hungry leopard prowling in new territory"; this name is traditionally equated to a pillager (or raider) and is commonly associated with the proverb "the miserably hungry leopard prowling in new territory, neither knows nor respects which goat is destined for sacrifice to a deity" implying that the ravages involved in war and raiding naturally involve gross disrespect for the adversary's norms and territorial bounds, or that a newcomer would not be expected to immediately know and adhere to the rules of the place that is new [*Ganda*].

Lugumira (m) *[luh-guh-mih-rah]* That is firm (or solid) in/ at; that is faithful in/ at; that is brave (or courageous) in/ at; that is daring in/ at; that has the nerve (or boldness to do) in/ at; this name is sometimes associated with the proverb "'the elderly person is patiently bearing the hunger'--so one says in commiseration even when the elder has just eaten something" implying that the elderly tend to always be sympathized with and are perpetually expected to be in some kind of pain or want, be it physical, physiological, or psychological [*Ganda*].

Lugwana (m) *[luh-gwaah-nah]* That is befitting; that ought to be; this name is sometimes associated with the proverb "kin relationships ought to go along with eating--if a related person leaves your home while hungry, then this relative will not come back" implying that treats are an important aspect of cultivating relations not only with friends, but also with kin; this name is also sometimes associated with the proverb "the stomach ought to be fed" implying that good nourishment is a paramount aspect of good health, wellbeing, and resourcefulness [*Ganda*].

Lukhanyo (m) *[luh-kah-ndjh-oh]* Light [*Xhosa*] (Thipa 1987: 114).

Lukka (m) *[luhk-kah]* That which descends; one who descends; this name is sometimes associated with the proverb "one who is going down to the lake does not leave the fish basket behind" [*Ganda*].

Lukuba (m) *[luh-kuh-bah]* That which strikes (or beats, or hits); this name is sometimes associated with the proverbs "that which strikes the nose, renders the eyes tearful" and "that which strikes the eye, leaves the nose sniffling" implying that an affliction that reigns misery on a person in a family or other social unit causes the other members in the unit to feel the pain, to be compassionate, and to suffer; this name is also sometimes associated with the proverb "that which strikes the child, also wants to strike the mother" implying that a father who beats his child is likely to beat its mother, that one will likely manifest his or her behavioral characteristics in whatever environment, or that an affliction that strikes the child is also inclined to strike its mother [*Ganda*].

Lul (m) *[luhl]* To cry: a name given to one whose previously born siblings died [*Nuer*] (Evans-Pritchard 1948: 167).

Lulama (m) *[luh-lah-mah]* To be meek [*Xhosa*] (Neethling 1994: 92).

Lulina (f) *[luh-lih-nah]* That which has (or contains, or is connected with); this name is sometimes associated with the proverb "'death is ridden with greed!'--(so one says) when it has just killed a relative (or a brother, or a sister)" and the name, in this context, is would be given to a child who is gravely sick, or one born into a family that has recently had a death or many deaths; this name is also sometimes associated with the proverb "death has a multitude of ways of killing; each one dies in his or her own way"--(so one says upon hearing of the death of a stranger) [*Ganda*].

Lulu (m) *[loo-loo]* A nickname-abbreviation for *Lulama*: "To be meek" [*Xhosa*] (Neethling 1994: 92).

Lunanga (m) *[luh-nahn-gah]* Wisdom [*Rega*].

Lungelo (m) *[luhn-geh-loh]* "(Social and political) rights" [*Zulu*] (Herbert 1997: 11).

Lungu (m) *[luhn-guh]* Species of vegetable that resembles squash (or cucumbers) and is eaten in cooked form; this name is sometimes associated with the proverb "'may the vegetable marrow plant be ever so sweet'--(one who says that) takes seeds out of the fruit (to plant in his own garden)" implying that good things are fostered to multiply [*Ganda*].

Lunyonga (m) *[luh-ndjh-ohn-gah]* Driver [*Rega*].

Lusala (m) *[luh-sah-lah]* That cuts (or cuts up, or slaughters, or divides, or apportions, or decides); this name is sometimes associated with the proverb "the cutting of the fiber from the plantain trunk renders scattered the tiny ants that had built in the trunk" implying that when the owner of a household dies, his dependents become disunited, or they stop gathering or living together; this name is also sometimes associated with the proverb "an old proverb is a devising precedent for a new one" implying that literary and academic works, laws, and societal values build on past works and stipulations as references [*Ganda*].

Lusambya (m) *[luh-sahm-bjah]* The unifier [*Rega*].

Lusowaanya (f) *[luh-soh-oh-waah-ndjh-ah]* That causes to have a tiff (or small quarrel); this name is commonly associated with the proverb "sickness (or death) brings about petty quarrels" implying that sicknesses or deaths bring about suspicion as to who the perpetrators, suspected of poisoning or witchcraft, are [*Ganda*].

Lusungu (m) *[luh-suhn-guh]* Insect [*Rega*].

Lutala (m) *[luh-tah-lah]* Where the "head of birds" (i.e. *Penge*) sleeps [The *Rega*].

Luthando (m) *[luh-sth-ahn-doh]* Love [*Xhosa*] (Neethling 1994: 92).

Lutimba (m) *[luh-tihm-bah]* A net; curtain; drape; screen; this name is sometimes associated with the proverb "an old hunting net will catch and kill an animal even where there is no game track" implying that old methods were often fashioned through extensive experience and practice, they do not lose their usefullness altogether, they can make astonishing gains, therefore they should never be easily dismissed as outmoded and worthless [*Ganda*].

Lutonde (f) *[luh-tohn-deh]* Star [*Rega*].

Lutta (m) *[luht-tah]* "It kills"; that which kills; this name is sometimes associated with the proverb "that which kills the one who supports you, thoroughly saps away your strength" implying that the loss of one you depend on for your material or emotonal wellbeing is indeed an unbearable blow on you; this name is also sometimes associated with the proverb "that which kills the cow, allows for the dog to travel" implying that just like the dog that will scent out and rush to get the leftover meat and bones from the hapless cow, people will sense and hasten to take advantage of circumstances that may have greatly disadvantaged others; this name is also sometimes associated with the proverb "that which goes on to kill a dog, (first) blocks its nose" implying that just like this example whereby the dog is unable to smell out and is therefore doomed, the malfunctioning of a crucial body part can easily lead to death [*Ganda*].

Luvuyo (m) *[luh-vuh-yoh]* Joy [*Xhosa*] (Thipa 1987: 111).

Luwambya (m) *[luh-wahm-bjah]* That causes to capture (or take prisoner, or appropriate, or commandeer) that causes to reserve an item for purchase; this name is commonly associated with the proverb "the one who (habitually) requests for goods to be reserved for him till he can later pay is in effect helping reserve goods for those customers who pay for the items there and then" implying that a merchant's interest is mostly in immediate buyers much more than in those who demand goods that it is uncertain they will pay for [*Ganda*].

Luwanga (m) *[luh-wahn-gah]* Skeleton; jaw; bones; jawbone (of the king or other important person traditionally removed and preserved following the person's death; this name is sometimes associated with the proverb "the jawbone of a dog is only despised when the dog is resting peacefully and quietly by the fireplace" implying that just like the dog which looks so docile when its jaws are closed as it rests quietly by the fireplace, a person may in threatening or other circumstances turn out to be one of fiery and aggressive character just like such a dog that is in actuality a tireless and fierce hunter that would make one wince upon the appearance of its teeth--therefore nothing or nobody that is apparently insignificant or useless is to be easily dismissed, as synonymous with "appearances are deceiving" [*Ganda*].

Luwangalwambwa (m) *[luh-wahn-gah-lwahm-bwah]* The jawbone of a dog; this name is often equated to a fearless warrior, and is commonly associated with the proverb "the jawbone of a dog is only despised when the dog is resting peacefully and quietly by the fireplace" implying that just like the dog which looks so docile when its jaws are closed as it rests quietly by the fireplace, a person may in threatening or other circumstances turn out to be one of fiery and aggressive character just like such a dog that is in actuality a tireless and fierce hunter that would make one wince upon the appearance of its teeth--therefore nothing or nobody that is apparently insignificant or useless is to be easily dismissed, as synonymous with "appearances are deceiving" [*Ganda*].

Luyijja (m) *[luh-yihj-jah]/* **Luwijja** (m) *[luh-wihj-jah]* Stone anvil; this name is sometimes associated with the proverb "the stone anvil that is instrumental in forging the needle, also helps forge the knife" implying that a mother's position in the world is paramount, as synonymous with "the hand that rocks the cradle, rules the world" [*Ganda*].

Luyindi (m) *[luh-yihn-dih]* A species of small bean; this name is commonly associated with the proverbs "the small bean is inedible while it is in the raw green state" and "the small bean is not eaten while it is still green" that advise prudence, patience, and some lenience to allow for persons or situations to reasonably develop and mature before they are with seriousness and heavy criticism dealt with (e.g. dealing with youngsters, newcomers, new employees, and new businesses) [*Ganda*].

Lwabaaga (m) *[lwaah-baah-gah]* "The day one butchers (an animal)"; this name is commonly associated with the proverbs "the day a poor man butchers his animal, is when he gets a friend" and "the day a servant butchers his animal, is when he gets a father and a mother" implying that opportunists who claim to be relatives or friends will flock around even one in servitude or poverty that has just acquired or potentially has something to give away [*Ganda*].

Lwakasi (m) *[lwah-kah-sih]* Monday [*Bashi*].

Lwakulya (m) *[lwah-kuh-ljaah]* Because (or on account of) eating; a need to eat; a time of eating; this name is commonly associated with the proverbs which dramatise that greed or passion blinds reasoning: "the need to eat leads the rat (blindingly) into the calabash" (i.e. to where it is easily caught and killed) and "the need to eat makes one lose the needle" (i.e. when busy with needlework, on notice that the food is ready, drops what he or she is doing) [*Ganda*].

Lwamulungi (m) *[wah-muh-luhn-jih]* That of the good one (or the virtuous one, or the handsome one, or the beautiful one); this name is commonly associated with the proverb "the funeral rites of one who was good are praisingly talked about endlessly (or cannot pass without being praised)" [The *Ganda*].

Lwazi (m) *[lwaah-zih]* Rock; rocky terrain; this name is sometimes associated with the proverb "a chiefship (or a chief) that likes you, entices you to even build on hardy (or infertile) ground" implying that being a favorite of the rulers is so cherished that it would make anyone maintain that closeness even if it means forgoing some personal needs (which you would anyway be able to obtain when living close to a ruler who likes you) [*Ganda*].

Lwokya (m) *[lwoh-tch-ah]* That burns or scars; this name is commonly associated with the proverb "that which burns the house, points the pied wagtail to take on to the roadway" i.e. the wagtail's dwelling in the thatched roof is destroyed upon the hut getting burnt down, such that it is forced to go and seek a habitation elsewhere--it is implied in the proverb that a calamity (such as death) that comes upon a house (or social unit), inevitably creates problems for members of the unit [*Ganda*].

Lwungu (m) *[lwuhn-guh]* Species of vegetable that resembles squash (or cucumbers) and is eaten in cooked form; this name is sometimes associated with the proverb "'may the vegetable marrow plant be ever so sweet'--(one who says that) takes seeds out of the fruit (to plant in his own garden)" implying that good things are fostered to multiply [*Ganda*].

-M-

Maanyi (m) *[maah-ndjh-ih]* Strength; power; energy; this name is sometimes associated with the proverb "that which kills the one who supports you, thoroughly saps away your strength" implying that the loss of one you depend on for your material or emotonal wellbeing is indeed an unbearable blow on you; this name is also sometimes associated with the proverbs "friendship overpowers (or rules) even a person of strength" and "friendship breaks down even a person of strong will" which imply that creating friendship with people allows for many advantages, for even persons of strong character can be more easily acquired from and compromised with, and their opinions more easily swayed through negotiating with them in a friendly manner [*Ganda*].

Mabe (m) *[maah-beh]* That are bad [*Kongo*].

Maddu (m) *[mahd-duh]* Strong desire; yearning; craving; this name is sometimes associated with the proverb "'death is ridden with greed!'--(so one says) when it has just killed a relative (or a brother, or a sister)" and the name, in this context, would be given to a child who is gravely sick, or one born into a family that has recently had a death or many deaths [The *Ganda*].

Madira (f) *[mah-dih-rah]* The mother associated with enemies: a name such as given to one born out of wedlock or infidelity [*Sotho*] (Thipa 1987: 112).

Maditaba (f) *[mah-dih-tah-bah]* The mother associated with controversy: a name such as given to one born out of wedlock or infidelity [*Sotho*] (Thipa 1987: 112).

Madube (f) *[maah-duh-beh]* The mother associated with a zebra [*Ndebele*] (Hemans 1968: 74).

Magulu (m) *[mah-guh-luh]* Legs; this name is sometimes associated with the proverb "a demonstration of prowess does not restrict the legs--it is confined to the mouth" which implies that those who boast or display enthusiasm would not necessarily stand up and fight, and not run away from the real situation (as with the example of war whereby one can boast with his mouth, but he is still with the convenience of the legs with which he can flee as he demonstrates his cowardice and non-commitment when the fighting begins) [*Ganda*].

Makerere (f) *[mah-keh-eh-reh-reh]* Acts of getting up early (and starting off for work or on a journey); the first things done in the morning (after having gone to bed with the intention of doing them); this name is commonly associated with the proverb "to be early is not the same for everybody" e.g. for the cock it tends to be 4-4.30 a.m., partridges 3 a.m., buffaloes 3.30-4 a.m., and times that people get up usually depend on whether their major occupations are in the mornings, evenings, or nights [*Ganda*].

Makgotso (f) *[mah-kgoh-tsoh]* The mother associated with peace [*Sotho*] (Thipa 1987: 114).

Makhosazane (f) *[mah-koh-sah-zah-neh]* Girls [The *Zulu*] (Koopman 1987: 148).

Makito (f) *[mah-kih-toh]* Doubt [*Rega*].

Makitshutshu (f) *[mah-kih-tsh-uh-tsh-uh]* "The exhausted one": an honorary praise name usually bestowed on one who has become the guardian and tutor of her grandchildren, and which name intimates that her breasts have been sucked to depletion by her children and grandchildren [*Chaga*] (Raum 1967: 125, 126).

Makulinga (f) *[mah-kuh-lihn-gah]* "The uniter (of the men/ women)": an honorary praise name usually bestowed on one whose sons or daughters are married [*Chaga*] (Raum 1967: 125).

Malandela (m) *[mah-lahn-deh-lah]* "The follower": the name of the father of the first ancestor (*Zulu*) of the *Zulu* ethnics [*Zulu*] (Koopman 1987: 156).

Mali (m) *[mah-lih]* A nickname-abbreviation for *Malizole*: "Let there be peace" [*Xhosa*] (Neethling 1994: 92).

Maliashi (f) *[mah-ljah-tsh-ih]* "Nice smell" [*Rega*].

Malimao (m) *[mah-lih-mah-woh]* "Limes" (from the *Kiswahili* language) [*Fipa*] (Willis 1982: 229).

Malindy (f) *[mah-lihn-dee]* A nickname-abbreviation for *Lindiwe*: "The one waited for" [*Xhosa*] (Neethling 1994: 92).

Malinga (f) *[mah-lihn-gah]* "A girl does not belong to one person" [*Rega*].

Malizo (m) *[mah-lih-zoh]* A nickname-abbreviation for *Malizole*: "Let there be peace" [*Xhosa*] (Neethling 1994: 92).

Malizole (m) *[mah-lih-zoh-leh]* "Let there be peace" [*Xhosa*] (Neethling 1994: 92).

Malungwana (f) *[mah-luhn-gwah-nah]* One who frequently experiences pain [*Xhosa*] (Neethling 1985: 89).

Malupenga (f/m) *[mah-luh-pehn-gah]* Trumpet [*Lamba*] (Doke 1931: 146).

Malusi (m) *[mah-luh-sih]* Shepherd [*Xhosa*] (Thipa 1987: 114).

Mamello (f) *[mah-mehl-loh]* The mother associated with perseverance [The *Sotho*] (Thipa 1987: 114).

Mampho (f) *[mahm-poh]* The mother associated with a gift (or the greatest gift) *[Sotho]* (Thipa 1987: 109).

Mandlenkosi (m) *[mah-nd-lehn-koh-sih]* "Strength of a chief" [The *Xhosa*] (Wainwright 1986: 297).

Mandlovu (f) *[mah-ndh-loh-vuh]* The mother associated with an elephant *[Ndebele]* (Hemans 1968: 74).

Mandwa/ Mmandwa (m) *[mmahn-dwah]* A spirit medium; oracle; a speaking medium between the people and a deity; the human mouthpiece (or representative) of a deity; a deity affiliated witchdoctor; this name is sometimes associated with the proverb "a bad spiritual priest brings abuse upon himself by the person who consults him" which applies to poor workmanship *[Ganda]*.

Mandwambi/ Mmandwambi (m) *[mmahn-dwaahm-bih]* A bad/ or ineffectual spirit medium (or speaking medium between the people and a deity); this name is commonly associated with the proverb "a bad spiritual priest brings abuse upon himself by the person who consults him" which applies to poor workmanship *[Ganda]*.

Mangwenya (f) *[mah-ndgh-weh-ndjah]* The mother associated with a crocodile *[Ndebele]* (Hemans 1968: 74).

Mankomo (f) *[mah-nkoh-moh]* The mother associated with cattle *[Ndebele]* (Hemans 1968: 74).

Mannangwa (f) *[mahn-nahn-gwah]* **Mannyangwa** (f) *[mahn-ndjh-ahn-gwah]* Wonders; the extraordinary; this name is commonly associated with the proverb "the wonderfully extraordinary is like sweet potatoes growing on a deserted homestead" i.e. such a deserted homestead is expected to have grass, perhaps some maize and gourd vine plants, but not sweet potatoes growing in the garden *[Ganda]*.

Mantwa (f) *[mahn-twah]* The mother associated with war: a name such as given to one born out of wedlock or infidelity *[Sotho]* (Thipa 1987: 112).

Mapula (f) *[mah-puh-lah]* Rain: a name such as given to one born during a period of rainfall *[Sotho]* (Herbert 1990: 5).

Masannganzira (m) *[mah-sahn-ndgh-ahn-zih-rah]* Crossroads; intersection; this name is commonly associated with the proverbs "'crossroads' kill the one who greets and the one who is greeted" and "'crossroads' kill the one who builds on them and the one they are looking for" in that one who is at or builds on crossroads is in a high population flow and interacting location (i.e. a highly public place), so such a person is visibly vulnerable to enemies, to legal action for obstruction, may obstruct and tend traffic toward accidents, etc.--it is implied in the proverb that it is very risky to be in the public eye; this name is also sometimes associated with the proverb "the one who happens to come across you at the crossroads considers you a traveler (or a stranger)" i.e. since crossroads are generally considered a location in which people from all directions meet and move through *[Ganda]*.

Maseneko/ Maseeneeko (m) *[mah-seh-eh-neh-eh-koh]* Faking; bluffing; for the sake of appearances; this name is commonly associated with the proverb "the situation of being temporarily attached is like the leg of a cricket--it breaks off when you casually touch it" and the name tends to be given to children who are alarmingly sick, or to those whose prior born siblings died [*Ganda*].

Masika (f) *[mah-sih-kah]* A name given to a first born daughter [*Mande*].

Masindi (f) *[mah-sihn-dih]* A nickname-abbreviation for *Sindiswa*: "The one who escaped" [*Xhosa*] (Neethling 1994: 92).

Masoka (f) *[mah-soh-kah]* "Good" [*Rega*].

Masupa (f) *[mah-soo-pah]* Bottles [*Rega*].

Maswabi (m) *[mah-swah-bih]* Regret; shame: a name such as given to one born out of wedlock or infidelity [*Sotho*] (Thipa 1987: 112).

Mateboho (f) *[mah-teh-boh-hoh]* The mother associated with gratitude [The *Sotho*] (Thipa 1987: 110).

Mathabo (f) *[mah-tah-boh]* The mother associated with joy [*Sotho*] (Thipa 1987: 111).

Mathapelo (f) *[mah-tah-peh-loh]* The mother associated with prayer [The *Sotho*] (Thipa 1987: 109, 110).

Mathda (f) *[mah-sth-dah]* "My friend" [*Nuer*] (Evans-Pritchard 1948: 169).

Mathe (m) *[mah-teh]* Saliva [*Sotho*] (Thipa 1987: 116).

Matshepo (f) *[mah-tsh-eh-poh]* "The mother associated with hope" [*Sotho*] (Thipa 1987: 114).

Mavumirizi (m) *[mah-vuh-mih-rih-zih]* That involve insults (or invectives); this name is commonly associated with the proverb "continued insults do not kill the one they speak of" which is synonymous with "hard words break no bones" and "sticks and stones may break my bones, but words will not hurt me" [*Ganda*].

Mayinja (m) *[mah-yihn-jah]* Rocks; stones; phonograph records; this name is sometimes associated with the proverb "an oarsman whose gaze wanders, steers the canoe onto the rocks" which advises against carelessness that involves engaging in distracting activity that would lead those with responsible duties to disaster [*Ganda*].

Mayirikiti (m) *[mah-yih-rih-kih-tih]* The trees of a species which bear red blossoms and have hook looking thorns on the trunk and branches: the Red-hot Poker tree; rashes of a kind that is irritating; this name is commonly associated with the proverb "the Red-hot Poker trees (which are unflowered and unsightly most of the time) crown themselves with a red bloom during the sowing season" i.e. the trees paradoxically bloom in the season when there are piles of ugly refuse and burnt out vegetation, including little greened stumps of savanna, the proverb implying that the unsightly can bloom into beauties so should not easily be dismissed [*Ganda*].

Mayoza (f) *[mah-yoh-zah]* A nickname-abbreviation for *Mayoza*: "To delight" [*Xhosa*] (Neethling 1994: 92).

Mazambi (f/m) *[mah-zahm-bih]* One that is not in good shape at birth [The *Rega*].

Mazozo (f/m) *[mah-zoh-zoh]* A nickname-abbreviation for *Nokuzola* i.e. "The calm and meek one," *Ntombizodwa* i.e. "Only girls," *Zolani* i.e. "Be calm," *Zoleka* i.e. "To be calm," and *Zoliswa* i.e. "To make calm"/ "one who calms" [*Xhosa*] (Neethling 1994: 92).

Mazzi (f/m) *[mahz-zih]* Water; this name is sometimes associated with the proverb "water obtained through begging, does not quench the thirst" implying that begging is unlikely to make one rich or adequate, that personal involvement in work is paramount to success and wellbeing; this name is also sometimes associated with the proverb "a situation where drinking water is limited results in discrimination, the herdsmen saying, 'Bring the nursing (or mothering) cows that they may drink first'" implying that precedence is given to elders, that those who possess little are meticulous when it comes to choosing heirs, and that it is favorites who are given things that are in short supply; this name is also sometimes associated with the proverb "a miser is (like) the frog which hides its young (i.e. the tadpoles) in the water" implying that the stingy hardly expose their treasures [*Ganda*].

Mbathalala (m) *[mbah-sth-ah-lah-lah]* "Great Fever" [*Xhosa*] (Thipa 1986: 288).

Mbazzi (m) *[mbahz-zih]* Ax; this name is sometimes associated with the proverb "the one who vainly boasts 'I am well accustomed to being involved in war,' is like the elder (or weakling) who goes to war with an ax for which he is exclusively called upon to use in helping divide the (bovine) booty acquired by the warriors (for which work he is rewarded inferior, such as hump or neck, portions of the meat)" [*Ganda*].

Mbidde (m) *[mbihd-deh]* A species of banana employed in making beer; this name is sometimes associated with the proverb "that which the banana beer lures you into, you cannot resist" implying that alcohol dangerously fashions the distasteful acts of a drunkard [*Ganda*].

Mbilizi (f/m) *[mbih-lih-zih]* Name given to a first born child after twin siblings [*Rega*].

Mbiro (m) *[mbih-roh]* Speed; this name is sometimes associated with the proverb "a slow pace (or run away) is better than hiding" meaning that during war it is better to flee at a slow pace than to hide so as to reduce the chances of getting captured, and that putting in some effort or working little is better than doing nothing about it at all; this name is also sometimes associated with the proverb "running away does not put to end a dispute" implying that people still hold grudges against those they have not seen for so long, and people who fled years back are still held accountable and tried for offenses they committed [*Ganda*].

Mbirontono (m) *[mbih-rohn-toh-noh]* Slow pace; slow run; this name is commonly associated with the proverb "a slow pace (or run away) is better than hiding" meaning that during war it is better to flee at a slow pace than to hide so as to reduce the chances of getting captured, and that putting in some effort or working little is better than doing nothing about it at all [*Ganda*].

Mbu (m) *[mbuh]* A nickname-abbreviation for *Mbulelo*: "Gratitude" [*Xhosa*] (Neethling 1994: 92).

Mbuga (m) *[mbuh-gah]* Court of law; chief's enclosure; fountain that cattle drink from; this name is sometimes associated with the proverb "a chiefship (or a chief) that likes you, entices you to even build on hardy (or infertile) ground" implying that being a favorite of the rulers is so cherished that it would make anyone maintain that closeness even if it means forgoing some personal needs (which you would anyway be able to obtain when living close to a ruler who likes you); this name is also sometimes associated with the proverb "the place of a chief where you are so much liked, is worth more than hunters' traps put together" meaning that being in the good books of, or being a favorite of the rulers is a highly cherished asset, given the numerous advantages [*Ganda*].

Mbugombi (m) *[mbuh-gohm-bih]* Barkcloths that are bad (or in poor condition); this name is commonly associated with the proverb "barkcloths (for sale) that are bad (or in poor condition) are despisingly unwanted at the market place" implying that one is expected to act or show one's best while in public [*Ganda*].

Mbulakaayo (m) *[mbuh-lah-kaah-yoh]* "I am missing the uproar (or clamor)" [*Ganda*].

Mbulekayo (m) *[mbuh-leh-kah-yoh]* "I leave (or abandon) them there" [The *Ganda*].

Mbulelo (m) *[mbuh-leh-loh]* Gratitude [*Xhosa*] (Neethling 1994: 92; Thipa 1987: 110).

Mbulidde (f) *[mbuh-lihd-deh]* "I have taken/ or been given (high) office"; "I have eaten (or consumed) it" [*Ganda*].

Mbuubi (m) *[mbuuh-bih]* Name-title of a chief (of *Buvuma* county) [*Ganda*].

Mbuula (m) *[mbuuh-lah]* A proposal; an intention; a bachelor; a poor boy; a poor kid [*Ganda*].

Mbuule (m) *[mbuuh-leh]* That is thrashed (or beaten, or beaten hard, or thrown to the ground); (cattle) that is raided; that is proposed (or intended); that is associated with bachelorhood (or losing one's wife through separation or desertion); that is associated with a poor boy (or a poor kid) [The *Ganda*].

Mbuulidde (f) *[mbuuh-lihd-deh]* "I have preached"; "I have told (or said)"; "I have indoctrinated"; "I have espoused teachings" [*Ganda*].

Mbuuliro (f) *[mbuuh-lih-roh]* (Method of) preaching; (way) of telling (or saying); doctrine; place where teachings are espoused; place where preaching is done [*Ganda*].

Mbuulo (m) *[mbuuh-loh]* Masses; large quantities [*Ganda*].

Mbuusi (m) *[mbuuh-sih]* That causes to be doubtful (or to suspect, or to vacillate); one who suspects (or has doubts about); one who flits (or flutters about) [*Ganda*].

Mbuyiselo (m) *[mbuh-yih-seh-loh]* Reward/ compensation/ recompense: a name given to one who has lost two or more preceding siblings to death, the name implying that this child serves as welcome restitution, by the action of God or the ancestors, for the deceased [*Xhosa*] (Thipa 1986: 290).

Mbuzimulanga (m) *[mbuh-zih-muh-lahn-gah]* "The outcry (or clamor, or wailing) of a goat; this name is commonly associated with the proverb "the wailing of a goat is even devoid of tears" which mirrors worthless effort as is compared to the frequent goat wailing which is not of benefit to the goat owner (and, in humor, a wailing goat does not even let out tears); this proverb also mirrors one who does not have any intention of providing anything, though pretends to be greatly compassionate [*Ganda*].

Mbwa (m) *[mbwah]* Dog; dogs; a species of small fly; this name is sometimes associated with the proverb "that which kills the cow, allows for the dog to travel" implying that just like the dog that will scent out and rush to get the leftover meat and bones from the hapless cow, people will sense and hasten to take advantage of circumstances that may have greatly disadvantaged others; this name is also sometimes associated with the proverb "the jaw-bone of a dog is only despised when the dog is resting peacefully and quietly by the fireplace" implying that just like the dog which looks so docile when its jaws are closed as it rests quietly by the fireplace, a person may in threatening or other circumstances turn out to be one of fiery and aggressive character just like such a dog that is in actuality a tireless and fierce hunter that would make one wince upon the appearance of its teeth--therefore nothing or nobody that is apparently insignificant or useless is to be easily dismissed, as synonymous with "appearances are deceiving"; this name is also sometimes associated with the proverb "the ears of a butcher heed to 'the dog is stealing your meat', but if you ask him for some meat, he does not give you any" meaning that the willingness of people to respond to a situation depends on level of convenience much more than on kindness and compassion [*Ganda*].

Mbwabwa (m) *[mbwah-bwah]* That is large and spread out; that is expansive [*Ganda*].

Mbwawe (m) *[mbwah-weh]* That is caused to be large and spread out; that is caused to be expansive [*Ganda*].

Mbweyunye (f) *[mbweh-yuh-ndjh-eh]* "I very eagerly await (or anticipate) it"; "I hurriedly in eagerness rush (or flee) to it"; "I hastily go for it" [The *Ganda*].

Mbyalwa (m) *[mbjah-lwah]* "They are spread out (or laid out) to (or for) me"; "they are in abundance given to me"; "they are increased (or multiplied) for me" [*Ganda*].

Mcanukeliwe (f) *[mkah-nuh-keh-lih-weh]/ Mcanukelwa* (m) *[mkah-nuh-keh-lwah]* "Be annoyed with her": a name such as given to a newborn whose mother is expressing that she is aware that her in-laws do not like her [*Zulu*] (Turner 1992: 49).

Mcebisi (m) *[muh-tch-eh-bih-sih]* Counselor [*Xhosa*] (Thipa 1987: 114).

Mdingi (m) *[muh-dihn-gih]* "One who lacks": a name such as given by a father to a child born at a time he was short of money [*Zulu*] (Koopman 1987:

152).

Mduduzi (m) *[muh-duh-duh-zih]* "The comforter": a name such as is given to a newborn who metaphorically solaces the family since his preceding sibling was stillborn; or a name such as is given to one born during or following circumstances of discomfort, pain, or beravement [The *Zulu*] (Koopman 1987: 151, 152).

Mehlo (f/m) *[meh-loh]* "Eyes (that are striking)" [The *Zulu*] (Koopman 1987: 150).

Mende/ Mmende (f/m) *[mmehn-deh]* A pigmoid (or colored) field mouse; kind of banana used for making beer [*Ganda*].

Menha (m) *[meh-ndh-ah]*/ *Menya* (m) *[meh-ndjh-ah]* To break; to break (the law) [*Soga*].

Mer (m) *[mehr]* Eye tear: a name given to one whose previously born siblings died [*Nuer*] (Evans-Pritchard 1948: 167).

Met (m) *[meht]* To decieve: a name given to one born to a father who while wooing the mother, boasted of the number of cattle he would provide as bride dowry, but this turned out to be a lie which went on to involve excuses when the time came for the father to hand over the cattle [*Nuer*] (Evans-Pritchard 1948: 167).

Meya (m) *[meh-yah]* Mayor (as adapted from the European word) [*Ganda*].

Mfanafuthi (m) *[mfah-nah-fuh-tih]* "Another boy": a name such as is given to one born into a family that already has a disproportionately large number of male children [*Zulu*] (Koopman 1987: 149).

Mfanakayise (m) *[mfah-nah-kah-yih-seh]* "(True) son of his father": a name such as is given to a newborn by its father who is expressing pride in himself as a new father, or pride in his child [*Zulu*] (Koopman 1987: 152).

Mfanobomvu (m) *[mfah-noh-bohm-vuh]* "Reddish complexioned boy" [*Zulu*] (Koopman 1987: 150).

Mfanufikile (m) *[mfah-nuh-fih-kih-leh]* "A boy has arrived" [*Zulu*] (Koopman 1987: 148).

Mfanukayise (m) *[mfah-nuh-kah-yih-seh]* "Father's son" [*Zulu*] (Koopman 1987: 148).

Mgoduyatsha (m) *[uhm-goh-duh-yah-tsh-ah]* "The feces are burning" [The *Xhosa*] (Neethling 1985: 89).

Mhletshwa (m) *[muh-leh-tsh-wah]* "The one who is whispered about": a name such as is given to a newborn by its mother who is telling her in-laws of an incident shortly before the birth of the child in which, unbenowest to them, she overheard the in-laws whispering unpleasant comments about her [*Zulu*] (Turner 1992: 50).

Micyo (m) *[mih-tch-oh]* "(Pleasant) dawnings" [*Ganda*].

Migereko (m) *[mih-geh-reh-koh]*/ *Migero* (m) *[mih-geh-roh]* Portions; shares; allotments [*Ganda, Soga*].

Miiro/ Miro (m) *[miih-roh]* Tracheas; windpipes [*Ganda*].

Mikalo (m) *[mih-kah-loh]* Dried or smoked meat; biltong [*Ganda*].

Mikiisesangwa (f) *[mih-kiih-seh-sahn-gwah]* "The original (or long term) representatives of a legislative body" [*Ganda*].

Mikira (m) *[mih-kih-rah]* Tails [*Ganda*].

Mikisa (f/m) *[mih-kih-sah]* Strokes of luck (or good luck); blessings; opportunities; chances; occasions [*Ganda, Soga*].

Milenge (m) *[mih-leh-ehn-geh]* Tears [*Rega*].

Milinganyo (m) *[mih-lih-ndgh-ah-ndjh-oh]* "Worries" [*Rega*].

Minaawa (m) *[mih-naah-wah]* Attacks; strikes; persistent goings after [The *Ganda*].

Mirembe (f/m) *[mih-rehm-beh]* Times of peace; periods; eras; epochs; this name is sometimes associated with the proverbs "eras are like the fingers on the hand--each subsequent one is different from the one past" and "it is times that bring changes" implying that conditions are never stagnant and so change with time, and that each generation of people is in ways inferior or superior to the foregone one [*Ganda*].

Miriika (f) *[mih-riih-kah]* Very high interest; usury; extortions; exacting payments from; demands of fulfillment of commitments by; putting pressure on [*Ganda*].

Mirimbe (m) *[mih-rihm-beh]* That are caused to attach to themselves; that are caused to lean on themselves; that are caused to be dependent on themselves; that are caused to be attached; that are caused to overlap [*Ganda*].

Mirundi (m) *[mih-ruhn-dih]* Times; occasions; kinds; types; categories [The *Ganda*].

Misaalenyooka (m) *[mih-saah-leh-ndjh-oh-oh-kah]* "The leading troublemakers"; "the leading smoking guns (of an epidemic, or battle); "the uppermost rages (of an epidemic, or battle)"; "the guiding fumes of smoke"; the leading swarms"; "the first ones to get to the signals of smoke" [*Ganda*].

Misaka (m) *[mih-sah-kah]* Movings around to obtain food for purchase or in exchange for services; foragings for food; diggings up (or ferretings out) of information [*Ganda*].

Misango (m) *[mih-sahn-goh]* Accusations; crimes; court cases; this name is sometimes associated with the proverb "a boy who is insolent, will upon maturing commit big offenses" [*Ganda*].

Misanvu (m) *[mih-sahn-vuh]* Sevens; branches (or parts of a tree) spread out to block a road or a path; obstacles; obstructions [*Ganda*].

Misigula (m) *[mih-sih-guh-lah]* Uprootings; deracinations; seductions (of women); leadings astray [*Ganda*].

Misinga (m) *[mih-sihn-gah]* Pig irons [*Ganda*].

Miti (m) *[mih-tih]* Trees; this name is sometimes associated with the proverbs "the young trees make the forests firm" and "the young trees are the forest" implying that children are the foundation and hope for the future so they ought to be carefully and adequately nourished, nurtured, and trained [*Ganda*].

Miwabo (f) *[mih-wah-boh]* Goings astray; goings out of control; wanderings [*Ganda*].

Miwanda (m) *[mih-wahn-dah]* (Modes of) spitting; roads [*Ganda*].

Miwunda (m) *[mih-wuhn-dah]* Decorations; adornments; ornaments; decorations (of a gourd) with patterns of beads; embellishments *[Ganda]*.

Miyiggo (m) *[mih-yihg-goh]* Hunts *[Ganda]*.

Miyingo (m) *[mih-yihn-goh]* The locks to the kraal gate; that are overwhelming; that are excessive; that are too great; the joints (of a body or a machine) *[Ganda]*.

Miyonga (m) *[mih-yohn-gah]* Burnt out remains of food; sparks from a fire; fucus cloths *[Ganda]*.

Miziisa (m) *[mih-ziih-sah]* Tendons of the back *[Ganda]*.

Mizimbo (m) *[mih-zihm-boh]* Modes of building (or construction); houses; swellings up; modes of anger (or fury) *[Ganda]*.

Mkhetheni (f/m) *[muh-keh-teh-nih]* "Single him out": a name such as given to a newborn by its father who is voicing his anger and bitterness against his parents for paying the bride dowry for all three of his brothers, but exclusively not providing his dowry for which he worked on his own and saved in order to pay *[Zulu]* (Turner 1992: 52).

Mlandeli (m) *[muh-lahn-deh-lih]* "The follower": a name such given to one whose preceding sibling was stillborn *[Zulu]* (Koopman 1987: 151).

Mlindi (m) *[uhm-lihn-dee]* The one who waits *[Xhosa]* (Neethling 1994: 92).

Mmaali (m) *[mmaah-lih]* Wealth; possessions; money; this name is sometimes associated with the proverb "'my possessions were destroyed' (one says), but then he goes on to buy a waterpot" which is applied to one who often complains about losses incurred, but then continues to invest in things that are easily destroyed (as with the example of waterpots which are easily cracked and destroyed) *[Ganda]*.

Mmabatho (f) *[mmah-bah-toh]* The mother of one named *Batho* *[Sotho]* (Thipa 1987: 116).

Mmale (m) *[mmah-leh]* Mud fish *[Ganda]*.

Mmalefa (f) *[mmah-leh-fah]* The mother of one named *Lefa* *[Sotho]* (Thipa 1987: 116).

Mmalerato (f) *[mmah-leh-rah-toh]* The mother of one named *Lerato* [The *Sotho*] (Thipa 1987: 116).

Mmamohau (f) *[mmah-moh-hahw]* The mother of one named *Mohau* [The *Sotho*] (Thipa 1987: 116).

Mmango (m) *[mmahn-goh]* Spears; the shaft of spears *[Ganda]*.

Mmanyanngenda (m) *[mmah-ndjh-ah-ndgh-ehn-dah]* "If I had known (or foreseen)"; this name is commonly associated with the proverb "'if I had known (or foreseen) I would have gone (to war)'--(says the one who remained home) as he sees the boys coming back with the raided (cattle)" which applies to deep regret *[Ganda]*.

Mmembe (m) *[mmehm-beh]* Crust on burnt food *[Ganda]*.

Mmengo/ Mengo (m) *[mmehn-goh]* Lower millstones; grind stones; scales for weighing sacks (or bags of produce) such as of sugar and coffee berries *[Ganda]*.

Mmere (m) *[mmeh-reh]* Food; this name is sometimes associated with the proverb "one who has plenty of food at home is (paradoxically) still killed by famine starvation conditions while on the road traveling" implying that those who have much become blind to the fact that conditions away from home can be far different from those at home; this name is also sometimes associated with the proverb "a visitor that gets to eat satisfactorily, makes the food tell it" implying that the amount of uneaten leftover food indicates the extent of satisfaction; this name is also sometimes associated with the proverb "a woman who is a diligent farmer brings forth food, while the weak (or lazy) one brings forth grass weeds"; this name is also sometimes associated with the proverb "a woman who is a diligent farmer causes you (the husband) to eat with your shield over the food" which dramatizes a very hard working wife who is able to give her husband so much to eat that he even has to shield her away from bringing more food [*Ganda*].

Mmese (m) *[mmeh-seh]* Rat; a mouse; this name is sometimes associated with the proverb which dramatizes that greed or passion blinds reasoning-- "the need to eat leads the rat (blindingly) into the calabash" i.e. to where it is easily caught and killed; this name is also sometimes associated with the proverb "the tears of a rat come when it is caught in a trap" i.e. the sorrowing tears come belatedly, as the rat dies; this name is also sometimes associated with the proverbs "a rat gets to the level of stealing things in the house only after it has finished digging hideouts (holes)" and "once you see a rat biting at a bountiful load, then it has surely dug up a sufficient number of holes" implying that one who goes to carry out daring or unpalatable acts usually has strongly armed himself or established a getaway to which he may retreat when things do not go as planned; this name is also sometimes associated with the proverb "a thief is like a rat--he can only be caught with the use of enticing bait" [*Ganda*].

Mmoloki (f) *[mmoh-loh-kih]* Guardian; keeper [*Sotho*] (Thipa 1987: 114).

Mmoneng (m) *[mmoh-neh-ndgh]* "See him!": a name such as given to a newborn by its mother to point out that she wishes everybody to perceive and pray for the product of her pregnancy which was so much talked about prior to the birth [*Sotho*] (Herbert 1990: 9).

Mmonero/ Monero (f) *[mmoh-neh-roh]* Sightings; signs; signals; symbols; feelings of regret [*Ganda*].

Mmundu (m) *[mmuhn-duh]* Gun; rifle; this name is sometimes associated with the proverb "where a gun points is where it kills (or conquers)" which is more so related to the past whereby the spear based local military technology was no match for the gun power of the colonialists, and the slave and ivory raiders [*Ganda*].

Mmunye (m) *[mmuh-ndjh-eh]* Eye; pupil of the eye [*Ganda*].

Mnce (m) *[uhmn-tch-eh]* A nickname-abbreviation for *Mncedist*: "Helper" [*Xhosa*] (Neethling 1994: 92).

Mncedist (m) *[uhmn-tch-eh-dih-st]* Helper [*Xhosa*] (Neethling 1994: 92).

Mnukwa (m) *[muh-nuh-kwah]* "The suspect": a name such as given to a newborn by its father who is publicly venting his frustration and anger, as he denies the suspicions of practicing witchcraft cast upon him by neighbors [*Zulu*] (Turner 1992: 54).

Modi (m) *[moh-dih]* A name denoting misfortune that is commonly given to one who lost more than one older sibling (usually brother) to death [*Bari*] (Whitehead 1947: 45).

Modisa (m) *[moh-dih-sah]* Shepherd [*Sotho*] (Thipa 1987: 114).

Modupe (m) *[moh-duh-peh]* Soft rain: a name such as given to one born during a period of rainfall [*Sotho*] (Herbert 1990: 5).

Moeletsi (m) *[moh-yeh-leh-tsih]* Counselor [*Sotho*] (Thipa 1987: 114).

Moferefere (m) *[moh-feh-reh-feh-reh]* Confusion; conflict: a name such as given to one born out of wedlock or infidelity [*Sotho*] (Thipa 1987: 112).

Mogga (m) *[mohg-gah]* "The one who holds the twins"/ "the one who is held by twins": a name commonly given to one whose immediately preceding siblings are twins [*Bari*] (Whitehead 1947: 45).

Mohau (m) *[moh-hahw]* Mercy [*Sotho*] (Thipa 1987: 116).

Mohlouwa (m) *[moh-lohw-wah]* "The hated one": a name such as given to one born out of wedlock or infidelity [*Sotho*] (Thipa 1987: 112).

Mokera (m) *[moh-keh-rah]* Burning; burning down; incinerating; roasting [*Ganda*].

Moleboheng (f) *[moh-leh-boh-heh-ndgh]* "Thank (the Lord) for her birth" [*Sotho*] (Thipa 1987: 110).

Molelekeng (f) *[moh-leh-leh-keh-ndgh]* "Disown (or sack) her": a name such as given to one born out of wedlock or infidelity [*Sotho*] (Thipa 1987: 112).

Moma/ Mmoma (m) *[mmoh-mah]* That is highly adept (or highly proficient); expert [*Ganda*].

Momboze (m) *[mohm-boh-zeh]* That recounts (or narrates, or mentions) [The *Ganda*].

Mombwe/ Mmombwe (m) *[mmohm-bweh]* That is held as security for the payment of a debt; that is striped [*Ganda*].

Monde (m) *[mohn-deh]* Patience [*Xhosa*] (Neethling 1994: 92).

Monde (m) *[mohn-deh]* Perseverance [*Xhosa*] (Thipa 1987: 114).

Mondes (f) *[mohn-dehs]/ Monde* (f) *[mohn-deh]* Nicknames-abbreviations for *Nomonde*: "Patience" [*Xhosa*] (Neethling 1994: 92).

Mondli (m) *[mohn-dlih]* The provider [*Zulu*] (Turner 1992: 43).

Mondo/ Mmondo (m) *[mmohn-doh]* The serval cat [*Ganda*].

Monnaotsile (m) *[moh-nah-woh-tsih-leh]* "A man has come": a name commonly given to a first born male amongst several older female siblings [The *Sotho*] (Herbert 1990: 17).

Monwa (f) *[moh-nwah]* A nickname-abbreviation for *Monwabisi*: "Giver of joy" [*Xhosa*] (Neethling 1994: 92).

Monwabisi (f) *[moh-nwah-bih-sih]* "Giver of joy" [*Xhosa*] (Neethling 1994: 92).

Moongo (f) *[moh-ohn-goh]* "Nursing mother": an honorary praise name usually bestowed on one who has half a dozen or more children, including an eldest son who has proved his might and mettle through adult initiation and other achievements [*Chaga*] (Raum 1967: 125).

Mosa (f) *[moh-sah]* "Son": an inappropriate 'cross-name' is a form of derogatory-protection name usually given to one born following the deaths of several of her previously born siblings--such (normally temporary) names are intended to confuse the ancestral spirits through making them believe that the parents do not care for the newborn and therefore their taking it away (by dealing it a hand of death as happened to other children in the family) would not hurt or serve as punishment [*Sotho*] (Herbert 1990: 5, 6).

Mosidi (f) *[moh-sih-dih]* Grinder [*Sotho*] (Herbert 1990: 10).

Motheo (f) *[moh-teh-woh]* Foundation: a name such as given to a newborn by its mother who before the pregnancy was ignorant of God, and so considers the newborn the foundation of her relationship with God, including of her salvation whereby she became a born again Christian [The *Sotho*] (Herbert 1990: 10).

Motlalentwa (m) *[moh-tlah-lehn-twah]* The one who brings war: a name such as given to one born out of wedlock or infidelity [*Sotho*] (Thipa 1987: 112).

Moyakazi (m) *[moh-yah-kah-zih]* Wind; dust: a name given to one born during dusty, windy, or drought conditions [*Xhosa*] (Thipa 1986: 289).

Moyo (m) *[moh-yoh]* Heart [*Ndebele*] (Hemans 1968: 74).

Mpaalikamanya (f) *[mpaah-lih-kah-mah-ndjh-aah]* "I give to the one who will know it"; "give me (or tell me) the one who will know it" [*Ganda*].

Mpaalikanya (f) *[mpaah-lih-kah-ndjh-ah]* "I give to the one who will increase (or abound, or will cause to be abundant)"; "give me (or tell me) the one who will increase (or abound, or will cause to be prolific)" [*Ganda*].

Mpaalikiraba (f) *[mpaah-lih-tch-ih-rah-bah]* "I give to the one who will see it (or perceive it, or find it, or get it)"; "give me (or tell me) the one who will see it (or perceive it, or find it, or get it)" [*Ganda*].

Mpaalugamba (f) *[mpaah-luh-gaahm-bah]* "I give to the one who says (or tells) it"; "give me the one who says (or tells) it" [*Ganda*].

Mpabulimu (f) *[mpah-buh-lih-muh]* "I give to those that have within themselves" [*Ganda*]

Mpabulungi (m) *[mpah-buh-luhn-jih]* "I give effectively (or properly, or nicely, or well)"; "I give to goodness (or quality, or beauty)" [*Ganda, Soga*]

Mpaggwa (m) *[mpahg-gwah]* Bullheaded and obstinate person; person with large and protruding ears [*Ganda*].

Mpaka (m) *[mpah-kah]* Argument; dispute; strife; contest; competition; game; this name is sometimes associated with the proverb "unceasing arguments result in the beating of the hated one" implying that it is often the disliked ones that are scapegoated for even the offenses of the favorites, as exemplified by a disliked wife bearing the blame for a favorite co-wife [The *Ganda*].

Mpalanyi (m) *[mpah-lah-ndjh-ih]* That foments hostility (or feuding, or mutual disliking) [*Ganda*].

Mpalata (m) *[mpah-laah-tah]* (Having) balding on the head [*Ganda*].

Mpalikitenda/ Mpaalikitenda (m) *[mpaah-lih-tch-ih-tehn-dah]* "I give to the one who will praise it"; "give me the one who will commend it" [*Ganda*].

Mpamulungi (f) *[mpah-muh-luhn-jih]* "I give to the good (or virtuous) one"; "I give to the beautiful (or handsome) person" [*Ganda, Soga*].

Mpande (m) *[mpaahn-deh]* Seed that resembles a peanut; fragment; piece; this name is sometimes associated with the proverb "one coffee seed that falls from the basket causes the whole basketfull to be spilled" implying that as in this instance of one stooping down to pick up the one fallen seed, one individual can cause suffering to a whole community, concentrating on the trivial and losing sight of the great things is counterproductive, and the proverb is also synonymous with "penny wise, pound foolish" [*Ganda*].

Mpanga (m) *[mpahn-gah]* Skull [*Bashi*].

Mpangaala (m) *[mpaahn-gaah-lah]* "I live long"; "I have a long life"; that lives for a long time [*Ganda*].

Mpangi (m) *[mpahn-jih]* Furrow (made with a hoe); plot of land [*Ganda*].

Mpanju (m) *[mpahn-juh]* "Give me a house"; "I give to the house" [*Ganda*].

Mpasa (m) *[mpah-sah]* Ax; "I get married"; mode of marrying [The *Ganda, Soga*].

Mpata/ Mpaata (m) *[mpaah-tah]* (Having) balding on the head [*Soga*].

Mpawulo (m) *[mpah-wuh-loh]* Cowry shell with the top removed [*Soga*].

Mpeera (f) *[mpeh-eh-rah]* Reward; salary; pay; wage [*Ganda*].

Mpeka (m) *[mpeh-kah]* A charm worn by mother on behalf of her child; braces [*Ganda*].

Mpeke (m) *[mpeh-keh]* Grain; seed; peel [*Ganda*].

Mpembe (m) *[mpehm-beh]* Crusts (on burnt food); burnt portions adhering to the pans; (formations of) crusts or scabs; coagulations; swarmings; abundances [*Ganda*].

Mpendo (m) *[mpehn-doh]* Long stick with a stick attached to the end that is used to grasp things which are out of arm's reach [*Ganda*].

Mpengere (m) *[mpehn-geh-reh]* Corn nuts; popcorn; dry sorghum millet eaten when the preferred food is scarce [*Ganda, Soga*].

Mpera (m) *[mpeh-rah]* The brandishing of weapons and morale boosting (before the war) as a token of loyalty, bravery, and determination; this name is sometimes associated with the proverbs "a demonstration of prowess does not restrict the feet--it does not prevent the warrior from fleeing (during the actual fight)" and "a demonstration of prowess does not restrict the legs--it is confined to the mouth" which imply that those who boast or display enthusiasm would not necessarily stand up and fight, and not run away from the real situation (as with the example of war whereby one can boast with his mouth, but he is still with the convenience of the feet or legs with which he can flee as he demonstrates his cowardice and non-commitment when the fighting begins) [*Ganda*].

Mpewo (m) *[mpeh-woh]* Wind; breeze; draft; air; atmosphere; cold; cold air [*Ganda*].

Mphikeleli (f/m) *[mpih-keh-leh-lih]* "The stubborn one": name such as given to a newborn by it's maternal grandfather to register his annoyance at his daughter who, after not heeding his warning following bearing her first child, has also borne this second one of wedlock [*Zulu*] (Turner 1992: 52).

Mphikeni (m) *[mpih-keh-nih]* The denial: a name such as given by a mother to a newborn to reflect that the alleged father of this child denies that he is the parent [*Zulu*] (Turner 1992: 48).

Mpho (m) *[mpoh]* "Gift" [*Sotho*] (Thipa 1987: 109).

Mpiiga (m) *[mpiih-gah]* Envy; jealousy; this name is sometimes associated with the proverb "jealousy against jealousy does not make the village prosperous" implying that heated jealousy between two prominent leaders in the village will involve so much friction and disorder that the entire community will unlikely settle down and thrive [*Ganda*].

Mpiima (m) *[mpiih-mah]* Dagger; knife; this name is sometimes associated with the proverb "it is not the meat cutting knife that does the cheating, it is the spirit of the one who cuts (or the distributor) that does it" [*Ganda*].

Mpiimerebera (m) *[mpiih-meh-eh-reh-beh-rah]* "The dagger (or knife) that is not firm" [*Ganda*].

Mpijja (m) *[mpij-jah]* Stone anvil; stone anvils [*Ganda*].

Mpindi (m) *[mpihn-dih]* The name of a species of small bean.

Mpindimuti (m) *[mpihn-dih-muh-tih]* "Small beans are (like) a tree"; "small beans are (like) a cowardly person" [*Ganda*].

Mpinga (m) *[mpihn-gah]* The top of the hill; to frustrate; to spoil things for [*Ganda*].

Mpingi (m) *[mpihn-jih]* Traps intended for birds and small animals [*Ganda*].

Mpingu (m) *[mpihn-guh]* A naval fleet; a fleet of canoes; a pair of handcuffs [*Ganda, Soga*].

Mpiri (m) *[mpih-rih]* Species of poisonous snake; the puff adder [*Ganda*].

Mpisi (m) *[mpih-sih]* Hyena; hyenas;this name is sometimes associated with the proverb "even the most indulging glutton cannot eat everything, otherwise the hyena would eat bananas" [*Ganda*].

Mpiso (m) *[mpih-soh]* Sewing (or hypodermic) needle; this name is sometimes associated with the proverb "the stone anvil that is instrumental in forging the needle, also helps forge the knife" implying that a mother's position in the world is paramount, as synonymous with "the hand that rocks the cradle, rules the world"; this name is also sometimes associated with the proverb "a rich person is so heartless, greedy, usurping and uncharitable just like the gargantuan lake which will not give back even the needle that has accidentally fallen into it"; this name is also sometimes associated with the proverb "a grown up (or mature person) will not brandish a needle and then not use it" implying that the earnest requests of elders are often sincere so they ought to be taken seriously, and that one of strong character acts deliberately and according to principles [*Ganda*].

Mpitiro (m) *[mpih-tih-roh]* Path; passage [*Ganda*].

Mpologoma (f/m) *[mpoh-loh-goh-mah]* Lion; lioness [*Ganda, Soga*].

Mpona (f/m) *[mpoh-nah]* "I escape from"; "I get rid of"; "I become cured (or healed)"; "I escape"; "I become saved" *[Ganda]*.

Mponye (m) *[mpoh-ndjh-eh]* "I have escaped from"; "I have got rid of"; "I have become cured (or healed)"; "I have escaped"; "I have become saved" *[Ganda]*.

Mpoza (m) *[mpoh-zah]* Justification; explanation; rationale; defense [The *Ganda]*.

Mpozaaki (f/m) *[mpoh-zaah-tch-ih]* "What grounds do I have for a plea of defense (or for justification, or for explanation)?"; "what am I pleading for?"; "of what use will my plea (or explanation, or justification) be?" [The *Ganda]*.

Mpumbu (m) *[mpuhm-buh]* Sawdust; rotted and dried patch in wood; dust looking substance produced by worms or insects that bore; powdery coating found on some leaves and peanuts *[Ganda]*.

Mpumelelo (m) *[mpuh-meh-leh-loh]* Success *[Xhosa]* (Neethling 1994: 92; Thipa 1987: 114).

Mpumi (m) *[mpuh-mih]* A nickname-abbreviation for *Mpumelelo*: "Success" *[Xhosa]* (Neethling 1994: 92).

Mpumy (f) *[muh-mee]* Nickname-abbreviation for *Nompumelelo*: "Success" *[Xhosa]* (Neethling 1994: 92).

Mpungu (m) *[mpuhn-guh]* Eagle; opening; gap; space; this name is sometimes associated with the proverb "the eagle kills for others" i.e. the eagle often lets its captured prey drop *[Ganda]*.

Mpuulo (m) *[mpuuh-loh]* Acts of thrashing (or beating); acts of beating hard; acts of throwing to the ground; acts of raiding cattle; that is proposed (or intended); that involve losing one's wife through separation or desertion; that involve the large mallet employed in the second stage beating in processing barkcloth; that involve the flail, a heavy stick employed in separating grains from husks *[Ganda]*.

Mpuuna (f) *[mpuuh-naah]* One who makes or reacts with indistinct sounds; one who responds with a grunt (or groan) *[Ganda]*.

Mqo (m) *[uhm-qoh]* A nickname-abbreviation for *Mqokeleli*: "Gatherer" *[Xhosa]* (Neethling 1994: 92).

Mqokeleli (m) *[uhm-qoh-keh-leh-lih]* "Gatherer" *[Xhosa]* (Neethling 1994: 92).

Msayinelwa (f/m) *[muh-sah-yih-neh-lwah]* "Having signed for": a name such as given to a newborn by it's maternal uncle to serve as a constant reminder of the family dispute that took place when the mother was pregnant with this child; consequently, the namer who is the mother's eldest brother, forbid his brothers from entering the homestead again, and even made them sign a letter agreement which is alluded to in the name [The *Zulu]* (Turner 1992: 52).

Msuri (m) *[muh-suh-rih]* "The rich one" *[Chaga]* (Raum 1967: 340).

Mtholephi (m) *[muh-toh-leh-pih]* "Where did you get him from?": name such as given to a newborn by it's maternal grandparents disgruntled over their daughter who had left home to seek employment, returned home less than a year later with a heavy pregnancy, and she was unable to name with certainty the father of the child or his whereabouts [*Zulu*] (Turner 1992: 51).

Mubaazi (m) *[muh-baah-zih]* Butcher; flayer; surgeon; this name is sometimes associated with the proverb "the ears of a butcher heed to 'the dog is stealing your meat', but if you ask him for some meat, he does not give you any" meaning that the willingness of people to respond to a situation depends on level of convenience much more than on kindness and compassion [*Ganda*].

Mubango (m) *[muh-bahn-goh]* Hump on the back; a projecting part; the shaft of a spear [*Ganda*].

Mubazzi (m) *[muh-bahz-zih]* Carpenter [*Ganda*].

Mubbi (m) *[muhb-bih]* Thief; this name is sometimes associated with the proverb "a thief uses his (long) fingers manipulatively while purchasing" which situation is contrasted with the honest person who uses his money to purchase; this name is also sometimes associated with the proverb "a thief is like a rat--he can only be caught with the use of enticing bait"; this name is also sometimes associated with the proverb "a thieving person (or child) is not readily placed in the care someone to be brought up" [*Ganda*].

Mubeezi (f/m) *[muh-beh-eh-zih]* Helper; assistant [*Ganda, Soga*].

Mubembe (m) *[muh-behm-beh]* A member of the *Bembe* ethnic group; one associated with the *Bembe* ethnics [*Bashi*].

Mubi (m) *[muh-bih]* The bad one; bad person; ugly person; this name is sometimes associated with the proverb "even a defective (or bad, or ugly) child is given birth to--when you give birth to a crippled one, you do not throw it away"; this name is also sometimes associated with the proverb "an ugly one who chats (thereby making a pleasant impression) is worth more than (or is preferable to) a good looking one who is aloof and conceited"; this name is also sometimes associated with the proverb "a bad tiller blames the hoe" which is synonymous with "a bad workman blames his tools" [The *Ganda*].

Mubialiwo (m) *[muh-bjah-lih-woh]* "The bad person is present" [*Soga*].

Mubiina (m) *[muh-biih-nah]* Collection together; a pile up.

Mubiito (m) *[muh-biih-toh]* Favorite; person who is especially pleasing [The *Ganda*].

Mubikkula (m) *[muh-bihk-kuh-lah]* That uncovers (or takes the lid off, or reveals); that opens (such as a book) [*Ganda*].

Mubinge (m) *[muh-bihn-geh]* That is driven away (or chased) [*Ganda*].

Mubiru (m) *[muh-bih-ruh]* A log to slide a canoe over [*Ganda*].

Mubisi (f) *[muh-bih-sih]* Sweet banana juice; honey; that which is fresh (or raw, or uncooked, or green, or unripe); one who is naive; one who is uncultured [*Ganda*].

Mubumbi (m) *[muh-buhm-bih]* Potter; molder; this name is sometimes associated with the proverb "a potter drying his pots is only bragging when he says 'When it comes to my wares, I just stand here on the drying shelves and toss them down (without them cracking)'" [*Ganda*].

Mubuuke (m) *[muh-buuh-keh]* One who is jumped over (or left out) [*Ganda*].

Mubuya (m) *[muh-buh-yah]* That is silly (or stupid) [*Ganda*].

Mubyowuwo/ Mubiowuwo (f/m) *[muh-bjoh-oh-wuh-woh]* "The person of your family is bad"; "the one of yours is bad"; "it is your comrade that is bad"; "the one that is bad (or ugly) is one of your kindred" [*Soga*].

Mudde (m) *[muhd-deh]* "(You all) come back (or return)" [*Ganda*].

Muddogwaluyiira (m) *[muhd-doh-gwah-luh-yiih-rah]* The new grass that sprouts after the old grassy area is burnt out; this name is commonly associated with the proverb "the luxuriant green grass that grows following the slashing and burning is looked forward to by even the one who does not own a goat" implying that good weather that will guarantee a good food crop and bountiful feeding conditions for the animals is looked forward to by, and is to the benefit of, both those who are and those who are not farmers [*Ganda*].

Muddu (m) *[muhd-duh]* Servant; member of the cultivator social class as opposed to the aristocratic cattle keeping class; captive; this name is sometimes associated with the proverb "the day a servant butchers his animal, is when he gets a father and a mother" implying that opportunists who claim to be relatives or friends will flock around even one in servitude that has just acquired or potentially has something to give away; this name is also sometimes associated with the proverb "a serf who becomes a member of the clan becomes (i.e. gets to take on the honorary title of) the 'father of twins' (i.e. *Ssaalongo*)" whereby aside from family connection, an one can traditionally become a clan member through such means as adoption, assimilation, long term residence, capture, and blood ritual; "the serf (or servant) that is obedient, gets the honor of holding the head dress of his king into battle" whereby traditionally, the *Mugabe*, the one in charge of the entire army, is invested with this honor as a symbol of homage and confidence --it is implied that a low class person can get to achieve immense authority through complying with the demands of superiors [*Ganda*].

Mudhasi/ Mudhaasi (m) *[muh-dhaah-sih]* A courageous fighter; a soldier; policeman; Chief of police; Commander-in-Chief [*Soga*].

Mudhungu (m) *[muh-tdh-uhn-guh]* That is of the wilderness (or wasteland, or desert); that is associated with *Ddungu* the God associated with hunters and animals [*Soga*].

Mudiima (m) *[muh-diih-mah]* That cultivates with the use of a hoe [*Soga*].

Mudondo (m) *[muh-dohn-doh]* Umbilical cord; navel; infant with a large umbilical cord or navel [*Soga*].

Mudondoli (m) *[muh-dohn-doh-lih]* That has gone bad; (beer) that has turned sour [*Ganda*].

Mudongo (m) *[muh-dohn-goh]* Harp player; musician [*Ganda*].

Mudungu (m) *[muh-duhn-guh]* That is of the wilderness (or wasteland, or desert); that is associated with *Ddungu* the God associated with hunters and animals [*Ganda*].

Mufumba (m) *[muh-fuhm-bah]* One who cooks; back muscle [*Soga*].

Mufumbe (m) *[muh-fuhm-beh]* Cooked [*Ganda*].

Mufumbiro (f/m) *[muh-fuhm-bih-roh]* One that is in (or that is of) the kitchen; one that cooks [*Soga*].

Mufume (m) *[muh-fuh-meh]* One that tells or recounts a legend (or a tradition, or a tale) [*Ganda*].

Mufumu (m) *[muh-fuh-muh]* Magician; medicine man; doctor [*Ganda*].

Mufumula (m) *[muh-fuh-muh-lah]* That probes; that digs up [*Ganda*].

Mufuumuula (m) *[muh-fuuh-muuh-lah]* That expels (or drives away, or pursues, or fires from employment) [*Ganda*].

Mugaanyi (m) *[muh-gaah-ndjh-ih]* One who causes to refuse [*Ganda*].

Mugaati (m) *[muh-gaah-tih]* Bread; loaf [*Ganda*].

Mugaba (m) *[muh-gah-bah]* That is donated/ or given (by God) [*Ganda*].

Mugabanseko (m) *[muh-gah-bahn-seh-koh]* "The distributor of laughter": a name such as given to one who is joked about or who often makes people laugh [*Ganda, Soga*].

Mugabi (m) *[muh-gah-bih]* Generous person; liberal person; one who distributes; distributor; this name is sometimes associated with the proverb "it is not the meat cutting knife that does the cheating, it is the spirit of the one who distributes it that does it" [*Ganda*].

Mugabira (m) *[muh-gah-bih-rah]* That gives away (or gives away, or gives as a present, or distributes, or designates) for/ or in/ or on behalf of others [*Soga*].

Mugabuzi (f/m) *[muh-gah-buh-zih]* That gives or entertains lavishly or pays for or provides a commendable meal [*Ganda*].

Mugagga (m) *[muh-gahg-gah]* The wealthy one; this name is sometimes associated with the proverb "a rich person is so heartless, greedy, usurping and uncharitable just like the gargantuan lake which will not give back even the needle that has accidentally fallen into it"; this name is also sometimes associated with the proverb "one who has plenty of food at home is (paradoxically) still killed by famine starvation conditions while on the road traveling" implying that those who have much become blind to the fact that conditions away from home can be far different from those at home; this name is also sometimes associated with the proverb "a rich person never ceases to be congratulated on account of achievements (or luckiness)" implying that the wealthy are flattered much more than the poor since they have more authority and also the potential to give much [*Ganda*].

Mugalagala (m) *[muh-gah-lah-gah-lah]* A page (or boy) residing in the palace and serving the king [*Ganda*].

Mugalu (m) *[muh-gah-luh]*/ *Mugalula* (m) *[muh-gah-luh-lah]* One that raises (his head or a weapon) so as to strike [*Ganda*].

Mugalya (m) *[muh-gah-ljah]* "You (all) eat them"; "you (all) consume them" [*Ganda*].

Mugamba (m) *[muh-gahm-bah]* That says/ or talks/ or tells (a lot) [*Ganda*].

Mugambajjolo (m) *[muh-gahm-bahj-joh-loh]* Chiseling [*Ganda*].

Mugambe (m) *[muh-gahm-beh]* One that is told (or said) to *[Ganda]*.

Mugambi (m) *[muh-gahm-bih]* One who says (or says to, or tells) *[Ganda]*.

Mugambwa (m) *[muh-gahm-bwah]* One who is said of (or told of) *[Ganda]*.

Mugana (m) *[muh-gah-nah]* One who relates (or tells) tales *[Ganda]*.

Mugana-Asuubira (m) *[muh-gah-naah-suuh-bih-rah]* "One who relates or tells tales expects (or hopes, or anticipates)" *[Ganda]*.

Muganda (m) *[muh-gahn-dah]* A person that works in the courtyard *[Bashi]*.

Muganda (m) *[muh-gahn-dah]* Bundle; bunch; brother; blood (or kin) relative; something terrible; terror; native of the kingdom (or territory) of *Buganda*; this name is sometimes associated with the proverb "'death is ridden with greed!'--(so one says) when it has just killed a relative (or a brother, or a sister)" and the name, in this context, would be given to a child who is gravely sick, or one born into a family that has recently had a death or many deaths *[Ganda]*.

Mugano (m) *[muh-gah-noh]* A swarming/ abundance (such as of grasshoppers, or ants, or termites); this name is sometimes associated with the proverb "a swarm of edible flying ants attracts every elder to come out of his house (or leaves not a single elder at home)" implying that there are things, such as the delicious flying ants, which will attract almost everybody *[The Ganda]*.

Muganwa (m) *[muh-gah-nwaah]* One who is told tales to *[Ganda]*.

Muganza (m) *[muh-gahn-zah]* Caretaker *[Ganda]*.

Muganza (m) *[muh-gahn-zah]* Name given to the younger of twins *[Rega]*.

Muganzi (f/m) *[muh-gahn-zih]* Darling; favorite; lover; sweetheart; this name is sometimes associated with the proverb "when the favorite (or beloved) one commits an offense you, the disliked one, become gleeful" implying that since a disliked person (as with this example of a disfavored co-wife) tends to frequently be scapegoated, she will jump with joy when it becomes clear that the favored one, who is hardly blamed for anything, has done wrong; this name is also sometimes associated with the proverb "an offense committed by a favorite is (often) paid for (or settled) by the disfavored one" which, similar to the foregone proverb, addresses the commonplace tendency for the disliked to be scapegoated for the offenses of the favored; this name is also sometimes associated with the proverb "a well loved person does not tumble into the baskets" implying that such a person is always welcome and, even if not expected at a meal, can easily join in *[Ganda]*.

Muganzi-Abuulirwa (f) *[muh-gahn-zih-ah-buuh-lih-rwah]* "Even a favorite (or a beloved) one can be told (or informed, or preached to)" *[Ganda]*.

Muganzi-Amalakuwona (f) *[muh-gahn-zih-ah-mah-lah-kuh-woh-nah]* "Let the favorite (or beloved one) get well first" *[Ganda]*

Muganzi-Atiibwa (f) *[muh-gahn-zjaah-tiih-bwah]* "The favorite (or beloved) one is feared (or respected)" *[Ganda]*.

Muganzirwazza (f) *[muh-gahn-zih-rwahz-zah]* "When the favorite (or beloved) one commits an offense; this name is commonly associated with the proverb "when the favorite (or beloved) one commits an offense you, the disliked one, become gleeful" implying that since a disliked person (as with this example of a disfavored co-wife) tends to frequently be scapegoated, she will jump with joy when it becomes clear that the favored one, who is hardly blamed for anything, has done wrong [*Ganda*].

Mugaya (m) *[muh-gah-yah]* Small bush having roots that are chewed while in their raw state; one that scorns or has contempt for [*Soga*].

Mugayangabo (m) *[muh-gah-yahn-gah-boh]* That scorns or has contempt for the shield (or fighting) [*Soga*].

Mugazi (m) *[muh-gah-zih]* That is broad (or wide, or thick) [*Ganda, Soga*].

Mugemuzi (f/m) *[muh-geh-muh-zih]* That gives; that entertains lavishly; that pays for (or provides a commendable meal) [*Ganda*].

Mugenyi (m) *[muh-geh-ndjh-ih]* Guest; stranger; visitor; this name is sometimes associated with the proverb "a visitor who stays long (or who does not leave) is made to tread out the beer" implying that the visitor who stays too long, often loses his "visitor" status and, gets to be treated like members of the household (such as doing jobs that a visitor would not normally do); this name is also sometimes associated with the proverb "a visitor that gets to eat satisfactorily, makes the food tell it" implying that the amount of uneaten leftover food indicates the extent of satisfaction; this name is also sometimes associated with the proverb "a visitor who arrives with a bag (or the visitor with luggage), you do not start off by vilifying him" which is synonymous with "no man is esteemed so well as he that comes full-handed" which implies that those with the potential to give materially are treated decently [*Ganda*].

Mugenzitazze (m) *[muh-gehn-zih-tahz-zeh]* "The departed one (or the traveler) has not returned" [*Ganda*].

Mugereko (m) *[muh-geh-reh-koh]* Allotment; portion; share [*Ganda, Soga*].

Mugerengejjo (m) *[muh-geh-rehn-gehj-joh]* A riddle; an obscure speech; a puzzling speech [*Ganda*].

Mugerere (m) *[muh-geh-reh-reh]* That is apportioned for (or assigned for, or distributed for) [*Ganda, Soga*].

Mugeresi (m) *[muh-geh-reh-sih]* One that assesses the value of; that apportions [*Ganda, Soga*].

Mugerwa (m) *[muh-geh-rwah]* That is measured/ or standardized; of medium / or average height [*Ganda*].

Mugga (m) *[muhg-gah]* Water well; river; large stream.; this name is sometimes associated with the proverb "the feeling of satisfaction (or fullness) after eating does not even last the time it takes to cross a river" implying that feelings or conditions of satiety rarely last long [*Ganda*].

Muggala (m) *[muhg-gah-lah]* One who closes (the entrances); the closer; gatekeeper; one who brings to an end; "the closer (of the womb)" i.e. the last born child; a basket trap having a hole at the bottom, and is used to capture lake fish [*Ganda*].

Muggale (f) *[muhg-gah-leh]* "(It is) closed (or brought to an end, or discontinued, or enclosed)" [*Ganda*].

Muggulu (m) *[muhg-guh-luh]* Of (or in) heaven (or the sky, or lightning) [*Ganda*].

Muggyaabaza (m) *[muhj-jaah-bah-zah]* "The newcomer causes to bear fruit" [*Ganda*].

Muggyabaza (m) *[muhj-jah-bah-zah]* "Newcomer, cause to bear fruit"; "newcomer, cause to count (or calculate, or reckon, or consider)" [*Ganda*].

Muggyankondo (m) *[muhj-jahn-kohn-doh]* One that takes out tree stumps [*Ganda*].

Mugimba (m) *[muh-jihm-bah]* One who takes by surprise [*Ganda*].

Mugimu (m) *[muh-jih-muh]* That is fertile (or fruitful, or with vigor, or with vitality); this name is sometimes associated with the proverbs "the fruitfulness of a person is evident at the time when, as a baby, the person is still wrapped on its mother's back in infant clothing" and "that a child is (or will be) strong and healthy, is evident at the time when, as a baby, it is still wrapped in infant clothing" which imply that a lot can be told about the future of one that is still an infant [*Ganda*].

Muginga (m) *[muh-jihn-gah]* One that forges (or falsifies, or camouflages, or makes up); one who clowns; stupid person; fool [*Ganda*].

Mugoba (m) *[muh-goh-bah]* One that navigates; steersman; driver (of a vehicle); this name is sometimes associated with the proverbs "an oarsman (has to concentrate so) does not gnaw at a bone" and "an oarsman whose gaze wanders, steers the canoe onto the rocks" which advise against carelessness that involves engaging in distracting activity that would lead those with responsible duties to disaster [*Ganda*].

Mugobe (m) *[muh-goh-beh]* That is pursued (or followed, or chased) [The *Ganda, Soga*].

Mugogo (f/m) *[muh-goh-goh]* A necklace made from the flowering stem of the plantain; stalk of a plantain tree; pair; couple; collar; one afflicted with spinal congenital paralysis [*Ganda, Soga*].

Mugole (f/m) *[muh-goh-leh]* Bride; mistress of the house; newly appointed or graduated person; bridegroom; new coming arrival; newly ordained priest or minister [*Ganda, Soga*].

Mugolooba (f) *[muh-goh-loh-oh-bah]* The setting of the sun; the coming to an end of the day; getting dark [*Ganda*].

Mugolozi (m) *[muh-goh-loh-zih]* One who straightens out or corrects; one that irons out dents [*Ganda, Soga*].

Mugoma (m) *[muh-goh-mah]* Drummer [*Ganda, Soga*].

Mugomba (m) *[muh-gohm-bah]* A clumsy (or awkward) person; bungler; big and ugly [*Ganda*].

Mugonja (m) *[muh-gohn-jah]* A species of large banana eaten after being baked or boiled [*Ganda*].

Mugonza (m) *[muh-gohn-zah]* One that softens (or appeases, or makes obedient, or flatters) [*Ganda, Soga*].

Mugowa/ Mugoowa (m) *[muh-goh-oh-wah]* Of (or associated with) Goan-

East Indian ethnicity [*Ganda*].

Mugoya (m) *[muh-goh-yah]* Blind worm [*Ganda, Soga*].

Mugula (m) *[muh-guh-lah]* One that buys or purchases; a purchase [*Ganda*].

Mugule (m) *[muh-guh-leh]* That is purchased (or bought); big and ugly looking cloud (that presages a heavy downpour of rain) [*Ganda*].

Muguluka (m) *[muh-guh-luh-kah]* One that gallops or flies; to ignore (or neglect, or pay no attention to) [*Ganda, Soga*].

Muguluma (m) *[muh-guh-luh-mah]* One who assumes an air of self importance; one who overrates himself [*Ganda*].

Mugulumali (m) *[muh-guh-luh-mah-lih]* That is high (or tall, or lofty) [The *Ganda*].

Mugulusi (m) *[muh-guh-luh-sih]* One that causes to gallop (or fly, or frolic); ignoring (or neglecting, or paying no attention to) [*Soga*].

Muguma (m) *[muh-guh-mah]* Shaft of a spear; sharpened stick for killing lungfish [*Ganda*].

Mugumya (m) *[muh-guh-mjah]* One who makes firm (or establishes); "the one who keeps them together (or firm)" [*Ganda*].

Mugunzi (m) *[muh-guhn-zih]* A discoverer; inventor; founder; an originator [*Ganda*].

Muguzi (m) *[muh-guh-zih]* A buyer; a purchaser; a customer; this name is commonly associated with the proverb "the one who has an item set aside for him to buy later, is not (necessarily) its eventual buyer" implying that a merchant's interest is mostly in immediate buyers much more than in those who demand goods that it is uncertain they will pay for [*Ganda*].

Mugwanya/ Mugwaanya (m) *[muh-gwaah-ndjh-ah]* One who makes suitable (or fitting) [*Ganda*].

Mugwe (m) *[muh-gweh]* "That you may (all) fall/ or fail" [*Ganda, Soga*].

Mugweri (m) *[muh-gweh-eh-rih]* Of (or associated with) *Bugweri* [*Soga*].

Mugwira/ Mugwiira (m) *[muh-gwiih-rah]* Foreigner; alien [*Ganda*].

Mugwisa/ Mugwiisa (m) *[muh-gwiih-sah]* One that causes to fall (or to deteriorate) [*Ganda*].

Mujaasiagulannyago (m) *[muh-jaah-sih-ah-guh-lahn-ndjh-ah-goh]* "The courageous fighter (or the soldier, or the Commander-in-Chief) buys the spear" [*Ganda*].

Mujabi (m) *[muh-jah-bih]* One who talks very fast; jabberer [*Ganda*].

Mujaguzo (m) *[muh-jah-guh-zoh]* A celebration; a festival; jubilee; party; rejoicing; exultation [*Ganda*].

Mujambula (m) *[muh-jahm-buh-lah]* Strong and aggressive person; a rebel; a terrorist; rogue [*Ganda*].

Mujasi/ Mujaasi (m) *[muh-jaah-sih]* Courageous fighter; soldier; policeman; Chief of police; Commander-in-Chief [*Ganda*].

Mujeemera (f) *[muh-jeh-eh-meh-rah]* One who rebels against [*Ganda*].

Mujeere (m) *[muh-jeh-eh-reh]* That is made miserable (or wretched, or destitute) [*Ganda*].

Mujobe (f/m) *[muh-joh-beh]* One who is soaked; one who is wet all over; one who becomes messy [*Ganda*].

Mujumbi (m) *[muh-juhm-bih]* A torrent (of rain); rag; barkcloth kilt worn by hunters [*Ganda*].

Mujumbula (m) *[muh-juhm-buh-lah]* That takes great interest in; that is diligent in; that is zealous about; that causes to be zealous about; that causes to quarrel (or to become furious, or to become vexed) [*Ganda*].

Mujuna (m) *[muh-juh-nah]* That helps (or assists) [*Ganda*].

Mujunga (m) *[muh-juhn-gah]* Tassel [*Ganda*].

Mujuzi (m) *[muh-juh-zih]* That causes to fill (or fill up); that makes full [The *Ganda*].

Mujwala (m) *[muh-jwah-lah]* Adorned; well dressed [*Ganda*].

Mukaabya (m) *[muh-kaah-bjah]* "One who causes them to weep (or mourn, or sing [i.e. birds], or roar [i.e. animals], or sound)"; name-title of the king [*Ganda*].

Mukaaku (m) *[muh-kaah-kuh]* A barkcloth tree from which the bark has not yet been removed; first bark removed from the barkcloth tree [*Ganda*].

Mukaawa (m) *[muh-kaah-wah]* That is bitter (or sour, or unpleasant to the taste); that is enraged (or quarrelsome); a situation that has become serious (or bad) [*Ganda, Soga*].

Mukaaya (m) *[muh-kaah-yah]* That causes to be bitter (or sour, or unpleasant to the taste); that causes to become enraged (or quarrelsome); that causes a situation to become serious (or bad) [*Ganda*].

Mukabagolomola (f) *[muh-kaah-bah-goh-loh-moh-lah]* "The spouse of the ones who sets (boats or canoes) afloat" [*Ganda*].

Mukadde (f/m) *[muh-kahd-deh]* Elder; parent; old person; that is old; elder of the church; minister; this name is sometimes associated with the proverb "a settled old court case is a precedent for a new one" implying that laws, literary and academic works, and societal values build on past works and stipulations as references; this name is also sometimes associated with the proverb "an elderly person will (or can) go on a hunt, but when asked to go to war he will refuse" which mirrors the commonplace lame excuse--since the man is confident of his hunting speed, he should not bring up the excuse of being too advanced in years to participate in war; this name is also sometimes associated with the proverb "the one who vainly boasts 'I am well accustomed to being involved in war,' is like the elder (or weakling) who goes to war with an ax for which he is exclusively called upon to use in helping divide the (bovine) booty acquired by the warriors (for which work he is rewarded inferior, such as hump or neck, portions of the meat)"; this name is also sometimes associated with the proverb "a swarm of edible flying ants attracts every elder to come out of his house (or leaves not a single elder at home)" implying that there are things, such as the delicious flying ants, which will attract almost everybody [*Ganda*].

Mukadde-Ayigga (m) *[muh-kahd-deh-ah-yihg-gah]* "The elder is hunting"; "the elder would hunt"; this name is commonly associated with the proverb "an elderly person will (or can) go on a hunt, but when asked to go to war he will refuse" which mirrors the commonplace lame excuse--since the man is confident of his hunting speed, he should not bring up the excuse of being too advanced in years to participate in war [*Ganda*].

Mukajanga/ Mukaajanga (m) *[muh-kaah-jahn-gah]* Royal executioner; rascal; cruel person [*Ganda*].

Mukakanya/ Mukakkanya (m) *[muh-kahk-kah-ndjh-ah]* That causes to sit down (or go down, or come down, or to take a seat, or to move to a lower position); that causes to become mild (or to calm down); that causes (such as an illness or a difficult situation) to subside [*Ganda*].

Mukalazi (m) *[muh-kah-lah-zih]* That angers (or makes irascible, or irritates); that causes to become obstinate (or reluctant) [*Ganda*].

Mukalo (m) *[muh-kah-loh]* Dried or smoked meat; biltong [*Ganda*].

Mukama (m) *[muh-kah-mah]* Lord; God; boss; master; employer; title for a hereditary ruler (or king); this name is sometimes associated with the proverb "the serf (or servant) that is obedient, gets the honor of holding the head dress of his king into battle" whereby traditionally, the *Mugabe*, the one in charge of the entire army, is invested with this honor as a symbol of homage and confidence--it is implied that a low class person can get to achieve immense authority through complying with the demands of superiors [*Ganda*].

Mukamba (m) *[muh-kahm-bah]* A name given to a child born with the umbilical cord tied around it [*Rega*].

Mukamba (m) *[muh-kahm-bah]* Having acidity (or bitterness) [*Ganda*].

Mukambata (m) *[muh-kahm-baah-tah]* That makes acidic (or bitter); that is harsh (or severe, or furious, or cruel, or angry, or fierce) [*Ganda, Soga*].

Mukambilwa (m) *[muh-kahm-bih-lwah]* One who suspects another [*Rega*].

Mukanda (m) *[muh-kaahn-dah]* A permanent (or long term) dweller; invitation [*Ganda*].

Mukandikwa (m) *[muh-kahn-dih-kwah]* "The one they falsely accuse" [The *Rega*].

Mukanga (m) *[muh-kahn-gah]* That terrifies or scares; a terrorist [*Ganda*].

Mukangula (m) *[muh-kahn-guh-lah]* That raises (the voice); that disturbs (or creates an uproar); that raises (a price) [*Ganda*].

Mukasakkiriza (m) *[muh-kah-sahk-kih-rih-zah]* "*Mukasa* agrees (or consents, or is willing, or approves)"; "*Mukasa* do agree (or consent, or be willing, or approve)"; an attempt to gather (or to produce, or to collect); foraging with difficulty [*Ganda*].

Mukazi (f) *[muh-kah-zih]* Wife; woman; skillful (or commendable) woman; the one who abstains; this name is sometimes associated with the proverb "a wife is like an old cooking pot--you do not store it at a friend's house"; this name is also sometimes associated with the proverb "a woman who is a diligent farmer brings forth food, while the weak (or lazy) one brings forth grass weeds" which applies to an agricultural society in which women are the backbone of the food needs of the family; this name is also sometimes associated with the proverb "a woman who is a diligent farmer causes you (the husband) to eat with your shield over the food" which dramatises a very hard working wife who is able to give her husband so much to eat that he even has to shield her away from bringing more food; this name is also sometimes associated with the proverb "a woman who is a diligent cult-ivator is the one that gets to see the chicken dancing with joy" implying that such a woman provides plenty of nourishment to the chickens by digging so much, insofar as she uncovers so many insects in the soil, she encourages insect feeding presence on her heavy yields and harvest garbage and, she throws away into her garden a lot of leftover food that would attract bugs as well as the chickens [*Ganda*].

Mukeba (m) *[muh-keh-bah]* Trap; circumvention [*Ganda*].

Mukebezi (m) *[muh-keh-beh-zih]* Examiner; inspector [*Ganda*].

Mukebu (m) *[muh-keh-buh]* The name of a species of tree [*Ganda*].

Mukedi (m) *[muh-keh-dih]* The name of a species of wild fig tree; of (or ass-ociated with) the *Kedi* ethnics [*Ganda, Soga*].

Mukeeka (m) *[muh-keh-eh-kah]* Mat [*Ganda*].

Mukeera (m) *[muh-keh-eh-rah]* That gets up early; that does early; that does all the time; dawning; letting up (of the rain) [*Ganda*].

Mukembo (m) *[muh-kehm-boh]* Monkey; strut about in a proud and pompous manner; doubling one's effort [*Ganda, Soga*].

Mukengo (f) *[muh-kehn-goh]* That is noticed (or perceived); that is scented; that is suspected [*Ganda*].

Mukessi (m) *[muh-kehs-sih]* Spy [*Ganda*].

Mukibe (m) *[muh-tch-ih-beh]* "In the jackal" [*Ganda*].

Mukiibi (m) *[muh-tch-iih-bih]* That causes to go alongside of; that causes to sneak alongside of; that causes to skirt; that comes in or enters using the back door(s) [*Ganda*].

Mukiiko (m) *[muh-tch-iih-koh]* Assembly; parliament; representative body; council; congress [*Ganda*].

Mukiise (m) *[muh-tch-iih-seh]* Representative; member of a representative body [*Ganda*].

Mukimba (m) *[muh-kihm-bah]* Blacksmith's charges; a tree that resembles the laburnum; one who attacks [*Ganda*].

Mukindikira (m) *[muh-kihn-dih-kih-rah]* A tuck in of a garment at the waist [*Ganda*].

Mukisa (f/m) *[muh-kih-sah]* Blessing; fortune; luck; opportunity; umbilical cord of cattle; this name is sometimes associated with the proverb "good luck is (like) a flea--you would not kill it by sitting on it"; this name is also sometimes associated with the proverb "good luck is (like) a flea--it finds the bed (i.e. one of its favorite environments) already made" implying that those with inborn luck excessively find themmselves in favorable situations; this name is also sometimes associated with the proverb "good luck is (like) a flea--it does not get burnt in the house" implying that people who often es-cape or get away with it are compared to the flea which often jumps and es-capes away from burning situations [*Ganda*].

Mukka (m) *[muhk-kah]* Breath; air which one breathes; smoke; vapor; steam; this name is sometimes associated with the proverb "too much air bursts the inner tube of a soccer ball" which is related to the story of the frog that in wanting to become as big as a cow, blew himself up and consequently burst --it is implied that "pride goeth before a fall" and advises against unreasonable overindulgence [*Ganda*].

Mukkuto (f) *[muhk-kuh-toh]* Feeling of satisfaction (or of fullness) after eating; this name is sometimes associated with the proverb "the feeling of satisfaction (or fullness) after eating does not even last the time it takes to cross a river" implying that feelings or conditions of satiety rarely last long; this name is also sometimes associated with the proverb "eating to satisfaction makes one lazy, starving makes one ill" implying that one ought to do things in the right measure or in moderation [*Ganda*].

Mukodo (m) *[muh-koh-doh]* Miser; stingy person; this name is sometimes associated with the proverb "a miser is (like) the frog which hides its young (i.e. the tadpoles) in the water" implying that the stingy hardly expose their treasures [*Ganda*].

Mukulu (f/m) *[muh-kuh-luh]* Adult; elder; grown up; head; superior; person in charge; this name is sometimes associated with the proverb "the gray hairs of the elderly never kneel down without a reason" implying that the earnest requests of elders are often sincere so they ought to be taken seriously; this name is also sometimes associated with the proverb "if the owner does not at all participate in checking on and looking after the goats in the pen, the animals will die from a disease" implying that one has to adequately take control and care of one's property or family for there to be the necessary cleanliness and order; this name is also sometimes associated with the proverbs "the master (or father) that does not eat in his home village, causes his children to not get enough nourishment" and "the master (or father) that eats in his home village, allows for his children to get adequately fed" which imply that the presence of a father is essential to the growth and wellbeing of the children; this name is also sometimes associated with the proverb "a grown up (or mature person) will not brandish a needle and then not use it" implying that the earnest requests of elders are often sincere so they ought to be taken seriously, and that one of strong character acts deliberately and according to principles [*Ganda*].

Mukumbu (m) *[muh-kuhm-buh]* Elephant's skin [*Rega*].

Mukwano/ Mukwaano (f) *[muh-kwaah-noh]* Friendship; friend; romantic love; this name is sometimes associated with the proverb "kin relationships improve further with friendship" implying that it is counterproductive to be genetically related without liking each other; this name is also sometimes associated with the proverb "the friendship with one who lives across the bay does not die as long as the two people visit (and take presents to) each other" implying that contact is essential in the sustenance of friendship; this name is also sometimes associated with the proverbs "friendship overpowers (or rules) even a person of strength" and "friendship breaks down even a person of strong will" which imply that creating friendship with people all-ows for many advantages, for even persons of strong character can be more easily acquired from and compromised with, and their opinions more easily swayed through negotiating with them in a friendly manner; this name is also sometimes associated with the proverb "friendship between children is broken up by laughter" implying that unlike adults who can more readily take jokes and ignore those laughing at them, children are very sensitive at their peers laughing at them (such as when one falls down) [*Ganda*].

Mukwanogwenyanja (m) *[muh-kwaah-noh-gwehn-ndjh-ahn-jah]* "A friend of the lake"; "the friendship of the lake"; this name is commonly associated with the proverb "the friendship with one who lives across the bay does not die as long as the two people visit (and take presents to) each other" imply-ing that contact is essential in the sustenance of friendship [*Ganda*].

Mukyawe/ Mukyaawe (m) *[muh-tch-aah-weh]* Hated one; enemy; this name is sometimes associated with the proverb "unceasing arguments result in the beating of the hated one" implying that it is often the disliked ones that are scapegoated for even the offenses of the favorites, as exemplified by a dis-liked wife bearing the blame for a favorite co-wife; this name is also some-times associated with the proverb "when the favorite (or beloved) one com-mits an offense you, the disliked one, become gleeful" implying that since a disliked person (as with this example of a disfavored co-wife) tends to frequently be scapegoated, she will jump with joy when it becomes clear that the favored one, who is hardly blamed for anything, has done wrong; this name is also sometimes associated with the proverbs "an offense committed by a favorite is (often) paid for (or settled) by the disfavored one" and "an offense is committed by a loved one, then the disliked one bears the abuse" which, similar to the foregone proverb, address the commonplace tendency for the disliked to be scapegoated for the offenses of the favored [*Ganda*].

Mulakanikwa (m) *[muh-lah-kah-nih-kwah]* "The one they plot over" [*Rega*].

Mulanga (f/m) *[muh-lahn-gah]* One that plays a harp (or organ, or piano); an outcry; an appeal; an announcement; this name is sometimes associated with the proverb "the wailing of a goat is even devoid of tears" which mirrors worthless effort as is compared to the frequent goat wailing which is not of benefit to the goat owner (and, in humor, a wailing goat does not even let out tears) [*Ganda*].

Mulangira (m) *[muh-lahn-gih-rah]* A prince; this name is sometimes ass-ociated with the proverb "a prince is not to be thrown a stone at" [*Ganda*].

Mulema (m) *[muh-leh-mah]* A lame person; a cripple; this name is some-times associated with the proverb "even a defective (or bad, or ugly) child is given birth to--when you give birth to a crippled one, you do not throw it away"; this name is also sometimes associated with the proverb "a crippled person knows how he manages to get ahead" [*Ganda*].

Mulenzi (m) *[muh-lehn-zih]* Noble; boy; young man; this name is sometimes associated with the proverb "a boy who is insolent, will upon maturing commit big offenses" [*Ganda*].

Mulima (m) *[muh-lih-mah]* One who cultivates; this name is sometimes associated with the proverb "a woman who is a diligent farmer brings forth food, while the weak (or lazy) one brings forth grass weeds"; this name is also sometimes associated with the proverb "a woman who is a diligent farmer causes you (the husband) to eat with your shield over the food" which dramatizes a very hard working wife who is able to give her husband so much to eat that he even has to shield her away from bringing more food; this name is also sometimes associated with the proverb "a woman who is a diligent cultivator is the one that gets to see the chicken dancing with joy" implying that such a woman provides plenty of nourishment to the chickens by digging so much, insofar as she uncovers so many insects in the soil, she encourages insect feeding presence on her heavy yields and harvest garbage and, she throws away into her garden a lot of leftover food that would attract bugs as well as the chickens [*Ganda*].

Mulonda (f/m) *[muh-lohn-dah]* Name given to a second born child after twin siblings, the first born after named *Mbilizi* [*Rega*].

Mulungi (f) *[muh-luhn-jih]* "(He/ she is) the good (or virtuous) one"; "(she is) the beautiful one"; this name is sometimes associated with the proverb "the funeral rites of one who was good are praisingly talked about endlessly (or cannot pass without being praised)"; this name is also sometimes associated with the proverb "an ugly one who chats (thereby making a pleasant impression) is worth more than (or is preferable to) a good looking one who is aloof and conceited"; this name is also sometimes associated with the proverb "a beautiful woman is the sister of many" which implies that many are eager to claim relationship to one that is good looking, and is synonymous with "a fair face is half a portion, a pretty face is a good recommendation" [*Ganda*]

Muluvu (m) *[muh-luh-vuh]* Gluttonous one; this name is sometimes associated with the proverb "even the most indulging glutton cannot eat everything, otherwise the hyena would eat bananas" [*Ganda*].

Mulyammamba (m) *[muh-ljahm-mahm-bah]* One that eats lungfish; this name is commonly associated with the proverb "just that one person that violates the clan and totemic taboo by eating mudfish, gives the entire clan a bad reputation" which implies that just one person can cause a family or a community to have a bad reputation [*Ganda*].

Mulyazzaawo (m) *[muh-ljahz-zaah-woh]* "The Eat-and-Put-Back"; this name is commonly associated with the proverb "those that 'eat-and-put-back' are like the white ants which eat and put back soil" which is advising people against wasting and instead to emulate the white ants by way of such actions as reforestation, recycling, and mutual hospitality [*Ganda*].

Mulyowansozi (m) *[muh-ljoh-wahn-soh-zih]* "The one who smoothes out difficulties for others"; this name is commonly associated with the proverb "the one who smoothes out difficulties for others is not done favors when he gets sick" implying that ingratitude is commonplace [*Ganda*].

Mumpi (m) *[muhm-pih]* Short one; this name is sometimes associated with the proverb "a short person does not see the locusts approaching" which implies that unimportant persons are not as readily listened too or taken seriously as those with authority *[Ganda]*.

Mun (m) *[muhn]* Earth: a name given to one whose previously born siblings died *[Nuer]* (Evans-Pritchard 1948: 167).

Munaku (f/m) *[muh-nah-kuh]* That is distraught (or in misery, or in poverty); this name is sometimes associated with the proverb "a poor person (or one in trouble) is (like) the wild yam (which is normally eaten during severe famine conditions)--it sprouts and grows up by its own efforts" *[Ganda]*.

Munakukaama (f/m) *[muh-nah-kuh-kaah-mah]* "A poor person (or one in trouble) is (like) the wild yam"; this name is commonly associated with the proverb "a poor person (or one in trouble) is (like) the wild yam (which is normally eaten during severe famine conditions)--it sprouts and grows up by its own efforts" *[Ganda]*.

Mundas (m) *[muhn-dahs]* A nickname-abbreviation for *Monde*: "Patience" *[Xhosa]* (Neethling 1994: 92).

Mungi (m) *[muhn-jih]* One that has a lot; a lot of it; this name is sometimes associated with the proverb "too much air bursts the inner tube of a soccer ball" which is related to the story of the frog that in wanting to become as big as a cow, blew himself up and consequently burst--it is implied that "pride goeth before a fall" and advises against unreasonable overindulgence; this name is also sometimes associated with the proverb "that which is in great number is feared (or respected)" which applies to such items as majority public opinion and large armies, and implies that there is power in numbers *[Ganda]*.

Muntukabani (m) *[muhn-tuh-kah-bah-nih]* "Child of whom?": a name such as given to a newborn whose father is expressing suspicion as to whether he is the parent *[Zulu]* (Turner 1992: 49).

Munyeera (m) *[muh-ndjh-eh-eh-rah]* Species of tiny ants that tend to gather in big numbers such as on uncovered animal meat or bones; this name is sometimes associated with the proverb "the cutting of the fiber from the plantain trunk renders scattered the tiny ants that had built in the trunk" implying that when the owner of a household dies, his dependents become disunited, or they stop gathering or living together *[Ganda]*.

Munywanyi (m) *[muh-ndjh-waah-ndjh-ih]* A close friend; this name is sometimes associated with the proverb "the day a poor man butchers his animal, is when he gets a friend" implying that opportunists who claim to be friends will flock around even one in poverty that has just acquired or potentially has something to give away *[Ganda]*.

Musajjaawaza (m) *[muh-sahj-jaah-wah-zah]* "A man struggles tremendously (or makes an effort), even when he is worn out"; this name is commonly associated with the proverb "a man struggles tremendously (or makes an effort), even when he is worn out" which implies that a man is expected to be strong willed even in the face formidable obstacles *[Ganda]*.

Musamba (m) *[muh-sahm-bah]* "Eye opener" [*Rega*].

Musango (m) *[muh-sahn-goh]* Accusation; crime; court case; this name is sometimes associated with the proverb "a settled old court case is a precedent for a new one" implying that laws, literary and academic works, and societal values build on past works and stipulations as references; this name is also sometimes associated with the proverb "running away does not put to end a dispute" implying that people still hold grudges against those they have not seen for so long, and people who fled years back are still held accountable and tried for offenses they committed; this name is also sometimes associated with the proverb "when the favorite (or beloved) one commits an offense you, the disliked one, become gleeful" implying that since a disliked person (as with this example of a disfavored co-wife) tends to frequently be scapegoated, she will jump with joy when it becomes clear that the favored one, who is hardly blamed for anything, has done wrong; this name is also sometimes associated with the proverbs "an offense committed by a favorite is (often) paid for (or settled) by the disfavored one" and "an offense is committed by a loved one, then the disliked one bears the abuse" which, similar to the foregone proverb, address the commonplace tendency for the disliked to be scapegoated for the offenses of the favored [*Ganda*].

Musazi (m) *[muh-sah-zih]* One who cuts; this name is sometimes associated with the proverb "a man whose occupation is cutting salt and extracting salt from it, depends on his knife for his livelihood" implying that every income earner fundamentally has a device on which his earnings depend [*Ganda*].

Musengelwa (m) *[muh-sehn-geh-lwah]* One that is respected [*Rega*].

Museveni (m) *[muh-seh-veh-nih]* War veteran; soldier; "of the seventh"; this name is sometimes associated with the proverb "that of uncertainty is like the trousers of the 7th Division (World War II) army soldier that are of intermediate length--'neither long enough nor short enough'" whereby a situation of significant doubtfulness became compared to the noted army uniform characteristic of the Ugandans that participated in the war; this name is also sometimes associated with the proverb "a poor soldier of the 7th Division (World War II) army is the one that goes to war without formally signaling goodbye" whereby such a poor soldier would be ashamed of not having anything material as a token gesture to give to his friends [*Ganda*].

Mushi (m) *[muh-shih]* A member of the *Bashi* ethnic group; one associated with the *Bashi* ethnics [*Bashi* and some other ethnics of East and Central Africa].

Musigire (m) *[muh-sih-gih-reh]* One that is entrusted with; deputy; an assistant; this name is sometimes associated with the proverb "the deputy of a chief settles small cases only (or cannot settle much)" [*Ganda*].

Musota (m) *[muh-soh-tah]* Snake; this name is sometimes associated with the proverbs "tears of a snake come with the application of a beating stick" and "the ear area of a snake responds to a beating stick" implying that bullheadedness, as compared with that of a snake, is not alleviated by sweet words, and the sorrowing tears come belatedly as the snake gets a thorough beating that may even cause it to die; this name is also sometimes associated with the proverb "a man of wrath is like the venomous viper" [*Ganda*].

Musukwa (m) *[muh-suh-kwah]* "The clean one" [*Rega*].

Muth'ungimele (m) *[muht-uhn-gih-meh-leh]* "The witchcraft has ceased to work on me": a name such as given to a newborn by it's father who is pointing out to potential sorcerers that, though in the *Inkandla* area they have moved in, most newcomers do not stay long for fear of becoming bewitched, their sorcery will not have any effect on him [*Zulu*] (Turner 1992: 54).

Muto (f/m) *[muh-toh]* Younger brother or sister; young person; child; this name is sometimes associated with the proverb "a boy who is insolent, will upon maturing commit big offenses" [*Ganda*].

Mutondo (m) *[muh-toh-ohn-doh]* Framework (for a house) [*Rega*].

Muumbilwa (m) *[muuhm-bih-lwah]* One who is often blamed for others' misdeeds [*Rega*].

Muungano (m) *[muuh-ndgh-ah-noh]* (Political) unity; (political) cooperation [*Pare, Swahili* and several other ethnics of eastern and central Africa] (Herbert 1997: 10; Omari 1970: 66).

Muwambi (m) *[muh-wahm-bih]* One who captures; captor; one who confiscates; one who asks a merchant to reserve an item which will be paid for and claimed at a later date; this name is commonly associated with the proverb "the one who has an item set aside for him to buy later, is not (necessarily) its eventual buyer" implying that a merchant's interest is mostly in immediate buyers much more than in those who demand goods that it is uncertain they will pay for [*Ganda*].

Muyiisa (m) *[muh-yiih-sah]* Brewer; beer maker; the one who brings it to the boil (or makes ready); this name is sometimes associated with the proverbs "the rooms in the house of the brewer never cease to harbor beer" and "the rooms in the house of the brewer never run out of beer" which is real or imagined, just like a rich person is expected to have aside adequate money for the entertainment of guests and for needy friends or kin [*Ganda*].

Muyise (m) *[muh-yih-seh]* One enabled to pass (through); this name is sometimes associated with the proverb "the one who happens to come across you at the crossroads considers you a traveler (or a stranger)" i.e. since crossroads are generally considered a location in which people from all directions meet and move through [*Ganda*].

Muzikawukho (m) *[muh-zih-kah-wuh-koh]* "There is no (real) family": name such as given to one born following a long succession of female siblings, the name implying that the family is still not yet complete without a reasonable number of male children [*Zulu*] (Koopman 1987: 149).

Muziwempi (m) *[muh-zih-wehm-pih]/ **Muziwenduku*** (m) *[muh-zih-wehn-duh-kuh]* "The home of the stick": a name such as given by a mother satirizing that the father of this newborn named so is well accustomed to excessively employing the stick in solving familial problems [*Zulu*] (Turner 1992: 47).

Mvumvu (f) *[mvuhm-vuh]* A nickname-abbreviation for *Nomvula*: "Rain"

[*Xhosa*] (Neethling 1994: 92).

Mvuyi (f) [*mvuh-yih*]/ **Mvuyo** (f) [*mvuh-yoh*] Nicknames-abbreviations for *Nomvuyo*: "Happiness" [*Xhosa*] (Neethling 1994: 92).

Mwaka (m) [*mwaah-kah*] Year; (new) season; a name commonly given to one born during the emergence of a new year or season; this name is sometimes associated with the proverb "the Red-hot Poker trees (which are un-flowered and unsightly most of the time) crown themselves with a red bloom during the sowing season" i.e. the trees paradoxically bloom in the season when there are piles of ugly refuse and burnt out vegetation, inc-luding little greened stumps of savanna, the proverb implying that the un-sightly can bloom into beauties so should not easily be dismissed [*Ganda*].

Mwami (m) [*mwaah-mih*] Chief; master; husband; this name is sometimes associated with the proverb "a chief that likes you, entices you to even build on hardy (or infertile) ground" implying that being a favorite of the rulers is so cherished that it would make anyone maintain that closeness even if it means forgoing some personal needs (which you would anyway be able to obtain when living close to a ruler who likes you) [*Ganda*].

Mwana (f/m) [*mwaah-nah*] Child; kid; youngster; son or daughter (of); this name is sometimes associated with the proverb "that which strikes the child, also wants to strike the mother" implying that a father who beats his child is likely to beat its mother, or that one will likely manifest his or her behavioral characteristics in whatever environment, or that an affliction that strikes the child is also inclined to strike its mother; this name is also sometimes associated with the proverb "an only child is heavily adorned with ornaments" implying that an only child is often overindulgently treat-ed, partly because it is the only child the parents have, and partly because there are more family resources available to a kid that does not have sib-lings; this name is also sometimes associated with the proverb "an only child is like a single rain cloud" implying that just like a single rain cloud that is unreliable since it will likely empty itself quickly and be followed by a hot and dry spell, the traditional African family prefers to have many children since the infant mortality rate is high; this name is also sometimes associated with the proverbs "the fruitfulness of a person is evident at the time when, as a baby, the person is still wrapped on its mother's back in in-fant clothing" and "that a child is (or will be) strong and healthy, is evident at the time when, as a baby, it is still wrapped in infant clothing" which im-ply that a lot can be told about the future of one that is still an infant [The *Ganda*].

Mwanomu/ Mwanoomu (f) [*mwaah-noh-oh-muh*] "One (and only) child"; this name is commonly associated with the proverb "an only child is heavily adorned with ornaments" implying that an only child is often overindulg-ently treated, partly because it is the only child the parents have, and partly because there are more family resources available to a kid that does not have siblings; this name is also commonly associated with the proverb "an only child is like a single rain cloud" implying that just like a single rain cloud that is unreliable since it will likely empty itself quickly and be followed by a hot and dry spell, the traditional African family prefers to have many children since the infant mortality rate is high [*Ganda*].

Mwavu (m) *[mwaah-vuh]* The poor one; this name is sometimes associated with the proverb "the day a poor man butchers his animal, is when he gets a friend" implying that opportunists who claim to be friends will flock around even one in poverty that has just acquired or potentially has something to give away; this name is also sometimes associated with the proverb "a poor soldier of the 7th Division (World War II) army is the one that goes to war without formally signaling goodbye" whereby such a poor soldier would be ashamed of not having anything material as a token gesture to give to his friends [*Ganda*].

Mwenebatende (m) *[mweh-neh-bah-tehn-deh]* The head of a group [*Rega*].

Mwenebatu (m) *[mweh-neh-bah-tuh]* One that is responsible [*Rega*].

Mwenge (m) *[mwehn-geh]* Banana based beer; liquor; this name is sometimes associated with the proverbs "the rooms in the house of the brewer never cease to harbor beer" and "the rooms in the house of the brewer never run out of beer" which is real or imagined, just like a rich person is expected to have aside adequate money for the entertainment of guests and for needy friends or kin; this name is also sometimes associated with the proverb "a visitor who stays long (or who does not leave) is made to tread out the beer" implying that the visitor who stays too long, often loses his "visitor" status and, gets to be treated like members of the household (such as doing jobs that a visitor would not normally do) [*Ganda*].

Mwenyi (m) *[mweh-ndjh-ih]* The owner [*Rega*].

Mwetaminwa (m) *[mweh-tah-mih-nwah]* One who is often blamed for others' misdeeds [*Rega*].

Mxolisi (m) *[muh-ksoh-lih-sih]* The peacemaker [*Xhosa*] (Thipa 1987: 114).

Mzwandile (m) *[uhm-zwahn-dih-leh]* "The home has expanded" [The *Xhosa*] (Neethling 1994: 92).

Mzwilili (m) *[muh-zwih-lih-lih]* "Canary": a name such as given to one who always loves to sing [*Zulu*] (Koopman 1987: 160).

-N-

Nabitali (f) *[nah-bih-tah-lih]* "People wearing special things" [*Rega*].

Nakataale (f) *[nah-kah-taah-leh]* A name commonly given to an unusually tall person [*Fipa*] (Willis 1982: 229).

Nakatuuce (f) *[nah-kah-tuuh-tch-eh]* "The Thin One" [*Fipa*] (Willis 1982: 229).

Nakimmenya (f) *[nnah-tch-ihm-meh-ndjh-ah]* "It breaks me down"; "it destroys me" [*Ganda*].

Nakimuli (f) *[nnah-tch-ih-muh-lih]* Flower [*Ganda, Soga*].

Nakimwero (f) *[nnah-tch-ih-mweh-eh-roh]* An abundance; that is profuse; profuseness [*Ganda*].

Nakinaalwa (f) *[nnah-tch-ih-naah-lwah]* That will delay (or linger, or be a long time, or be late) [*Ganda*].

Nakindiba (f) *[nnah-tch-ihn-dih-bah]* Hide; skin [*Ganda*].

Nakindirira/ Nnakindirira (f/m) *[nnah-kihn-dih-rih-rah]* A sewing in many places; sewing quickly; an embroidering [*Ganda*].

Nakinku (f/m) *[nnah-tch-ihn-kuh]* Expert; person with a lot of expertise and accomplishment in his or her occupation [*Ganda*].

Nakinnyogoga/ Nnakinyogoga (f) *[nnah-tch-ihn-ndjh-oh-goh-gah]* That is cold; that feels cold [*Ganda*].

Nakinobe (f) *[nnah-tch-ih-noh-beh]* (One associated with) a separation of the wife from the husband [*Ganda*].

Nakinsige/ Nnakinsige (f) *[nnah-tch-ihn-sih-geh]* The brown grass finch; "that is entrusted to me"; "that is given to me in confidence (or in trust)" [*Ganda*].

Nakinsigo/ Nnakinsigo (m) *[nnah-tch-ihn-sih-goh]* That is associated with seeds (or kidneys) [*Ganda*].

Nakintu (f) *[nnah-tch-ihn-tuh]* One associated with *Kintu* the legendary first king of and founder of the kingdom of *Buganda*; thing; matter; affair [*Ganda*].

Nakinyaga (m) *[nnah-kih-ndjh-ah-gah]* That plunders (or pillages, or robs, or steals, or seizes by force, or carries off); uncouth person; vulgarian; dirty (or messy) person; slob [*Ganda*].

Nakinyago (f) *[nah-kih-ndjh-ah-goh]* Plunder (or stolen goods, or goods seized by force); the rectum [*Ganda*].

Nakiranda (f) *[nnah-tch-ih-rahn-dah]* Creeping (plant); a creeping up (or climbing, or spreading); a traveling around; a flourishing; one that creeps up (or climbs up, or spreads); one that wanders around; one that flourishes [*Ganda*].

Nakire (f) *[nnah-tch-ih-reh]* Cloud [*Ganda*].

Nakiremba/ Nnakiremba (f) *[nnah-tch-ih-rehm-bah]* Scarf; head cloth; handkerchief; turban (or headdress) worn by muslims [*Ganda*].

Nakirembwe (f) *[nnah-kih-rehm-bweh]* A species of large ant [*Ganda*].

Nakirigya (f) *[nnah-tch-ih-rih-jah]* One that will be (or become) suitable (or appropriate, or fitting, or corresponding) [*Ganda*].

Nakirijja (f) *[nnah-tch-ih-rihj-jah]* One that is untidy (or slovenly); that is haphazard [*Ganda*].

Nakirindi/ Nnakirindi (f) *[nnah-tch-ih-rihn-dih]* A group; a flock; a band; a crowd; a throng [*Ganda*].

Nakirindisa/ Nnakirindisa (f/m) *[nnah-tch-ih-rihn-dih-sah]* "It causes one to wait" [*Ganda*].

Nakirize (f) *[nnah-tch-ih-rih-zeh]* One that has wept (or become tearful, or cried); one that has mourned [*Ganda*].

Nakirulu (f) *[nnah-tch-ih-ruh-luh]* That is greedy; that is gluttonous; greed [*Ganda*].

Nakirwadde (f) *[nnah-tch-ih-rwahd-deh]* That is sick; sickness; disease

[*Ganda*].

Nakisaka (f) *[nnah-tch-ih-sah-kah]* Thicket; bush; one that forages (for food); foraging; digging up (information); that digs up/ or ferrets out (information) [*Ganda*].

Nakisanje (f) *[nnah-tch-ih-sahn-jeh]* That has been caused to dry (or wither); a drying (or withering) of plantain leaves [*Ganda*].

Nakisi (f) *[nnah-tch-ih-sih]* Large country; big land [*Ganda*].

Nakisige (f) *[nnah-tch-ih-sih-geh]* Eyebrow [*Ganda, Soga*].

Nakisozi (f) *[nnah-tch-ih-soh-zih]* Big hill [*Ganda*].

Nakisula (f) *[nnah-tch-ih-suh-lah]* That spends the night; that remains (or stays, or dwells); salt in a rock (or lump) form [*Ganda*].

Nakisuula (f) *[nnah-tch-ih-suuh-lah]* That throws away (or disposes of, or drops, or loses, or throws down, or knocks over, or throws); "I threw it away"; "I disposed of it"; "I threw it"; "I dropped it"; "I let go of it" [The *Ganda*].

Nakisuule (f) *[nnah-tch-ih-suuh-leh]* That is thrown away (or disposed of, or dropped, or lost, or thrown down, or knocked over, or is thrown); "throw it away"; "dispose of it"; "throw it"; "drop it"; "let go of it" [*Ganda*].

Nakitaabajja (f) *[nnah-tch-ih-taah-bahj-jah]* "It frees (or releases, or lets go of) the newcomers"; "it frees (or releases, or lets go of) those that come/ arrive" [*Ganda*]

Nakitabajja (f) *[nnah-tch-ih-tah-bahj-jah]* That does not engage in carpentry work; that does not make out of wood using carpentry tools; that does not chop (or carve, or cut) [*Ganda*].

Nakitaka (f) *[nnah-tch-ih-tah-kah]* Earth (or mud) colored [*Ganda, Soga*].

Nakitanda/ Nnakitanda (f) *[nnah-tch-ih-tahn-dah]* That advances by climbing or clinging to an object; that spreads; that strides along; bed [*Ganda*].

Nakitende (f) *[nnah-tch-ih-tehn-deh]* That is praised (or commended, or spoken well of); that is described (or told about, or told of) [*Ganda*].

Nakitiibwa (f) *[nnah-tch-ih-tiih-bwah]* That is feared; honor; glory; prestige; dignity; respect; reverence; pomp [*Ganda*].

Nakitondo (f) *[nnah-tch-ih-tohn-doh]* Touchy; easily offended [*Ganda*].

Nakitowoolo (f) *[nnah-tch-ih-toh-woh-oh-loh]* That is relaxed; that has grown slack; that has become refreshed; that has recuperated; (a swelling) that has shrunk [*Ganda*].

Nakittabajja (f) *[nnah-tch-iht-tah-bahj-jah]/ Nakittaabajja* (f) *[nnah-tch-iht-taah-bahj-jah]* "It kills (or destroys, or ruins) the newcomers"; "it kills (or destroys, or ruins) those that come/ arrive" [*Ganda*].

Nakitto (f) *[nnah-tch-iht-toh]* Coldness; dampness (of the weather); (large) pillow/ cushion [*Ganda*].

Nakityo (f) *[nnah-tch-ih-tjoh]* A name given to one who has twin siblings [*Ganda*].

Nakiwala (f) *[nnah-tch-ih-wah-lah]* Tanner; one who scrapes (such as hides); rake; young human female; one who pulls or drags along [*Ganda*].

Nakiwu (f) *[nnah-tch-ih-wuh]* Leather hide; cushion; seat; a carpet made of animal hide; canoe middle seat where one sits to bale water out [*Ganda*].

Nakiyemba (f) *[nnah-tch-ih-yehm-bah]* That talks in a noisy and foolish manner; that talks nonsense; that rants [*Ganda*].

Nakiyenje/ Nnakiyenje (f/m) *[nnah-kih-yehn-jeh]* Cockroach; cricket [The Ganda].

Nakiyingi (f) *[nnah-tch-ih-yihn-jih]* A lot; in abundance; trapping for birds and small animals [*Ganda*].

Nakiyini (f) *[nnah-tch-ih-yih-nih]* One associated with the king's tanner; a hoe handle [*Ganda*].

Nakiyitabajja (f) *[nnah-tch-ih-yih-taah-bahj-jah]* "It calls forward those who come (or those that arrive)"; "it calls forward the newcomers" [*Ganda*].

Nakiyuka (f) *[nnah-tch-ih-yuh-kah]* Anger; harshness; fury; one that is ill tempered; one that is harsh; that has become old; that has lost one's beauty [*Ganda*].

Nakiyumba (f) *[nnah-tch-ih-yuhm-bah]* Large house [*Ganda*].

Nakizza (f/m) *[nnah-kihz-zah]* That brings back; that is associated with a birth which follows that of twin siblings [*Ganda*].

Nakkadde/ Nnakadde (f) *[nnahk-kahd-deh]* That is venerable and old; that is worn out; that is aged [*Ganda*].

Nakkazi (f) *[nnahk-kah-zih]* (Big) woman; (big) wife [*Ganda*].

Nakkoba (f) *[nnahk-koh-bah]* Large belt [*Ganda*].

Nakkomo (f) *[nnahk-koh-moh]* Limit; end [*Ganda*].

Nakkonde (f) *[nnahk-kohn-deh]* Large fist; heavy punch [*Ganda*].

Nakku (f/m) *[nnahk-kuh]* A (large) piece of firewood [*Ganda*].

Nakkungu/ Nnakkungu (f/m) *[nnahk-kuhn-guh]* Arrogance; one who be- haves like a dignitary [*Ganda*].

Nakomo (f) *[nnah-koh-moh]* Copper; bracelet [*Ganda*].

Nakoojo (m) *[nnah-koh-oh-joh]* The little boy (of the children): a name us- ually given to a boy born following the mother giving birth to four boys in a row [*Ganda*].

Nakoolya (f) *[nnah-koh-oh-ljah]* "What you eat" [*Ganda*].

Nakubulwa (f) *[nnah-kuh-buh-lwah]* Lacking; (one) at loss for; losing; be- ing at loss for [*Ganda*].

Nakukaawa (f) *[nnah-kuh-kaah-wah]* Becoming bitter (or sour, or unplea- sant to the taste); becoming quarrelsome (or enraged); (a situation) beco- ming serious/ bad [*Ganda*].

Nakulabye (f) *[nnaah-kuh-lah-bjeh]* "I saw (or perceived, or found) you"; "I greeted you" [*Ganda*].

Nakulembi/ Nnakulembi (f) *[nnah-kuh-lehm-bih]* "I grew bad ones"; "bad ones grew on me" [*Ganda*].

Nakulima (f/m) *[nnah-kuh-lih-mah]* A good cultivator; digging; cultivating; backbiting [*Ganda*].

Nakungi/ Nnakungi (f) *[nnah-kuhn-jih]* That makes repeated exclamations of astonishment; that expresses amazement at; that marvels at; that admires [*Ganda*].

Nakunja (f) *[nnah-kuhn-jah]* One who finishes dressing a hide/ skin [The Ganda].

Nakuni/ Nnakuni (f) *[nnahk-kuh-nih]* That of darkness (or growing darkness); that of obscurity (or blocking); that of thickly luxuriant growth [The Ganda].

Nakutanya/ Nnakutanya (f) *[nnah-kuh-tah-ndjh-ah]* That becomes the source of an inadvertence/ accident; that causes to become infested (or to fester, or to become septic); that causes to deteriorate; that makes worse [The Ganda].

Nakuwanda/ Nnakuwanda (f) *[nnah-kuh-wahn-dah]* That spits out; that blurts out; that throws out [Ganda].

Nakuya (f) *[nnah-kuh-yah]* That makes dirty (or messes up, or crumples) [Ganda].

Nakuyita (f) *[nnah-kuh-yih-tah]* That passes (by/ around); that calls forth (or invites); that names (or describes) as [Ganda].

Nakweyama (f) *[nnah-kweh-yah-mah]* Vowing; making a vow [Ganda].

Nakyaawa/ Nnakyaawa (f) *[nnah-tch-aah-wah]* "That which the person gives"; that hates; that detests [Ganda].

Nakyabula (f) *[nnah-tch-ah-buh-lah]* That disappeared (or became lost, or went astray); that became lacking (or missing); that became lost to [Ganda].

Nakyagaba (f) *[nnah-tch-ah-gah-bah]* "What he (i.e. God) apportions/ or gives away/ or gives as a present" [Ganda].

Nakyajja (f) *[nnah-tch-ahj-jah]* "It came"; "it arrived"; "it happened" [The Ganda].

Nakyali (f) *[nnah-tch-ah-lih]* That was [Ganda].

Nakyamu (f) *[nnah-tch-aah-muh]* That is false (or wrong, or incorrect); that is crooked (or disfigured, or bent) [Ganda].

Nakyanja (f) *[nnah-tch-ahn-jah]* One that spreads out (or unfolds); one that submits (such as a bill or proposal); one that brings up a matter; a spreading out; an unfolding; the presenting (of a bill or proposal); the bringing up of a matter [Ganda].

Nakyanzi (f) *[nnah-tch-ahn-zih]* Container used to capture the milking from cows [Ganda].

Nakyawa/ Nnakyawa (f) *[nnah-tch-ah-wah]* That of hating (or detesting, or loathing); that one gives [Ganda].

Nakyazirana/ Nnakyazirana (f) *[nnah-tch-ah-zih-rah-nah]* One who carries out tasks as soon as possible [Ganda].

Nakyazze (f) *[nnah-tch-ahz-zeh]* Visitor; that which has come [Ganda].

Nakyejjwe/ Nnakyejjwe (m) *[nnah-tch-ehj-weh]* That is made up/ or invented (such as stories or lies); that is ascribed falsely [Ganda].

Nakyekoledde/ Nnakyekoledde (f) *[nnah-tch-eh-koh-lehd-deh]* "I did it (or do it exclusively) by myself"; that does for oneself; that works for oneself; that makes trouble for oneself; that gets oneself into a fix; that hurts oneself [Ganda].

Nakyeyuwa (f) *[nnah-tch-eh-yuh-wah]* That pours itself (or oneself); that disgraces itself (or oneself) [*Ganda*].

Nakyobula/ Nnakyobula (f) *[nnah-tch-oh-buh-lah]* That which you lose (or lack); that which becomes missing (or lacking).

Nakyomu (f) *[nnah-tch-oh-oh-muh]* That of (or belonging to) one [*Ganda*].

Nakyomubi (f) *[nnah-tch-oh-oh-muh-bih]* Belonging to the bad (or ugly) person [*Ganda*].

Nakyonda (f) *[nnah-tch-ohn-dah]* A plaiting; a twining; a twisting [The *Ganda*].

Nakyongo (f) *[nnah-tch-ohn-goh]* That is brainy [*Ganda*].

Nakyoto (f) *[nnah-tch-oh-toh]* Fireplace; hearth [*Ganda*].

Nakyoya (f) *[nnah-tch-oh-yah]* Feather; (single) hair on the body [*Ganda*].

Nakyuma (f) *[nnah-tch-uuh-mah]* Iron; metal; factory; machinery; machine; tool; device [*Ganda*].

Nalaaki (m) *[nnah-laah-kih]* That becomes choked up; that wheezes; that gasps [*Ganda*].

Nalebe (f) *[nnah-leh-beh]* That is soft and pliable; that feels weak; that feels tired; that is slack [*Ganda*].

Naligaba (f) *[nnah-lih-gah-bah]* "I gave it away"; "I gave it as a present"; "I apportioned it" [*Ganda*].

Naliggya (f) *[nnah-lihj-jah]* The adze, a knife with a curved blade; that is new; that becomes exhausted; that gets burned; that gets cooked; that takes away; that takes out [*Ganda*].

Naliisaanga (f) *[nnah-liih-saahn-gah]* "I used to feed (them)"; "I used to enable (them) to eat"; "I used to cater to (their) nutritional needs" [*Ganda*].

Nalikka (f/m) *[nnah-lihk-kah]* That goes down; that comes down; that sinks [*Ganda*].

Nalimanga (m) *[nnah-lih-mahn-gah]* " I used to cultivate (or farm, or dig)"; "I used to backbite (or slander behind one's back)" [*Ganda*].

Nalisanga (f) *[nah-lih-saahn-gah]* "I found it"; "I came upon it"; "I met with it" [*Ganda*].

Nalongo/ Nnaalongo (f) *[nnaah-lohn-goh]* Mother of twins; honorific title for a woman; wife [*Ganda, Soga*].

Nalu (f/m) *[nah-luh]* A name given to a fifth born [*Nuba*] (Seligman 1932: 387).

Nalubaale/ Nnalubaale (f) *[nnah-luh-baah-leh]* One of the names of Lake Victoria (or *Nnyanza*); that is associated with the heavens (or a deity, or space, or the skies) [*Ganda*].

Nalube (f) *[nnah-luh-beh]* One who jeers (or boos, or shouts at, or shouts down); the jackal [*Ganda*].

Nalubega (f) *[nnah-luh-beh-gah]* Serving or helping of food; of the backside; of a portion; to spy; to detect [*Ganda*].

Nalubimbi (f) *[nnah-luh-bihm-bih]* A day's cultivation [*Ganda*].

Naluboobi (f) *[nnah-luh-boh-oh-bih]* A species of millipede [*Ganda*].

Nalubowa (f) *[nnah-luh-boh-wah]* Security held for the payment of a debt; that seizes/ or confiscates/ or appropriates [*Ganda*].

Nalubuga (f) *[nah-luh-buh-gah]* Co-heir of an important person; one associated with the queen sister *[Ganda]*.

Nalubunga (f) *[nnah-luh-buhn-gah]* An aimless wander around; a ramble *[Ganda]*.

Nalubuula (f) *[nnah-luh-buuh-lah]* A mass; large quantities; proposal; an intention; a proclamation; a preaching *[Ganda]*.

Nalubuzi (m) *[nnah-luh-buh-zih]* A goat (more so in a pitiable state) *[Ganda]*.

Nalubwama (f) *[nnah-luh-bwaah-mah]* That greets; that welcomes (or receives gladly, or greets enthusiastically); one that crouches down *[Ganda]*.

Nalufu/ Nnalufu (f) *[nnah-luh-fuh]* Fog; mist *[Ganda]*.

Naluga (f) *[nnah-luh-gah]* Cane; walking stick; cane for administering a beating; a species of creeping plant *[Ganda]*.

Nalugala (f) *[nnah-luh-gah-lah]* Of the framework structure built around an anthill to capture edible flying ants *[Ganda]*.

Naluggya (f) *[nnah-luhj-jah]* Yard; courtyard *[Ganda]*.

Nalugo/ Nnalugo (f) *[nnah-luh-goh]* Leopard; enclosure for keeping cattle *[Ganda]*.

Nalugonda (f) *[nnah-luh-gohn-dah]* Docile and obedient; yielding; pliable; able to be softened *[Ganda]*.

Nalugooti/ Nnalugooti (f/m) *[nnah-luh-goh-oh-tih]* One that is tall and thin; one that is excessively thin, and moves unsteadily *[Ganda]*.

Nalugulu (f) *[nnah-luh-guh-luh]* (With a peculiarity of) the leg *[Ganda]*.

Nalugumbula (m) *[nnah-luh-guhm-buh-lah]* One that runs into (such as a hostile animal); one that falls prey to; one that is a victim of; one that contracts (an illness) *[Ganda]*.

Nalugunju (f) *[nnah-luh-guhn-juh]* A species of large mongoose; a species of wild cat *[Ganda]*.

Nalugwa (f) *[nnah-luh-gwah]* That of a happening (or an occurrence, or a fall); that of a failure *[Ganda]*.

Nalugya (f) *[nnah-luh-jah]* That is fitting (or suitable, or appropriate); that fits in (or has room); that corresponds to; that is equivalent to *[Ganda]*.

Nalukadde (f) *[nnah-luh-kahd-deh]* That is old (or aged, or worn out) [The Ganda].

Nalukenge (f) *[nnah-luh-kehn-geh]* Examining; scrutinizing; a look around; being careful (or watchful); perceiving; noticing; being suspicious of; scenting; smelling; one that is perceptive; swelling of the feet *[Ganda]*.

Nalukola (m) *[nnah-luh-koh-lah]* That works (or functions, or operates, or acts as); "I worked it"; "I operated it" *[Ganda]*.

Nalukoobyo (f) *[nnah-luh-koh-oh-bjoh]* Being last in line; coming last; being at the end *[Ganda]*.

Nalukoola (m) *[nnah-luh-koh-oh-lah]* That of an uninhabited country (or wasteland, or wilderness, or desert); weeding out; uprooting; the leaf of a tree *[Ganda]*.

Naluku (f) *[nnah-luh-kuh]* A piece of firewood *[Ganda]*.

Nalukuuma (f) *[nnah-luh-kuuh-mah]* Watching over; guarding; protecting; maintaining; keeping *[Ganda]*.

Nalukwago (f) *[nnah-luh-kwaah-goh]* Scratching; clawing.

Nalukwakkula (f/m) *[nnah-luh-kwahk-kuh-lah]* A seizing; grasping; snatching away; taking away *[Ganda]*.

Nalulungi/ Nnalulungi (f) *[nnah-luh-luhn-jih]* Beautiful girl; beautiful woman *[Ganda, Soga]*.

Naluma/ Nnaluma (f/m) *[nnah-luh-mah]* That bites (or pinches, or pains, or aches, or hurts); "I bit (or pinched, or ached, or hurt, or pained)" *[Ganda]*.

Nalumaga/ Nnalumaga (f) *[nnah-luh-mah-gah]* One who scatters; one that characteristically glances from side to side (in a single or sudden movement) *[Ganda]*.

Nalumansi (m) *[nnah-luh-mahn-sih]* That scatters (or sprinkles, or pours); a scattering (or sprinkling, or pouring); that acts in a vain and ostentatious manner; that puts on airs *[Ganda]*.

Nalumenya/ Nnalumenya (f/m) *[nnah-luh-meh-ndjh-ah]* That breaks (or breaks into, or destroys); that captures (a stronghold); that bends at the joint; that refutes (or counters, or retracts); that mentions (or refers to); "I broke (or destroyed, or countered) it" *[Ganda]*.

Nalumoso (m) *[nnah-luh-moh-soh]* Filching; stealing little by little; a showy manner; making a spectacle of oneself *[Ganda]*.

Nalumu (f/m) *[nnah-luh-muh]* Once; on one occasion *[Ganda]*.

Nalunga/ Nnalunga (f) *[nnah-luhn-gah]* That of seasoning (or flavoring, or adding salt to) *[Ganda]*.

Nalungu/ Nnalungu (f) *[nnah-luhn-guh]* (That is associated with) a deserted area/ or wasteland *[Ganda]*.

Nalunguulu/ Nnalunguulu (m) *[nnah-luhn-guuh-luh]* (That is associated with) becoming bruised and swollen *[Ganda]*.

Nalungwa/ Nnalungwa (f) *[nnah-luhn-gwah]* That is seasoned (or flavored, or added salt to); "it falls upon me"; "it occurs to me"; "it happens"; "it fails on me" *[Ganda]*.

Nalunkuuma (f) *[nnah-luhn-kuuh-mah]* "That watches over (or protects) me" *[Ganda]*.

Nalusa (f) *[nnah-luh-sah]* A species of marsh grass; a marshy area; permission; a permit *[Ganda]*.

Nalusiba (f) *[nnah-luh-sih-bah]* That ties (or imprisons, or binds, or fastens, or locks); that binds (or obliges); that reserves (or preserves, or packs up) *[Ganda]*.

Nalusolo (f) *[nnah-luh-soh-loh]* Body rash; animal (in a piteous or emaciated state) *[Ganda]*.

Naluswa/ Nnaluswa (f/m) *[nnah-luh-swah]* That of the termite hill *[Ganda, Soga]*.

Nalutoogo/ Nnalutoogo (f) *[nnah-luh-toh-oh-goh]* Wide area of papyrus; papyrus patch *[Ganda]*.

Naluuma (m) *[nnah-luuh-mah]* Metal wire *[Ganda]*.

Naluutu (f) *[nnah-luuh-tuh]* A large amount; a large mass; one who pursues vigorously; one who beats a drum; one who becomes greedy *[Ganda]*.

Naluvumba (f) *[nnah-luh-vuhm-bah]* A rub; a massage; seizing; grasping; eating ravenously *[Ganda]*.

Naluvuuma (f) *[nnah-luh-vuuh-mah]* A rumbling sound; a hiss; a whizz; a rumble *[Ganda]*.

Naluwaayiro (m) *[nnah-luh-waah-yih-roh]* Piece (or portion) added; patch; graft; appendix or supplement (such as of a book); slander; false accusation *[Ganda, Soga]*.

Naluwaga (f) *[nnah-luh-wah-gah]* One related to the king; that supports (or backs up, or encourages); staunch supporter; prop post *[Ganda]*.

Naluwalo (f) *[nnah-luh-wah-loh]* A shift; a turn *[Ganda, Soga]*.

Naluwanda (f) *[nnah-luh-wahn-dah]* Spitting out; blurting out; throwing out *[Ganda]*.

Naluwemba (f) *[nnah-luh-wehm-bah]* Red cloth; a spread; a swarming; a covering up of *[Ganda]*.

Naluwembe (f/m) *[nnah-luh-wehm-beh]* A razor; a pampering; an embrace; a swarm all over *[Ganda]*.

Naluwo (f) *[nnah-luh-woh]* A species of tree that has medicinal properties; septic dermatitis *[Ganda]*.

Naluwooza (f) *[nnah-luh-woh-oh-zah]* The charging (or levying) of (such as of taxes, custom duties, tariffs, or dues) *[Ganda]*.

Naluwu (f) *[nnah-luh-wuh]* A skin carpet; a cushion; a seat *[Ganda]*.

Naluwugge (f) *[nnah-luh-wuhg-geh]* Sawdust; thin and dusty substance; ashy substance that forms on young plantain leaves *[Ganda]*.

Naluyange (f) *[nnah-luh-yahn-geh]* The egret; flower of the corn plant *[The Ganda]*.

Naluyiga (f) *[nnah-luh-yih-gah]* Learner; neophyte *[Ganda]*.

Naluyima (f) *[nnah-luh-yih-mah]* Of (or associated with) the aristocratic cattle keeping ethnics, the *Hima*; that stands up; that is situated *[Ganda]*.

Naluyinda (f) *[nnah-luh-yihn-dah]* (Weather) that is menacing (or threatening) *[Ganda]*.

Naluyulu (f) *[nnah-luh-yuh-luh]* A species of reed employed in making baskets *[Ganda]*.

Naluzze (f) *[nnah-luhz-zeh]* A return; a resurgence; "it has come back/ or gone back/ or returned" *[Ganda]*.

Nalwaambo (f) *[nah-lwaahm-boh]* A satirical name such as given by the family midwife to a newborn whose mother is "a scrounging woman" *[Fipa]* (Willis 1982: 230).

Nalwadda (f) *[nnah-lwahd-dah]* That is of long ago (or times past); that came back *[Ganda]*.

Nalwamba (m) *[nnah-lwahm-bah]* The filing tool; one with a peculiarity of the jaws *[Ganda]*.

Nalwatu (m) *[nnah-lwah-tuh]* That does openly (or publicly) *[Ganda]*.

Nalwemanyidde/ Nnalwemanyidde (m) *[nnah-lweh-mah-ndjh-ihd-deh]* "I am well accustomed to it"; this name is commonly associated with the proverb "the one who vainly boasts 'I am well accustomed to being involved in war,' is like the elder (or weakling) who goes to war with an ax for which he is exclusively called upon to use in helping divide the (bovine) booty acquired by the warriors (for which work he is rewarded inferior, such as hump or neck, portions of the meat)" [*Ganda*].

Nalwera/ Nnalwera (f) *[nnah-lweh-rah]* Copper; an abundance; profuseness; a flourishing [*Ganda*].

Nalweyiso (f) *[nnah-lweh-yih-soh]* The pushing of oneself forward (or ahead); conducting oneself; behaving; calling oneself; considering oneself [*Ganda*].

Nalwoluya (f) *[nnah-lwoh-luh-yah]* That is of the yard/ courtyard [*Ganda*].

Nalwoma (f) *[nnah-lwoh-mah]* One that is propped up (or shored up, or underpinned); one that is covered; one that props up (or covers, or shores up) [*Ganda*].

Nalwondooba/ Nnalwondooba (f) *[nnah-lwohn-doh-oh-bah]* That becomes impoverished; that becomes destitute; that suffers greatly [*Ganda*].

Nalyaaki (m) *[nnah-ljaah-tch-ih]* "What did I eat (or consume)?" [*Ganda, Soga*].

Nalyakungabo (f/m) *[nnah-ljah-kuhn-gah-boh]* "I profited from the shield"; "I profited from the war" [*Ganda*].

Nalyambe (f) *[nnah-ljahm-beh]* One associated with the curved garden knife: a name usually given to one who is so lucky that her harvests are always plentiful [*Ganda*].

Nalyankuma (f) *[nnah-ljahn-kuh-mah]* "I ate while I was making the fire"; "I ate while blowing on the fire to keep it going" [*Ganda*].

Nalyazi (f) *[nnah-ljaah-zih]* A large rock [*Ganda*].

Namaaba (f/m) *[nnah-maah-bah]* Of the time of the ceremony of distributing the goods and installing the heir to the deceased; of the time of finalizing funeral rites; that is overwhelming (or ruinous); that involves departing (or leaving); weakness; sickness [*Ganda*].

Namaala (m) *[nnah-maah-lah]* Huge talons; big nails; big claws [*Ganda*].

Namaalwa (f) *[nnah-maah-lwah]* That is smeared; that is smeared on; that is plastered on [*Ganda*].

Namaato (f) *[nnah-maah-toh]* Boats; canoes; steamers; ships; brewing vats [*Ganda*].

Namabega (f) *[nnah-mah-beh-gah]* (With a peculiarity of) the back; behind [*Ganda*].

Namabwa/ Nnamabwa (m) *[nnah-mah-bwah]* Sores; open wounds [*Ganda, Soga*].

Namaga (f) *[nnah-mah-gah]* One who looks (or glances) about [*Ganda*].

Namagambe (f) *[nnah-mah-gahm-beh]* That are said (or told) of/ about [*Ganda*].

Namagambo (f) *[nnah-mah-gahm-boh]* Words; news relayed by word of mouth as opposed to through print or other public media; connected to a filthy or dirty word [*Ganda*].

Namaganda (f) *[nnah-mah-gahn-dah]* (Peculiarities) of the *Ganda* ethnics [*Ganda*].

Namaganngaali (f/m) *[nnah-mah-gahn-ndgh-aah-lih]* "The (glancing from side to side) peculiarities of the crested crane" [*Ganda*].

Namagembe/ Nnamagembe (f) *[nnah-mah-gehm-beh]* Lies; traps for large animals [*Ganda*].

Namagga (f) *[nnah-mahg-gah]* The black shouldered kite [*Ganda*].

Namaggwa (f) *[nnah-mahg-gwaah]* Thorns; spikes; spines [*Ganda*].

Namagina (f) *[nnah-mah-jih-nah]* Bristles on the back or hair on the spine (of an animal); manes [*Ganda*].

Namagoye (f/m) *[nnah-mah-goh-yeh]* Albino [*Ganda, Soga*].

Namaguzi/ Nnamaguzi (f/m) *[nnah-mah-guh-zih]* Merchandise; trade commodities [*Ganda*].

Namajala (f) *[nnah-mah-jah-lah]* Magnificence; showiness; making a display [*Ganda*].

Namakaaga (m) *[nnah-mah-kaah-gah]* (That involve) the sixes [*Ganda*].

Namakaga (m) *[nnah-mah-kah-gah]* Pride; assuredness; defiance; truculence; arrogance [*Ganda*].

Namakajjo (m) *[nnah-mah-kahj-joh]* (That are associated with) sugar cane [*Ganda*].

Namakibozi/ Nnamakibozi (f) *[nnah-mah-tch-ih-boh-zih]* That involve (fruits) becoming bruised and soft (or becoming excessively ripe); that involve festering (of an abscess); that involve rotting (or decaying) [*Ganda*].

Namakiika (m) *[nnah-mah-tch-iih-kah]* That are crosswise (or across); obliquely; that are put across (or placed sideways, or placed horizontally) [The *Ganda*].

Namakobe (f) *[nnah-mah-koh-beh]* Which relates to a species of creeping plant (or climbing yam) resembling ivy, and which produces edible fruits [*Ganda*].

Namakoola (f) *[nnah-mah-koh-oh-lah]* Weeding or uprooting period; leaves; foliage [*Ganda*].

Namakula (f) *[nnah-mah-kuh-lah]* (That of) food presented to the king; magnificent or wondrous; gorgeous looking; "(good) growth" [*Ganda*].

Namala (m) *[nnah-mah-lah]* The finisher; the finalist; "I finished"; that is sufficient for; the instep (or sole) of the foot [*Ganda*].

Namale (f) *[nnah-mah-leh]* Clouds; that sings well; that is associated with (*malenge* which are) small wind instruments (or reed pipes) made of bamboo [*Ganda*].

Namaleego (m) *[nnah-mah-leh-eh-goh]* That involve a difficult situation (or job); that involve hardship; that involve strain; that involve stretching (or tightening, or aiming) [*Ganda*].

Namalubi/ Nnamalubi (f/m) *[nnah-mah-luh-bih]* (That of) the deep waters; (that of) depths [*Ganda*].

Namalusu (m) *[nnah-mah-luh-suh]* Spit; saliva [*Ganda*].

Namalwa (f) *[nnah-mah-lwah]* Millet based beer [*Ganda*].

Namammonde (f) *[nnah-mahm-mohn-deh]* Species of mushrooms that grow amongst sweet potatoes; sweet potatoes [*Ganda*].

Namanda (f) *[nnah-mahn-dah]* Charcoals; coals [*Ganda, Soga*].

Namandwa/ Nammandwa (m) *[nahm-mahn-dwah]* A spirit medium; a speaking medium between the people and a deity [*Ganda*].

Namane (m) *[nah-mah-neh]* Calf [*Tswana*] (Herbert 1995: 3; Herbert 1990: 10).

Namasange (f) *[nnah-mah-sahn-geh]* That are met (or come upon, or found) [*Ganda*].

Namasole (f) *[nnah-mah-soh-leh]* Mother of the king; the queen mother [*Ganda*].

Namaswala (m) *[nnah-mah-swah-lah]* (That involve) disgrace (or shame) [*Ganda*].

Namata (f) *[nnah-mah-tah]* Milk [*Ganda*].

Namataka (f) *[nnah-mah-tah-kah]* The sole survivor [*Ganda*].

Namatama (f) *[nnah-mah-tah-mah]* Cheeks; with prominent cheeks; disgusting; sickening; things you get disgusted with [*Ganda*].

Namatiiti (m) *[nnah-mah-tiih-tih]* Beads; an abundance; timidness; fearfulness; frightfulness; tremblings; chilliness; coldness; pampering [*Ganda*].

Namatiko (f) *[nnah-mah-tih-koh]* Mushrooms [*Ganda*].

Namatiti (m) *[nnah-mah-tih-tih]* Becoming cold (or chilled); chilliness; coldness [*Ganda*].

Namatiwa (m) *[nnah-mah-tih-wah]* (That involve) acts of an exaggerated manner (or overdoing things, or trying to create an impression) [*Ganda*].

Namatovu (f) *[nnah-mah-toh-vuh]* Thistle [*Ganda*].

Namawagi/ Nnamawagi (f) *[nnah-mah-wah-jih]* That are firm (or well supported); encouragement; supporters [*Ganda*].

Namawejje (f) *[nnah-mah-wehj-jeh]* That are calm (or cool-headed, or well behaved) [*Ganda*].

Namawuba (f) *[nnah-mah-wuh-bah]* (One who is) overlooked (or missed); one who is unintentionally slipped by; loss of color; changing beyond recognition [*Ganda*].

Namawuuba (f) *[nnah-mah-wuuh-bah]* (One who) waves or swings about; bothered; one kept on the go; one caused to move about [*Ganda*].

Namayanja/ Nnamayanja (f) *[nnah-mah-yahn-jah]* Lakes; large bodies of water; a name usually given to one whose mother made a sacrifice or offering (to a deity) in River *Mayanja* [*Ganda*].

Namayega (f) *[nnah-mah-yeh-gah]* Feelings of being unwell [*Ganda*].

Namayengo (f) *[nnah-mah-yehn-goh]* Lake or ocean waves; the mix of water waves of lakes (or oceans); that is stirred and dissolved; that is diluted [*Ganda*].

Namayumba (m) *[nnah-mah-yuhm-bah]* Houses; homes [*Ganda*].

Namaziina (f) *[nnah-mah-ziih-naah]* Shreds of barkcloth; barkcloth rags;

ragged clothes [*Ganda*].

Namazime (f) *[nnah-mah-zih-meh]* That are extinguished; that are tarnished; that have lost luster [*Ganda*].

Nambaale (f) *[nnahm-baah-leh]* Wedge [*Ganda*].

Nambago (f/m) *[nnahm-bah-goh]* Hoe [*Soga*].

Nambajjwe (f/m) *[nnahm-bahj-jweh]* That is carved out; that is cut; that is chopped [*Ganda*].

Nambalirwa (f) *[nnaahm-bah-lih-rwah]* That is taken into consideration; one they are concerned about; one who is counted in/ for; taken account of [*Ganda*].

Nambasa (f) *[nnahm-bah-sah]* "I catch (something thrown) with"; "I grasp (or grab, or lay hold on) with" [*Ganda*].

Nambassa (f) *[nnahm-bahs-sah]* "I cause them to be killed"; "I cause them to be killed by means of" [*Ganda*].

Nambatuusa (m) *[nnahm-bah-tuuh-sah]* "I take them there"; "I enable them to arrive (safely)" [*Ganda*].

Nambatya (f) *[nnahm-bah-tjah]* "I am scared (or frightened) of them"; "I fear (or honor, or respect) them" [*Ganda*].

Nambawubye (f) *[nnahm-bah-wuh-bjeh]* "I have overlooked (or missed) them"; "I have slipped by them"; "I have misled them" [*Ganda*].

Nabedha (f) *[nahm-beh-eh-tdh-ah]* Princess; favorite girl [*Soga*].

Nambeere (f) *[nnahm-beh-eh-reh]* The female edible rat [*Ganda*].

Nambejja (f) *[nnahm-behj-jah]* Princess; favorite girl [*Ganda*].

Namberenge (f) *[nnahm-beh-reh-ehn-geh]* Corn nuts; popcorn; a name usually given to a very intelligent and daring child [*Ganda*].

Nambiggya (f/m) *[nnahm-bihj-jah]* "I take the things away (or out, or off)" [*Ganda*].

Nambira/ Nnambira (f) *[nnahm-bih-rah]* Bead; "I become warmed up"; "I become warmed over" [*Ganda*].

Nambirige (f) *[nnahm-bih-rih-geh]* That rolls (or turns over and over); that rolls on the ground; that plays about; that travels at a fast rate; that pushes back (or repels); that throws; that is hurled [*Ganda*].

Nambiro (f) *[nnaahm-bih-roh]* Sprinter; good runner; speed [*Ganda, Soga*].

Nambogo (f) *[nnahm-boh-goh]* The buffalo [*Ganda*].

Namboolanyi (f) *[nnahm-boh-oh-lah-ndjh-ih]* One that causes to repudiate each other; that causes a mutual antagonism based on alleged differences (such as those between family or clan); antagonisms; disavowals [*Ganda*].

Namboowa (f) *[nnahm-boh-oh-wah]* Of noble birth; free born; of the upper class [*Ganda*].

Nambooze (f) *[nnahm-boh-oh-zeh]/* ***Namboozi*** (f) *[nnahm-boh-oh-zih]* One that narrates (or recounts, or mentions); a good conversationalist [The *Ganda*].

Nambowooze (f) *[nnahm-boh-woh-oh-zeh]* Of noble birth; free born; of the upper class [*Ganda*].

Namboza/ Nnamboza (f) *[nnahm-boh-zah]* "I cause to be wet"; "I cause to rot (or to decay)"; "I cause (an abscess) to fester"; "I cause (fruit) to become excessively ripe (or to become bruised and soft)"; the mode of getting wet; the mode of rotting (or decaying); the mode of (an abscess) festering; the mode of (fruit) becoming excessively ripe (or becoming bruised and soft) [*Ganda*].

Nambozze (f) *[nnahm-bohz-zeh]* One that takes on an attractive appearance (especially of a young girl or bride) and whose skin is as fair and healthy as that of a baby [*Ganda*].

Nambubi (f) *[nnahm-buh-bih]* One associated with evil (or badness, or inferiority, or ugliness) [*Ganda*].

Nambuga (m) *[nnahm-buh-gah]* Court of law; chief's enclosure; council; fountain that cattle drink from; place of a chief [*Ganda*].

Nambuule (f) *[nnahm-buuh-leh]* That is thrashed (or beaten, or beaten hard, or thrown to the ground); (cattle) that is raided; that is associated with bachelorhood (or losing ones wife through separation or desertion); that is associated with a poor boy (or a poor kid) [*Ganda*].

Nambuulirwa/ Nnambuulirwa (f) *[nnahm-buuh-lih-rwah]* "I am told (or informed)"; "I am proclaimed to"; "I am preached to" [*Ganda*].

Nambuusi (f) *[nnahm-buuh-sih]* Jumper; flier; astronaut; one that causes to be doubtful (or to suspect, or to vacillate); one who suspects (or has doubts about); one who flits (or flutters about) [*Ganda*].

Nambuya (f) *[nnahm-buh-yaah]* State of chaos; a strong wind [*Ganda*].

Nambuyaga (f) *[nnahm-buh-yah-gaah]* State of chaos; strong winds [The *Ganda*].

Nambwa (f) *[nnahh-bwaah]* Dog [*Ganda*].

Nambwayo (f) *[nnahm-bwah-yoh]* That involves ferocity (or cruelty, or fury, or anger) [*Ganda*].

Namenya/ Nnamenya (f/m) *[nnahm-meh-ndjh-ah]* To break; to break (the law) [*Ganda*].

Namenyeka/ Nnammenyeka (m) *[nnahm-meh-ndjh-eh-kah]* A relaxation of one's demands (or conditions); broken; crushed; giving in [*Ganda*].

Namfumbambi (f) *[nnahm-fuhm-bahm-bih]* Bad method of cooking; badly cooking [*Ganda*].

Namicyo/ Namicho/ Namico (f) *[nnah-mih-tch-oh]* "(Pleasant) dawnings"; a name usually given to one born in the morning [*Ganda*].

Namiganda (f) *[nnah-mih-gahn-daah]* Bundles; bunches; terror [*Ganda*].

Namige/ Nnamige (m) *[nnah-mih-geh]* Courageous (or bold, or heroic) person [*Ganda*].

Namigga (f) *[nnah-mihg-gah]* Water wells; rivers; large streams [*Ganda*].

Namiggo (f) *[nnah-mihg-goh]* Stick; walking sticks; canes; crutches [The *Ganda*].

Namiiro/ Namiro (f) *[nnah-miih-roh]* Tracheas; windpipes [*Ganda*].

Namikka (f) *[nnah-mihk-kah]* The force of exhaled breath (that enhances trumpet blown music); breathes; vapors [*Ganda*].

Naminha (m) *[nnah-mih-nhah]/* **Naminya** (m) *[nnah-mih-ndjh-ah]* Lizards

[*Soga*].

Namirambo (f) *[nnah-mih-rahm-boh]* At rest; corpses: a name pertaining to a population depleting situation such as a war or an epidemic [*Ganda*].

Namirembe (f) *[nnah-mih-rehm-beh]* Throne; peace; name of a Goddess; a plant with small yellow flowers and greyish-green leaves [*Ganda*].

Namirimu (f) *[nnah-mih-rih-muh]* Work; tasks; employment [*Ganda*].

Namisango (f) *[nnah-mih-sahn-goh]* Accusations; crimes; court cases [The *Ganda*].

Namisanvu (f) *[nnah-mih-saahn-vuh]* Sevens; branches; branching parts of a tree spread out to block a road or path; obstacles; obstructions [*Ganda*].

Namitala (f) *[nnah-mih-tah-lah]* (Of) the lands (or villages); newly acquired lands; lands between two streams or swamps used as a measure of distance [*Ganda*].

Namitembo (f) *[nnah-mih-teh-ehm-boh]* Twine nets for carrying small water or milk pots; spider's webs [*Ganda*].

Namiwanda (f) *[nnah-mih-waahn-dah]* Acts of spitting; roads; paths [The *Ganda*].

Namiya (f) *[nnah-mih-yah]* Fishing baskets used to trap fish.

Namiyingo (f) *[nnah-mih-yihn-goh]* The locks to the kraal gates; overwhelming; excessive; too great [*Ganda*].

Namiyonga (f) *[nnah-mih-yohn-gah]* Burned out remains of food; sparks from a fire [*Ganda*].

Namizanga/ Nnamizanga (f) *[nnah-mih-zahn-gah]* "I used to induce to (or cause to) swallow using" [*Ganda*].

Nammale (f) *[nnahm-mah-leh]* Mud fish [*Ganda*].

Nammambi (m) *[nnahm-mahm-bih]* "A bad way of refusing to give (or grudging, or withholding)" [*Ganda*].

Nammande (f) *[nnahm-mahn-deh]* A name usually given to a first born girl [*Ganda*].

Nammembwa (f) *[nnahm-mehm-bwah]* That has been turned into a burnt food crust [*Ganda*].

Nammondo/ Namondo (f) *[nnahm-mohn-doh]* The serval cat [*Ganda*].

Nammuli (f) *[nnahm-muh-lih]* Reeds [*Ganda, Soga*].

Nampa (f) *[nnahm-pah]* Giver; "I give" [*Ganda*].

Nampagi (f/m) *[nnahm-pah-jih]* Pillar; post; pole [*Ganda*].

Nampala (f/m) *[nnahm-pah-lah]* Antelope; overseer [*Ganda, Soga*].

Nampamba (f) *[nnahm-pahm-bah]* "I appropriate"; "I put on reserve (an item that will be purchased)"; "I capture (or confiscate)"; "I take prisoner" [*Ganda*].

Nampanga (f) *[nnahm-pahn-gah]* That is associated with a rooster; that is associated with a large beetle; that is associated with jawbones of kings or other important persons which were traditionally removed at death and preserved [*Ganda*].

Nampawengwa (f) *[nnahm-pah-wehn-gwah]* "Give me the place where I (will) fall" [*Ganda*].

Nampeera/ Nnampeera (f) *[nnahm-peh-eh-rah]* Reward; salary; pay; wage [*Ganda*].

Nampenge (m) *[nnahm-pehn-geh]* Fringes; edges; corners of cloth; crests (or tufts) of birds [*Ganda*].

Nampewo (f) *[nahm-peh-woh]* Wind; breeze [*Ganda*].

Nampiima/ Nnampiima (f) *[nnahm-piih-mah]* Dagger; daggers [*Ganda*].

Nampijja (f) *[nnahm-pihj-jah]* Stone anvil [*Ganda*].

Nampoza (f) *[nnahm-poh-zah]* Justification; explanation; rationale; defense [*Ganda*].

Nampunta (m) *[nnahm-puhn-tah]* The (prickly) spicules of a species of tall grass [*Ganda*].

Nampuuma (m) *[nnahm-puuh-mah]* "I am at loss as to what to do"; "I am confused"; the mode of hissing (or making buzzing noises, or rumbling, or whistling, or rustling) [*Ganda*].

Nampwaayo/ Nnampwaayo (f) *[nnahm-pwaah-yoh]* "I become exhausted (or worn out, or weary)" [*Ganda*].

Nampyangu (f/m) *[nnahm-pjaahn-guh]* Conceitedness; deceitfulness [The *Ganda*].

Namubuya (f) *[nnah-muh-buh-yah]* Silly; stupid [*Ganda*].

Namudaala (f/m) *[nnah-muh-daah-lah]* A market stand [*Ganda*].

Namuddu (f) *[nnah-muhd-duh]* Captive; one related to a former captive; servant [*Ganda*].

Namuga (f) *[nnah-muh-gah]* Perfume; smell [*Ganda*].

Namugaanyi (f) *[nnah-muh-gaah-ndjh-ih]* One who causes to refuse (or to forbid, or to prevent, or to withhold, or to deny) [*Ganda*].

Namugaba (f) *[nnah-muh-gah-bah]* A give away; that is given as a present; that is divided (or distributed, or apportioned) [*Ganda*].

Namugabi (f) *[nnah-muh-gah-bih]* Generous person; liberal person; one who distributes; distributor [*Ganda*].

Namugala (m) *[nnah-muh-gah-lah]* Framework structure built around an anthill to facilitate the capturing of edible ants; blue starling [*Ganda*].

Namugamba (f) *[nnah-muh-gahm-bah]* "You (all) say (or say to, or tell)"; "I told him/ her" [*Ganda*].

Namugambe (f) *[nnah-muh-gahm-beh]* One who was (or is) told; one who was (or is) told of [*Ganda*].

Namugambi (f) *[nnah-muh-gahm-bih]* That says (says to, tells) [*Ganda*].

Namuganga (f) *[nnah-muh-gahn-gah]* Doctor; physician; a witchdoctor; magician; one that creates sparks [*Ganda*].

Namugaya (f) *[nnah-muh-gah-yah]* One that scorns; a small bush which has roots that are chewed while in their raw state [*Ganda, Soga*].

Namugayi (f) *[nnah-muh-gah-yih]* That is contemptuous; one that is scornful; despising [*Ganda*].

Namugazi (f) *[nnah-muh-gah-zih]* That is broad (or thick, or wide) [The *Ganda*].

Namugenyi (f) *[nnah-muh-geh-ndjh-ih]* Guest; stranger; visitor [*Ganda*].

Namugera (m) *[nnah-muh-geh-rah]* One that distributes (or apportions) [The *Ganda*].

Namugere (m) *[nnah-muh-geh-reh]* That is precise (or measured, or definite); (one with the peculiarity of) a large foot [*Ganda, Soga*].

Namugga (f) *[nnah-muhg-gah]* Water well; river; large stream [*Ganda*].

Namuggala (f/m) *[nnah-muhg-gah-lah]* That closes (the entrances); that shuts (or encloses, or brings to an end, or discontinues) [*Ganda*].

Namugulu (f) *[nnah-muh-guh-luh]* (With a peculiarity of) the leg [*Ganda*].

Namugunde (f/m) *[nnah-muh-guhn-deh]* One that is (or was) violently thrown down; that is (or was) hurled down; that is (or was) dashed down; that is (or was) stabbed [*Ganda*].

Namuguzi (f/m) *[nnah-muh-guh-zih]* Buyer; purchaser; customer [*Ganda*].

Namugwanga (f/m) *[nnah-muh-gwahn-gah]* A national; of the country (or nation); tribesman; indigenous; citizen; one that takes revenge [*Ganda*].

Namugwano (f) *[nnah-muh-gwaah-noh]* That is suitable (or fitting) [The *Ganda, Soga*].

Namugwanya (f) *[nnah-muh-gwaah-ndjh-ah]* That makes suitable (or fitting) [*Ganda*].

Namugwe (f) *[nnah-muh-gweh]* "Fall down"; which occurs; which falls down [*Ganda*].

Namujulirwa (f/m) *[nnah-muh-juh-lih-rwah]* Witness; martyr [*Ganda*].

Namujunga (m) *[nnah-muh-juhn-gah]* Tassel [*Ganda*].

Namujuzi (m) *[nnah-muh-juh-zih]* That causes to fill (or to fill up); that makes full [*Ganda*].

Namukaabya (f) *[nnah-muh-kaah-bjaah]* One who causes to weep (or to mourn, or to sing [i.e. birds], or to roar [i.e. animals], or to sound)"; one associated with the reign of King *Muteesa Mukaabya* [*Ganda*].

Namukadde (f/m) *[nnah-muh-kahd-deh]* Elder; parent; old person; elder of the church; minister [*Ganda*].

Namukambya (f) *[nah-muh-kahm-bjah]* That makes acidic (or bitter) [The *Ganda*].

Namukangula (m) *[nnah-muh-kahn-guh-lah]* That raises the voice; the creation of an uproar; that disturbs; a raise in price [*Ganda*].

Namukasa/ Nnamukasa (f) *[nnah-muh-kah-sah]* One affiliated with *Mukasa* the God associated with Lake Victoria; the grivet monkey; the vervet monkey [*Ganda, Soga*].

Namukaya (f) *[nah-muh-kaah-yah]* Skilled diver [*Ganda*].

Namukimba (f) *[nnah-muh-kihm-bah]* Blacksmith's charges; a tree that resembles the laburnum; one who attacks [*Ganda*].

Namukisa/ Nnamukisa (f) *[nnah-muh-kih-sah]* One endowed with luck; blessing; opportunity; chance [*Ganda, Soga*].

Namukoka (f/m) *[nnah-muh-koh-kah]* Water which flows in streams during or after rainfall [*Ganda*].

Namukumbi (f) *[nnah-muh-kuhm-bih]* One who (joyfully) struts around (or parades about, or shows off, or swaggers, or marches) [*Ganda*].

Namukundi (f) *[nnah-muh-kuhn-dih]* (With a feature of) the navel [*Ganda*].

Namukwa (f/m) *[nnah-muh-kwah]* Cattle tick [*Ganda*].

Namukwaya/ Nnamukwaya (f) *[nnah-muh-kwaah-yah]* Moving as quickly as lightning; making a rustling noise while moving; arc; spear; the spear warrior [*Ganda*].

Namulaalirwa/ Nnamulaalirwa (f) *[nnah-muh-laah-lih-rwah]* That gets congested in the lungs; that has difficulty in breathing; that hangs suspended for (or in); that gets stuck for (or in); that gets blocked/ or hindered for (or in); that adheres for (or in) [*Ganda*].

Namulangwa (m) *[nnah-muh-lahn-gwah]* The talked about one; one worth talking about; one who is announced (or advertised, or prophesied, or given notice of) [*Ganda*].

Namulege/ Nnamulege (f) *[nnah-muh-leh-geh]* That is tasted (or tried); that is caused to have an overdue pregnancy [*Ganda*].

Namuleme (f) *[nnah-muh-leh-meh]* One who does not budge; one who refuses to go [*Ganda*].

Namulengo (m) *[nnah-muh-lehn-goh]* Limited amount (or quantity); a pile (or heap); a unit of market food (such as nuts that are set out for sale by a merchant) [*Ganda*].

Namuli (f) *[nnah-muh-lih]* Glutton; eater [*Ganda, Soga*].

Namuligo (f) *[nnah-muh-lih-goh]* That is dirty (or filthy) [*Ganda*].

Namulima (f) *[nnah-muh-lih-mah]* Cultivation; one that cultivates; one who farms; one who backbites [*Ganda*].

Namulinde (f) *[nnah-muh-lihn-deh]* That is waited for/ or upon (with patience) [*Ganda*].

Namulindi (f) *[nnah-muh-lihn-dih]* Ambatch tree which is light wooded and grows in or near swamps; one associated with a deceased chief's grandson who participated in the chief's burial ceremonies [*Ganda*].

Namulindwa/ Nnamulindwa (f) *[nnah-muh-lihn-dwah]* That is protected (or waited upon) [*Ganda*].

Namulinzi (f) *[nnah-muh-lihn-zih]* One who spies out; one who goes in search of; one who waits for; one who keeps guard of [*Ganda*].

Namulira (f) *[nnah-muh-lih-rah]* That weeps (or cries, or mourns); mourning; crying; (with the peculiarity of a large) umbilical cord [*Ganda, Soga*].

Namulizi (f) *[nnah-muh-lih-zih]* That is tearful; that has a tendency to weep; mourner [*Ganda, Soga*].

Namulondo (f) *[nnah-muh-lohn-doh]* The throne; a species of mushroom [*Ganda, Soga*].

Namulunda (m) *[nnah-muh-luhn-dah]* A herdsman; a shepherd; a tender of farm animals [*Ganda*].

Namulunga (f) *[nnah-muh-luhn-gah]* Seasoned; flavored; salted [*Ganda*].

Namulwana (f) *[nnah-muh-lwaah-nah]* Fighter; one that fights or struggles towards a goal [*Ganda*].

Namumenya/ Nnamumenya (f/m) *[nnah-muh-meh-ndjh-ah]* That breaks (or breaks into, or destroys); that captures (a stronghold); that bends at the joint; that refutes (or counters, or retracts); that mentions (or refers to); "I broke (or destroyed, or countered) the person" [*Ganda*].

Namumwa (m) *[nnah-muh-mwah]* (One that has peculiarities of) the lips; beak [*Ganda*].

Namuna (m) *[nnah-muh-nah]* Compulsion; force [*Ganda*].

Namunene (f/m) *[nnah-muh-neh-neh]* Large; one who is big [*Ganda*].

Namunga (m) *[nnah-muhn-gah]* Aimless wander around; a ramble [*Ganda*].

Namungo/ Nnamungo (f/m) *[nnah-muhn-goh]* Large quantity; an abundance [*Ganda*].

Namunnungu (m) *[nnah-muhn-nuhn-guh]* That has cracked skin (on the feet) [*Ganda*].

Namunyomba (f) *[nnah-muh-ndjh-oh-ohm-bah]* One notorious for a characteristic way of quarreling (or speaking angrily) [*Ganda*].

Namunyonyi (f) *[nnah-muh-ndjh-oh-ndjh-ih]* Chicken [*Ganda*].

Namunyoro (f) *[nnah-muh-ndjh-oh-roh]* One of (or one associated with) the *Nyoro* ethnics [*Ganda*].

Namunywa (m) *[nnah-muh-ndjh-wah]* Close friend; that is victorious [The *Ganda*].

Namusaawa (f) *[nnah-muh-saah-wah]* One that clears away or cuts down; of the time [*Ganda, Soga*].

Namusaazi (f) *[nnah-muh-saah-zih]* Joker; one whose talk is not to be taken seriously [*Ganda, Soga*].

Namusobya (f/m) *[nnah-muh-soh-bjah]* Violator; wrongdoer; one at fault [*Ganda, Soga*].

Namusota/ Nnamusota (m) *[nnah-muh-soh-tah]* Snake [*Ganda, Soga*].

Namusubo/ Namusuubo (f/m) *[nnah-muh-suuh-boh]* One who plays on a swing; one who swings (or is swung) back and forth; the one of the playing swing [*Soga*].

Namusujja (f) *[nnah-muh-suhj-jah]* One that is feverish [*Ganda*].

Namusuutwa (f) *[nnah-muh-suuh-twah]* A favorite (or a beloved, or a heavily praised) person [*Ganda*].

Namutala/ Nnamutala (f/m) *[nnah-muh-tah-lah]* (One that is of) the land (or village); newly acquired land; land between two streams or swamps used as a measure of distance [*Ganda*].

Namutale (f/m) *[nah-muh-tah-leh]* Bird which follows cattle herds [*Ganda*].

Namutalira/ Nnamutalira (m) *[nnah-muh-tah-lih-rah]* That is tall (or lanky); a name-title of the one officially in charge of the king's xylophone resembling musical instrument (*ddinda*) made of wood [*Ganda*].

Namutanyi (f) *[nnah-muh-tah-ndjh-ih]* That causes to deteriorate; that makes worse; that causes to become infected (or to fester); that accidentally makes mistakes; that is the source of an inadvertence [*Ganda*].

Namutebi (f) *[nah-muh-teh-bih]* Markswoman; that shoots for a goal; one who outwits (or foils, or baffles) [*Ganda*].

Namutete (m) *[nnah-muh-teh-teh]* One associated with the chief that supervises elderly men guarding the rear of the palace and caring for the plantain gardens of the king's womenfolk [*Ganda*].

Namutibe (f) *[nnah-muh-tih-beh]* Beautiful; pampered; spoiled [*Ganda*].

Namutidde (f) *[nnah-muh-tihd-deh]* "You are frightened (or afraid)"; "you are respectful" [*Ganda*].

Namutinda (m) *[nnah-muh-tihn-dah]* The provision (or erecting) of a bridge (or ceiling, or trellis, or framework over) [*Ganda*].

Namuto (f) *[nnah-muh-toh]* The young one; child; young person [*Ganda*].

Namutunga (f) *[nah-muh-tuhn-gah]* One that sews (or threads, or attaches) [*Ganda*].

Namutwe/ Nnamutwe (f/m) *[nnah-muh-tweh]* (With a peculiarity of the) head; the leader; the one on top [*Ganda*].

Namuwanga (f) *[nnah-muh-waahn-gah]* One associated with the God *Muwanga* who is affiliated with creation and whose shrine was at *Nseke*; one who fits in (or installs, or establishes); "you must (or should) always give to him/ her" [*Ganda*].

Namuwawu (f) *[nnah-muh-wah-wuh]* Genuine; real [*Ganda*].

Namuwaya/ Nnamuwaya (f) *[nnah-muh-wah-yah]* The chatterer; a conversationalist; talker [*Ganda, Soga*].

Namuwemba/ Nnamuwemba (f/m) *[nnah-muh-wehm-bah]* (Reddish brown colored) sorghum or millet (for making beer); a spreadout [*Ganda*].

Namuwube (m) *[nnah-muh-wuh-beh]* That is unintentionally slipped by (or got by, or slipped out); one that is overlooked (or missed) [*Ganda*].

Namuwulya (f) *[nnah-muh-wuh-ljah]* One who pulls down (such as berries from a bush)/ or unstrings (such as beads from a string) [*Ganda*].

Namuyama (m) *[nnah-muh-yah-mah]* That greets; that welcomes (or receives gladly, or greets enthusiastically) [*Ganda*].

Namuyanja (f) *[nnah-muh-yahn-jah]* Native of the lakes (or islands); a wind; species of tall and wild tree; one who spreads out, unfolds, or begins; one who presents or submits (such as a bill or a proposal) [*Ganda*].

Namuyiga (f) *[nnah-muh-yih-gah]* Learner; neophyte [*Ganda*].

Namuyige (f) *[nnah-muh-yih-geh]* That is learned; that is trained; that is educated [*Ganda*].

Namuyigge/ Nnamuyigge (f) *[nnah-muh-yihg-geh]* **Namuyiggwa/ Nnamuyiggwa** (f) *[nnah-muh-yihg-gwah]* That is hunted for (or sought after) [*Ganda*].

Namuyimba (f/m) *[nnah-muh-yihm-bah]* Combination; joined together; one who joins together (or does in addition to, or ties together); one who sings [*Ganda*].

Namuyimbwa (f) *[nnah-muh-yihm-bwah]* That is sung about; that is combined (or joined together) [*Ganda*].

Namuyira (m) *[nnah-muh-yih-rah]* A rippling noise; gurgling (of water); rumbling/ or roaring (such as of a waterfall, or the sea, or a big fire); snorting; snoring; wheezing; purring [*Ganda*].

Namuyomba (f) *[nnah-muh-yohm-bah]* That is quarrelsome; that speaks angrily [*Ganda*].

Namuyondo (f) *[nnah-muh-yohn-doh]* Lace; braid; girdle; one that plaits or twines [*Ganda*].

Namuyonjo (f/m) *[nnah-muh-yohn-joh]* A chicken basket; a basket for carrying chickens [*Ganda*].

Namuyumba (f) *[nnah-muh-yuhm-bah]* House; of the house [*Ganda*].

Namuzinda (m) *[nnah-muh-zihn-dah]* A species of tall forest tree; African bread fruit [*Ganda*].

Namwa (m) *[nnah-mwah]* "I shaved" [*Ganda*].

Namwaagala (f) *[nnah-mwaah-gah-lah]* "I wanted (or desired) him/ her"; "I loved (or liked) him/ her"; that loves (or desires, or likes) [*Ganda*].

Namwabula (f) *[nnah-mwah-buh-lah]* One who leads (someone) in a hurry; one who rushes or does in a hurry [*Ganda*].

Namwama (m) *[nnah-mwaah-mah]* That greets; that welcomes; that receives gladly (or greets enthusiastically); that of a rushing forth (or rushing out, or dashing out, or bursting out); that of a flushing out (of an animal from the bush); a crouching down [*Ganda*].

Namwana (m) *[nnah-mwaah-nah]* (Associated with/ or having) a child [The *Ganda*].

Namwanda (f) *[nnah-mwahn-dah]* That is of ampleness; one that is swollen (or puffed); a spread across [*Ganda, Soga*].

Namwangu (f) *[nnah-mwahn-guh]* That is speedy [*Ganda, Soga*].

Namwanja (m) *[nnah-mwahn-jah]* Spreading out (or unfolding, or beginning); presenting/ submitting (such as a bill or proposal); bringing up (a matter); that spreads out (or unfolds, or begins); that presents/ submits (such as a bill or proposal); that brings up (a matter) [*Ganda, Soga*].

Nashibu (f) *[nah-shih-buh]* "The mother associated with the rainbow" [The *Rega*].

Ncediswa (f) *[uhn-tch-eh-dih-swah]* "The helped one" [*Xhosa*] (Neethling 1994: 92).

Ncepsi (f) *[uhn-tch-ehp-sih]* A nickname-abbreviation for *Nonceba*: "Mercy" [*Xhosa*] (Neethling 1994: 92).

Ncesh (f) *[uhn-tch-eh-tsh]* A nickname-abbreviation for *Ncediswa*: "The helped one" [*Xhosa*] (Neethling 1994: 92).

Ndelaukiwa (f/m) *[ndeh-lahw-kih-wah]* "I have met with bitterness": a name such given by the mother to one who is the product of a difficult and costly pregnancy and birth [*Chaga*] (Raum 1967: 297).

Ndhlalambi (f/m) *[ndh-lah-lahm-bih]* Bad drought; draining hunger: a name such as given to a child born during a persistently long drought or hunger period [*Ndebele*] (Hemans 1968: 74).

Ndileka (m) *[ndih-leh-kah]* To be dignified [*Xhosa*] (Neethling 1994: 92).

Ndils (m) *[ndih-ls]/ Ndish* (m) *[ndih-tsh]* Nicknames-abbreviations for *Ndileka*: "To be dignified" [*Xhosa*] (Neethling 1994: 92).

Ndiphiwe (f) *[ndih-pih-weh]* "(The child) has been given to us" [*Xhosa*] (Thipa 1987: 109).

Ndivuyeleni (m) *[ndih-vuh-yeh-leh-nih]* "Be joyful (over my birth)" [*Xhosa*]

(Thipa 1987: 111).

Ndlovu (m) *[ndloh-voo]* Elephant *[Ndebele]* (Hemans 1968: 74).

Ndoda (m) *[ndoh-dah]* Man *[Zulu]* (Koopman 1987: 148).

Neo (m) *[neh-woh]* Gift: a name such as given to a newborn by its parents to indicate that they consider the child a gift from God *[Tswana]* (Herbert 1997: 8; Herbert 1995: 3; Herbert 1990: 9); or a name such as given to a newborn by its mother to indicate that it is indeed the gift of a baby boy that she wished for, and for which she prayed to God *[Sotho]* (Herbert 1990: 9).

Ngabo (m) *[ndgh-ah-boh]* Shield; this name is sometimes associated with the proverb "a woman who is a diligent farmer causes you (the husband) to eat with your shield over the food" which dramatises a very hard working wife who is able to give her husband so much to eat that he even has to shield her away from bringing more food *[Ganda]*.

Ngec (m) *[ngeh-tch]* Francolin: a name given to a twin [The *Nuer*] (Evans-Pritchard 1948: 167).

Ngenzeni (f) *[ndgh-ehn-zeh-nih]* "What have I done?": a name such as given to a newborn by its mother who is pointing out to neighbors that the rumors in the neighborhood that are told of her are false and therefore should not merit the neighbors' jealousy and ill-feeling towards her *[Zulu]* (Turner 1992: 55).

Ngori (f) *[ndgh-oh-rih]* A name given to a fourth born *[Nuba]* (Seligman 1932: 387).

Ngozi (f/m) *[ngoh-zih]* Swaddling clothes; clothes used to cover an infantthis name is sometimes associated with the proverbs "the fruitfulness of a person is evident at the time when, as a baby, the person is still wrapped on its mother's back in infant clothing" and "that a child is (or will be) strong and healthy, is evident at the time when, as a baby, it is still wrapped in infant clothing" which imply that a lot can be told about the future of one that is still an infant *[Ganda]*.

Ngwana (m) *[ndgh-wah-nah]* "Daughter": an inappropriate 'cross-name' is a form of derogatory-protection name usually given to one born following the deaths of several of his previously born siblings--such (normally temporary) names are intended to confuse the ancestral spirits through making them believe that the parents do not care for the newborn and therefore their taking it away (by dealing it a hand of death as happened to other children in the family) would not hurt or serve as punishment *[Sotho]* (Herbert 1990: 5, 6).

Ngwanangwako (m) *[ndgh-wah-nah-ndgh-wah-koh]* "Child of the house": a 'special' protection name commonly given to a first born male amongst several older female siblings, or to a first child of a mother who has taken an unusually long time to have a child, or to one born following the deaths of several of his previously born siblings--'children of the house' are traditionally not to be touched by outsiders and they are to spend most of their time at home *[Sotho]* (Herbert 1990: 6, 16).

Ngwanenyana (m) *[ndgh-wah-neh-ndjh-ah-nah]* "Small daughter": an inappropriate 'cross-name' is a form of derogatory-protection name usually given to one born following the deaths of several of his previously born siblings-- such (normally temporary) names are intended to confuse the ancestral spirits through making them believe that the parents do not care for the newborn and therefore their taking it away (by dealing it a hand of death as happened to other children in the family) would not hurt or serve as punishment [*Sotho*] (Herbert 1990: 5, 6).

Ngwenya (m) *[ndgh-weh-ndjh-ah]* Crocodile [*Ndebele*] (Hemans 1968: 74; Koopman 1990: 336).

Nhial (m) *[ndjh-ahl]* Sky; rain: a name such as given to one born during a period of rain [*Nuer*] (Evans-Pritchard 1948: 167).

Nhlanhla (m) *[nlah-nlah]* "Luck": a name such as given to a newborn by its parents who express that they have had a gratifying state of affairs [*Zulu*] (Koopman 1987: 152).

Nhlanhla (m) *[nlah-nlah]* "Lucky" [*Zulu*] (Herbert 1997: 15).

Njala (m) *[ndjh-ah-lah]* Famine; hunger; this name is sometimes associated with the proverb "'the elderly person is patiently bearing the hunger'--so one says in commiseration even when the elder has just eaten something" implying that the elderly tend to always be sympathized with and are perpetually expected to be in some kind of pain or want, be it physical, physiological, or psychological; this name is also sometimes associated with the proverb "kin relationships go along with eating--if a related person leaves your home while hungry then this relative will not come back" implying that treats are an important aspect of cultivating relations not only with friends, but also with kin; this name is also sometimes associated with the proverb "one who has plenty of food at home is (paradoxically) still killed by famine starvation conditions while on the road traveling" implying that those who have much become blind to the fact that conditions away from home can be far different from those at home; this name is also sometimes associated with the proverb "eating to satisfaction makes one lazy, starving makes one ill" implying that one ought to do things in the right measure or in moderation [*Ganda*].

Njamombe (m) *[ndjh-ah-mohm-beh]* "Owner of the cattle" [*Chaga*] (Raum 1967: 340).

Njofu (m) *[ndjh-oh-fuh]* Elephant [*Chaga*] (Raum 1967: 340).

Nkanga (m) *[nkahn-gah]* A basket (or container) woven from grass and is used to store or carry a variety of food produce; this name is sometimes associated with the proverb "one who is going down to the lake does not leave the fish basket behind" [*Ganda*].

Nkatazo (f/m) *[nkah-tah-zoh]* Worry: a name given to a child whose alarming sickness warrants concern, or to a child born during worrying times [*Ndebele*] (Hemans 1968: 74).

Nkinzi (f) *[nkihn-zih]* A sewing in many places; a sewing quickly; an embroidering; needle; this name is sometimes associated with the proverb which dramatizes that greed or passion blinds reasoning: "the need to eat makes one lose the needle" (i.e. when busy with needlework, on notice that the food is ready, drops what he or she is doing) [*Ganda*].

Nkoko (f/m) *[nkoh-koh]* Chickens; hen; this name is sometimes associated with the proverb "a woman who is a diligent cultivator is the one that gets to see the chicken dancing with joy" implying that such a woman provides plenty of nourishment to the chickens by digging so much, insofar as she uncovers so many insects in the soil, she encourages insect feeding presence on her heavy yields and harvest garbage and, she throws away into her garden a lot of leftover food that would attract bugs as well as the chickens [*Ganda*].

Nkoligo (m) *[nkoh-lih-goh]* Piece of wood tied around the neck of a dog to prevent it from biting; this name is sometimes associated with the proverb "a skinny but freely strolling dog is better off than the one that is properly fed but is on a leash" implying that freedom is more essential and advantageous to wellbeing than material satisfaction devoid of liberty [*Ganda*].

Nkomo (m) *[nkoh-moh]* Cattle; beast; head of cattle [*Ndebele*] (Hemans 1968 : 74; Koopman 1990: 336).

Nkomokazikho (m) *[nkoh-moh-kah-zih-koh]* "There are no cattle": a name such as given to a newborn by its maternal grandparents as a reminder to the child's father that they continue to await the bride dowry which he has not as yet paid [*Zulu*] (Turner 1992: 50).

Nkomokazikho (m) *[nkoh-moh-kah-zih-koh]* "There are no cattle (in him)": a name such given to a newborn by the father to metaphorically imply that since it is not a girl, it would not (upon getting married) serve as compensation for the bride dowry that the father gave over to his wife's family [*Zulu*] (Koopman 1987: 151).

Nkosibonile (m) *[nkoh-sih-boh-nih-leh]* "God has seen": a name such as given by a preacher who suspects that this newborn named so is a result of infidelity on the part of his wife [*Zulu*] (Turner 1992: 48).

Nkosinathi (m) *[nkoh-sih-nah-tih]* "The Lord is with us" [*Xhosa*] (Thipa 1987: 109, 111).

Nkosivumile (m) *[nkoh-sih-vuh-mih-leh]* "The Lord has agreed" [*Xhosa*] (Thipa 1987: 109, 111).

Nkuba (m) *[nkuh-bah]* Rainfall; this name is sometimes associated with the proverb "an only child is like a single rain cloud" implying that just like a single rain cloud that is unreliable since it will likely empty itself quickly and be followed by a hot and dry spell, the traditional African family prefers to have many children since the infant mortality rate is high [*Ganda*].

Nkuli (f) *[nkuh-lih]/ Nonkuli* (f) *[nohn-kuh-lih]* Nicknames-abbreviations for *Nonkululeko*: "Freedom" [*Xhosa*] (Neethling 1994: 92).

Nkululeko (m) *[nkuh-luh-leh-koh]* Freedom; independence [*Xhosa*] (Herbert 1997: 11; Thipa 1986: 288).

Nkumbi (m) *[nkuhm-bih]* The hoe; the elephant snout fish; this name is sometimes associated with the proverb "a bad tiller blames the hoe" which is synonymous with "a bad workman blames his tools" [*Ganda*].

Nobantu (f) *[noh-bahn-tuh]* The mother associated with the people [*Xhosa*] (Thipa 1987: 116).

Nobulele (f) *[noh-buh-beh-leh]* "The kind and generous one" [The *Xhosa*] (Neethling 1985: 89).

Nobuntu (f) *[noh-buhn-tuh]* The mother associated with kindness [*Xhosa*] (Thipa 1987: 116).

Nocawe (f) *[noh-tch-ah-weh]* A name commonly given to one born on Sunday [*Xhosa*] (Thipa 1987: 108).

Nofefe (f) *[noh-feh-feh]* "The compassionate (or sympathetic) one" [*Xhosa*] (Neethling 1985: 89).

Nofezile (f) *[noh-feh-zih-leh]* The mother associated with fulfillment [The *Xhosa*] (Thipa 1987: 116).

Nogoqwashu (f) *[nohg-qwah-shoo]* One who is cruel and unkind [*Xhosa*] (Neethling 1985: 89).

Nokhephu (f) *[noh-keh-poo]* Snow: a name given to one born during snow conditions [*Xhosa*] (Thipa 1986: 289).

Nokuzola (f) *[noh-kuh-zoh-lah]* "The calm and meek one" [The *Xhosa*] (Neethling 1994: 92).

Nokwayiyo (f) *[noh-kwah-yih-yoh]* "Also one--a girl" [*Xhosa*] (Neethling 1994: 92).

Nolindipasi (f) *[noh-lihn-dih-pah-sih]* Rinderpest (as adapted from the European word) [*Xhosa*] (Thipa 1986: 288).

Nolita (f) *[noh-lih-tah]* "Light" [*Xhosa*] (Neethling 1994: 92).

Noluthando (f) *[noh-luh-tahn-doh]* Love [*Xhosa*] (Neethling 1994: 92).

Nomacece (f) *[noh-mah-tch-eh-tch-eh]* "The party goer": a name such as given to a newborn whose mother is habitually present at every gathering and ceremony in the area, including in many instances when she does not have any business there, that she actually went into labor and gave birth to this child at one of the meetings [*Zulu*] (Turner 1992: 55).

Nomalizo (f) *[noh-mah-lih-zoh]* Comforter [*Xhosa*] (Neethling 1994: 92); "the one who has consoled us"/ "the one who has made us cross": a name given to one who has lost two or more preceding siblings to death, the name implying that this child serves as solace, by the action of God or the ancestors, for the family of the deceased [*Xhosa*] (Thipa 1986: 290).

Nomasirayeli (f) *[noh-mah-sih-rah-yeh-lih]* Israel (as adapted from the country name) [*Xhosa*] (Neethling 1994: 92).

Nomawethu (f) *[noh-mah-weh-too]* "One of us" [*Xhosa*] (Neethling 1994: 92).

Nomawezo (f) *[noh-mah-weh-zoh]* Crossing [*Xhosa*] (Neethling 1994: 92).

Nombathalala (f) *[nohm-bah-sth-ah-lah-lah]* "Great Fever" [*Xhosa*] (Thipa 1986: 288).

Nombulelo (f) *[nohm-buh-leh-loh]* Gratitude [*Xhosa*] (Neethling 1994: 92).

Nombulelo (f) *[nohm-buh-leh-loh]* The mother associated with gratitude [*Xhosa*] (Thipa 1987: 110).

Nombuyiselo (f) *[noh-mbuh-yih-seh-loh]* Reward/ compensation/ recom-

pense: a name given to one who has lost two or more preceding siblings to
death, the name implying that this child serves as welcome restitution, by
the action of God or the ancestors, for the deceased [*Xhosa*] (Thipa 1986:
290).

Nomethetho (f) *[noh-meh-sth-eh-sth-oh]* "Make the law": a name such as
given to a newborn by it's mother's mother-in-law who is expressing that
this newly wedded daughter-in-law is uncharacteristically violating customary etiquette as she insistently does things in her way even in her mother-
in-law's homestead i.e. she makes her own rules though new brides are expected to maintain a low profile--for example, she refused to serve certain
visitors food, would not allow her brother-in-law to wear her husband's
clothes, and she was evasive when requested to help with certain household
chores [*Zulu*] (Turner 1992: 50).

Nomfazwe (f) *[nohm-fah-zweh]* The mother associated with war: a name
such as given to one born out of wedlock or infidelity [*Xhosa*] (Thipa 1987:
112).

Nomfazwe (f) *[nohm-fah-zweh]* War [*Xhosa*] (Thipa 1986: 288).

Nomonde (f) *[noh-mohn-deh]* Patience [*Xhosa*] (Neethling 1994: 92).

Nomonde (f) *[noh-mohn-deh]* The mother associated with perseverance
[*Xhosa*] (Thipa 1987: 114).

Nompeyazana (f) *[nohm-peh-yah-zah-nah]* A nickname-abbreviation for
Pheliswa: "Last child" [*Xhosa*] (Neethling 1994: 92).

Nompumelelo (f) *[nohm-puh-meh-leh-loh]* Success [*Xhosa*] (Neethling
1994: 92).

Nomthandazo (f) *[nohm-tahn-dah-zoh]* Prayer [*Xhosa*] (Neethling 1994:
92).

Nomthandazo (f) *[nohm-tahn-dah-zoh]* The mother associated with prayer
[*Xhosa*] (Thipa 1987: 109, 110).

Nomusa (f) *[noh-muh-sah]* kindness [*Zulu*] (Turner 1992: 43).

Nomvula (f) *[nohm-vuh-lah]* Rain: a name such as given to one born during
a period of rainfall [*Xhosa*] (Neethling 1994: 92; Thipa 1986: 289).

Nomvume (f) *[nohm-vuh-meh]* One who eventually becomes rewarded handsomely following her generous act of heeding to the requests of passers-by
[*Xhosa*] (Neethling 1985: 89).

Nomvuyo (f) *[nohm-vuh-yoh]* Happiness [*Xhosa*] (Neethling 1994: 92).

Nomvuyo (f) *[nohm-vuh-yoh]* The mother associated with joy [The *Xhosa*]
(Thipa 1987: 111).

Nomvuzo (f) *[nohm-vuh-zoh]* "Reward" [*Xhosa*] (Neethling 1994: 92).

Nomxolisi (f) *[nohm-ksoh-lih-sih]* The mother associated with peace [The
Xhosa] (Thipa 1987: 114).

Nomzamo (f) *[nohm-zah-moh]* The mother associated with exertion/ effort
[*Xhosa*] (Thipa 1987: 116).

Nonceba (f) *[nohn-tch-eh-bah]* "Mercy" [*Xhosa*] (Neethling 1994: 92).

Nonhlanhla (f) *[nohn-lah-nlah]* "Luck": a name such as given to a newborn
by its parents who express that they have had a gratifying state of affairs

[Zulu] (Koopman 1987: 152).

Nonhlanhla (f) *[nohn-lahn-lah]* The lucky one *[Zulu]* (Turner 1992: 43).

Nonkululeko (f) *[nohn-kuh-luh-leh-koh]* Freedom; independence *[Xhosa]* (Herbert 1997: 11; Neethling 1994: 92; Thipa 1986: 288).

Nontshaba (f) *[nohn-tsh-ah-bah]* The mother associated with enemies: a name such as given to one born out of wedlock or infidelity *[Xhosa]* (Thipa 1987: 112).

Nontuthuko (f) *[nohn-tuh-tuh-koh]* "Progress": a name such as given to a newborn by its parents who express that they have made considerable progress in their state of affairs *[Zulu]* (Koopman 1987: 152).

Nonyewe (f) *[noh-ndjh-eh-weh]* The mother associated with controversy: a name such as given to one born out of wedlock or infidelity *[Xhosa]* (Thipa 1987: 112).

Nopasika (f) *[noh-pah-sih-kah]* Passover/ Easter: a name given to one born during Passover or Easter *[Xhosa]* (Thipa 1986: 289).

Nosipho (f) *[noh-sih-poh]* Gift *[Xhosa]* (Neethling 1994: 92).

Nosipho (f) *[noh-sih-poh]* The mother associated with a gift (or the greatest gift) *[Xhosa]* (Thipa 1987: 109).

Nothemba (f) *[noh-tehm-bah]* The mother associated with hope *[Xhosa]* (Thipa 1987: 114).

Nothuli (f) *[noh-sth-uh-lih]* "Great Drought" *[Xhosa]* (Thipa 1986: 288).

Novukazingce (f) *[noh-vuh-kah-zihn-gkeh]* "The proud one" [The *Xhosa*] (Neethling 1985: 89).

Nozindaba (f) *[noh-zihn-dah-bah]* "Nosy parker": a nickname such as given to a girl who is habitually inquisitive and is present at the break out of a fight or other conflict in the area *[Zulu]* (Turner 1992: 55).

Nozolile (f) *[noh-zoh-lih-leh]* The mother associated with quietness (or humility) *[Xhosa]* (Thipa 1987: 116).

Nqobile (m) *[nkwoh-bih-leh]* "We have conquered" *[Zulu]* (Herbert 1997: 11).

Nsalamo (f/m) *[nsah-lah-moh]* Ring *[Lamba]* (Doke 1931: 146).

Nsandawunga (m) *[nsahn-dah-wuhn-gah]* "Scatterer of Gunpowder" [The *Lamba*] (Doke 1931: 146).

Nsapato (f/m) *[nsah-pah-toh]* Shoe *[Lamba]* (Doke 1931: 146).

Nsawo (m) *[nsah-woh]* Pocket; bag; this name is sometimes associated with the proverb "a visitor who arrives with a bag (or the visitor with luggage), you do not start off by vilifying him" which is synonymous with "no man is esteemed so well as he that comes full-handed" which implies that those with the potential to give materially are treated decently *[Ganda]*.

Nseko (f/m) *[nseh-koh]* Laugh; laughter; this name is sometimes associated with the proverb "friendship between children is broken up by laughter" implying that unlike adults who can more readily take jokes and ignore those laughing at them, children are very sensitive at their peers laughing at them (such as when one falls down) *[Ganda]*.

Nsiko (m) *[nsih-koh]* Bush; jungle; uncultivated land; this name is sometimes associated with the proverb "a thinned out dog is only despised when it is lying by the fireplace--when it gets into the wilds, it makes a remarkable transition from the weak and tired state" implying that just like a lazy looking dog that is actually a tireless hunter, nothing or nobody that is apparently insignificant or useless is to be easily dismissed, as synonymous with "appearances are deceiving"; this name is also sometimes associated with the proverb "do not despise the Red-hot Poker tree (which is unflowered and unsightly most of the time) in the burnt out bush--the time (of the sowing season) the savanna has not yet greened up is when the tree crowns itself with a bloom" i.e. the trees paradoxically bloom in the season when there are piles of ugly refuse and burnt out vegetation, including little greened stumps of savanna, the proverb implying that the unsightly can bloom into beauties so should not easily be dismissed [*Ganda*].

Nsizwazonke (m) *[nsih-zwah-zohn-keh]* "All men": a name such as given by the father to reflect that the mother of this newborn has been promiscuous with a number of young studs in the area; or a name given to a newborn with exclusively male siblings [*Zulu*] (Turner 1992: 47).

Ntambika (f/m) *[ntahm-bih-kah]* "Offerer of Food" [*Lamba*] (Doke 1931: 146).

Ntebaleng (m) *[nteh-bah-leh-ndgh]* "Forget about me": a name such as given to one born out of wedlock or infidelity [*Sotho*] (Thipa 1987: 113).

Nthabeleng (m) *[ntah-beh-leh-ndgh]* "Be joyful (over my birth)" [*Sotho*] (Thipa 1987: 111).

Nthofeela (m) *[ntoh-feh-eh-lah]* "A thing of naught": a name such as given to one born out of wedlock or infidelity [*Sotho*] (Thipa 1987: 112).

Ntobeka (m) *[ntoh-beh-kah]* To be submissive [*Xhosa*] (Neethling 1994: 92).

Ntobs (m) *[ntoh-bs]* Nickname-abbreviation for *Ntobeka*: "To be submissive" [*Xhosa*] (Neethling 1994: 92).

Ntombembi (f) *[uhn-tohm-behm-bih]* An ugly girl [*Xhosa*] (Neethling 1985: 89).

Ntombenkulu (f) *[ntohm-behn-kuh-luh]* "Big girl" [*Zulu*] (Koopman 1987: 150).

Ntombifikile (f) *[ntohm-bih-fih-kih-leh]* "A girl has arrived" [The *Zulu*] (Koopman 1987: 148).

Ntombikayise (f) *[ntohm-bih-kah-yih-seh]* "Girl of her father" [The *Zulu*] (Koopman 1987: 148).

Ntombizodwa (f) *[uhn-tohm-bih-zoh-dwah]* "Only girls" [*Xhosa*] (Neethling 1994: 92).

Ntombizonke (f) *[ntohm-bih-zohn-keh]* "All girls": a name such as given to one born into a family that exclusively has female children [*Zulu*] (Koopman 1987: 149).

Ntsika (m) *[ntsih-kah]* Pillar [*Xhosa*] (Thipa 1987: 114).

Ntsike (m) *[ntsih-keh]* A nickname-abbreviation for *Ntsikelelo*: "Blessing" [*Xhosa*] (Neethling 1994: 92).

Ntsikelelo (m) *[ntsih-keh-leh-loh]* Blessing [*Xhosa*] (Neethling 1994: 92).

Ntuthuko (m) *[ntuh-tuh-koh]* "Progress": a name such as given to a newborn by its father who has recently been selected a member of a political party (African National Congress--ANC) executive *[Zulu]* (Herbert 1997: 11).

Nyabol (f) *[ndjah-bohl]* A name given to one whose birth follows that of her twin siblings *[Nuer]* (Whitehead 1947: 46).

Nyaboth (f) *[ndjah-boh-sth]* "The one that goes ahead of the other": a name given to the older twin *[Nuer]* (Evans-Pritchard 1948: 167).

Nyacwiil (f) *[ndjah-tch-wiihl]* A name given to the second born following the birth of her twin siblings *[Nuer]* (Whitehead 1947: 46).

Nyadiet (f) *[ndjah-djeht]* Bird: a name given to a twin [The *Nuer*] (Evans-Pritchard 1948: 167).

Nyaduoth (f) *[ndjah-duh-woh-sth]* "The one who follows the other": a name given to the younger twin *[Nuer]* (Evans-Pritchard 1948: 167).

Nyagaak (f) *[ndjah-gaahk]* Quarrel: a name given to one born during a family dispute *[Nuer]* (Evans-Pritchard 1948: 167).

Nyageng (f) *[ndjah-geh-ndgh]* A name given to the second born following the birth of her twin siblings *[Nuer]* (Whitehead 1947: 46).

Nyaluaak (f) *[ndjah-luh-waahk]* Cattle byre: a name given to one born in a cow barn *[Nuer]* (Evans-Pritchard 1948: 167).

Nyamer (f) *[ndjah-mehr]* Eye tear: a name given to one whose previously born siblings died *[Nuer]* (Evans-Pritchard 1948: 167).

Nyangi (m) *[ndjh-aahn-gih]* "Brown complexioned man" *[Rega]*.

Nyanja/ Nnyanja (f/m) *[nndjh-ahn-jah]* Lake; large body of water; this name is sometimes associated with the proverb "one who is going down to the lake does not leave the fish basket behind"; this name is also sometimes associated with the proverb "a rich person is so heartless, greedy, usurping and uncharitable just like the gargantuan lake which will not give back even the needle that has accidentally fallen into it"; this name is also sometimes associated with the proverb "the friendship with one who lives across the bay does not die as long as the two people visit (and take presents to) each other" implying that contact is essential in the sustenance of friendship *[Ganda]*.

Nyapun (f) *[ndjah-poon]* Wild rice: a name given to one born in an environment of wild rice *[Nuer]* (Evans-Pritchard 1948: 167).

Nyapuol (f) *[ndjah-puh-wohl]* Pool of water: a name given to one born near a pool *[Nuer]* (Evans-Pritchard 1948: 167).

Nyatoot (f) *[ndjah-toh-oht]* A name given to the third born following the birth of her twin siblings *[Nuer]* (Whitehead 1947: 46).

Nyatot (f) *[ndjah-toh-oht]* A name given to the second born following the birth of her twin siblings *[Nuer]* (Evans-Pritchard 1948: 168).

Nyawec (f) *[ndjah-weh-tch]* Cattle camp: a name given to one born in a cow camp *[Nuer]* (Evans-Pritchard 1948: 167).

Nyibuol (f) *[ndjih-buh-wohl]* A name given to one whose birth follows that of her twin siblings *[Nuer]* (Evans-Pritchard 1948: 168).

Nyindo/ Nnyindo (m) *[nndjh-ihn-doh]* Nose; this name is sometimes associated with the proverbs "that which strikes the nose, renders the eyes tearful" and "that which strikes the eye, leaves the nose sniffling" implying that an affliction that reigns misery on a person in a family or other social unit causes the other members in the unit to feel the pain, to be compassionate, and to suffer; this name is also sometimes associated with the proverb "that which strikes the child, also wants to strike the mother" implying that a father who beats his child is likely to beat its mother, that one will likely manifest his or her behavioral characteristics in whatever environment, or that an affliction that strikes the child is also inclined to strike its mother [*Ganda*].

Nyinyar (f) *[ndjih-ndjh-arh]* An ox name [*Nuer*] (Evans-Pritchard 1948: 170).

Nzige (m) *[nzih-geh]* Locust; locusts; this name is sometimes associated with the proverb "a short person does not see the locusts approaching" which implies that unimportant persons are not as readily listened too or taken seriously as those with authority [*Ganda*].

Nzigire (f) *[nzih-giih-reh]* "I am delighted" [*Bashi*].

Nzogu (m) *[nzoh-guh]* Elephant [*Rega*].

-O-

Oupa (m) *[ohw-pah]* "Grandfather": a name commonly given by the named child's grandparent in honor of an ancestor or a late husband [*Afrikaans*] (Suzman 1994: 268, 270).

-P-

Pasika (m) *[pah-sih-kah]* Passover/ Easter: a name such as given to one born during Passover or Easter [*Xhosa*] (Suzman 1994: 270; Thipa 1986: 289).

Penge (m) *[pehn-geh]* "Head of birds" [*Rega*].

Pet (m) *[peht]* Month [*Nuer*] (Evans-Pritchard 1948: 167).

Phakatikwezinja (m) *[pah-kah-tih-kweh-zihn-jah]* "Among the dogs": a praise name such given to a newborn by the father to metaphorically imply that his son is the only true man among all other men who when compared to him are like dogs [*Zulu*] (Herbert 1997: 6).

Phel (f) *[pehl]*/ *Pheli* (f) *[peh-lih]* Nicknames-abbreviations for *Pheliswa*: "Last child" [*Xhosa*] (Neethling 1994: 92).

Pheli-Pheli (f) *[peh-lih-peh-lih]* A nickname-abbreviation for *Pheliswa*: "Last child" [*Xhosa*] (Neethling 1994: 92).

Pheliswa (f) *[peh-lih-swah]* Last born child [*Xhosa*] (Neethling 1994: 92).

Phongiphayo (f) *[pohn-gih-pah-yoh]* "But I give and get": a name such as given to a newborn by its paternal aunt and is intended as a satirical warning to the child's mother who was known to engage in prostitution--when confronted by her sister-in-law about the issue she retorted "I give the one I get from" [*Zulu*] (Turner 1992: 51).

Phumelele (m) *[puh-meh-leh-leh]* "May he be successful" *[Xhosa]* (Thipa 1987: 114).

Pita (f) *[pih-tah]* A name commonly given to a fourth born amongst several (at least four) female siblings that have fortunately survived death *[Bari]* (Whitehead 1947: 45).

Pitia (m) *[pih-tih-yah]* A name commonly given to a fourth born amongst several (at least four) male siblings that have fortunately survived death *[Bari]* (Whitehead 1947: 45).

Pitso (m) *[pih-tsoh]* Meeting *[Sotho]* (Thipa 1987: 116).

Poni (f) *[poh-nih]* A name commonly given to a second born amongst several (at least four) female siblings that have fortunately survived death *[Bari]* (Whitehead 1947: 45).

Pun (m) *[poon]* Wild rice: a name such as given to one born in an environment of wild rice *[Nuer]* (Evans-Pritchard 1948: 167, 169).

Puol (m) *[puh-wohl]* Pool of water: a name such as given to one born near a pool *[Nuer]* (Evans-Pritchard 1948: 167).

Puso (m) *[puh-soh]* "Government": a name such as given to one born during a political disturbance (Herbert 1995: 2), or to one born after his father was killed in a political disturbance *[Tswana]* (Herbert 1990: 8).

-Q-

Qhamukephi (m) *[kah-muh-keh-pih]* "Where do you come from?": a name such as given to a newborn whose father is expressing suspicion as to whether he is the parent *[Zulu]* (Turner 1992: 49).

Qondeni (f/m) *[kwohn-deh-nih]* "What is your intention?": a name such as given to a newborn by the mother expressing puzzlement as to what her husband, who with her in-laws constantly feuds with her, intends for her and the family in regard to the future *[Zulu]* (Turner 1992: 48).

Qukeza (m) *[tch-uh-keh-zah]* "Be diligent" *[Xhosa]* (Thipa 1987: 114).

-R-

Ralebitso (m) *[rah-leh-bih-tsoh]* The father of one named *Lebitso* *[Sotho]* (Thipa 1987: 116).

Ramathe (m) *[rah-mah-teh]* The father of one named *Mathe* *[Sotho]* (Thipa 1987: 116).

Ramohau (m) *[rah-moh-hahw]* The father of one named *Mohau* [The *Sotho*] (Thipa 1987: 116).

Rang (m) *[rah-ndgh]* A name given to one skilled at aiming and throwing the spear *[Nuer]* (Evans-Pritchard 1948: 169).

Rapitso (m) *[rah-pih-tsoh]* The father of one named *Pitso* *[Sotho]* (Thipa 1987: 116).

Ratsebe (m) *[rah-tseh-beh]* A name commonly given to a child with large ears *[Sotho]* (Herbert 1990: 5).

Reath (m) *[reh-yah-sth]* Drought: a name such as given to one born during a period of drought [*Nuer*] (Evans-Pritchard 1948: 167).

Refilwe (m) *[reh-fih-lweh]* "(The child) has been given to us" [*Sotho*] (Thipa 1987: 109).

Reoagile (m) *[reh-yoh-ah-gih-leh]* "We have built it": a name such as given to a newborn by its parents to imply that this child is a response to what they have longed for--a boy who will build up the family name [*Tswana*] (Herbert 1995: 3; Herbert 1990: 10, 17).

Rethabile (m) *[reh-tah-bih-leh]* "We are joyful" [*Sotho*] (Thipa 1987: 111).

Rier (m) *[rih-yehr]* The white pith of reeds [*Nuer*] (Evans-Pritchard 1948: 170).

Rolnyang (m) *[rohl-ndjh-ah-ndgh]* An ox name [The *Nuer*] (Evans-Pritchard 1948: 169).

Ruei (m) *[ruh-wehy]* Spittle: a name given to one born to a mother who because she had not conceived for so long, was subjected to a ritual in which the child's father's kinsfolk spit into a gourd and the collected spittle is rubbed on the mother's belly and a prayer offered to enable her to conceive [*Nuer*] (Evans-Pritchard 1948: 167).

Rupia (m) *[ruh-pih-yah]* "Rupee" (from the *Kiswahili* language) [The *Fipa*] (Willis 1982: 229).

Ruwalyako (m) *[ruh-wah-ljah-koh]* "My God" [*Chaga*] (Raum 1967: 340).

Ruwalyaumbe (m) *[ruh-wah-ljah-uhm-beh]* "God of the cattle" [The *Chaga*] (Raum 1967: 340).

-S-

Saalongo/ Ssaalongo (m) *[ssaah-lohn-goh]* The father of twins; this name is sometimes associated with the proverb "a serf who becomes a member of the clan becomes (i.e. gets to take on the honorary title of) the 'father of twins' (i.e. *Ssaalongo*)" whereby aside from family connection, an one can traditionally become a clan member through such means as adoption, assimilation, long term residence, capture, and blood ritual [*Ganda*].

Sabasaba (m) *[sah-bah-sah-bah]* "Seven-seven": this refers to independence day (July 7th in *Tanzania*) so the name is appropriate for one born on or associated with this day [*Pare, Swahili* and several other ethnics of eastern and central Africa] (Herbert 1997: 10; Omari 1970: 66).

Sabatha (f/m) *[sah-bah-sth-ah]* Sabbath (as adapted from the European word): a name such as given to one born on Saturday [*Xhosa*] (Thipa 1986: 289).

Sakhe (m) *[sah-keh]* A nickname-abbreviation for *Sonosakhe*: "His sin" [The *Xhosa*] (Neethling 1994: 92).

Sakhile (f/m) *[sah-kih-leh]* "We have (indeed) built": a name such as given to a newborn by its parents who express that they have made considerable progress in their state of affairs [*Zulu*] (Koopman 1987: 152).

Sam (m) *[sahm]* A nickname-abbreviation for *Samkelo*: "Acceptance" [The

Xhosa] (Neethling 1994: 92).

Samari (m) *[sah-mah-rih]* Scepter [*Chaga*] (Raum 1967: 340).

Samkelo (m) *[sahm-keh-loh]* "Acceptance" [*Xhosa*] (Neethling 1994: 92).

Sebolai (m) *[seh-boh-lahy]* Killer: a name such as given to one born out of wedlock or infidelity [*Sotho*] (Thipa 1987: 113).

Sebueng (m) *[seh-bweh-ndgh]* "Hold your tongue": a name such as given to one born out of wedlock or infidelity [*Sotho*] (Thipa 1987: 113).

Sekabemba/ Ssekabemba (m) *[sseh-kah-behm-bah]* A crust (on burnt food); burnt portion adhering to the pan; (formation of) a crust or scab; a coagulation; a swarming; an abundance; the name of a fetish [*Ganda*].

Sekabembe/ Ssekabembe (m) *[sseh-kah-behm-beh]* A crust (on burnt food); burnt portion adhering to the pan; (formation of) a crust or scab; a coaglation; a swarming; an abundance [*Ganda*].

Sekabira/ Ssekabira (m) *[sseh-kah-bih-rah]* Small forest; thicket of shrubs and small trees; grove; bead [*Ganda*].

Sekaboga (m) *[sseh-kah-boh-gah]* A ficus tree species [*Ganda*].

Sekabunga/ Ssekabunga (m) *[sseh-kah-buhn-gah]* That rambles or wanders around aimlessly [*Ganda*].

Sekabuuza/ Ssekabuuza (m) *[sseh-kah-buuh-zah]* One who often asks (or greets, or visits) [*Ganda*].

Sekaddakiro/ Ssekaddakiro (m) *[sseh-kahd-dah-tch-ih-roh]* That comes back during the night [*Ganda*].

Sekade/ Ssekade (m) *[sseh-kah-deh]* Small bell [*Ganda*].

Sekafuuwa/ Ssekafuuwa (m) *[sseh-kah-fuuh-wah]* That blows on (or plays a wind instrument such as a flute) [*Ganda*].

Sekaggo/ Ssekaggo (m) *[sseh-kahg-goh]* That beats with a small stick (in a children's game involving the use of sticks); a beater; that with a stick frequently whacks others [*Ganda*].

Sekaggya/ Ssekaggya (m) *[sseh-kahj-jah]* That uproots/ or picks (crops and takes them away) [*Ganda*].

Sekajoba/ Ssekajoba (m) *[sseh-kah-joh-bah]* That creates confusion or commotion; one who arranges for a great feast or banquet; that gets soaked; one who gets messy such as with mud or liquids; (small) crest of the crested crane bird; (small) tuft of hair on a shaven head [*Ganda*].

Sekajolo/ Ssekajolo (m) *[sseh-kah-joh-loh]* A species of small bird, the bee eater [*Ganda*].

Sekajugo/ Ssekajugo (m) *[sseh-kah-juh-goh]* A bell ringer; pen holder; small bell used as an ornament on the neck or on the drums [*Ganda*].

Sekakande/ Ssekakande (m) *[sseh-kah-kahn-deh]* The jungle; a (small) deserted stretch of land; (small) wasteland; that was forced (or compelled); that is caused to persist [*Ganda*].

Sekakoni/ Ssekakoni (m) *[sseh-kah-koh-nih]* Pipe stem euphorbia tree that is small; that has failed to cook; that is slow in cooking; that is stunted in growth; that has failed to ripen; that is silent; that refuses to answer; that sulks; that remains motionless [*Ganda*].

Sekalaala/ Ssekalaala (m) *[sseh-kah-laah-lah]* That is so calm [*Ganda*].

Sekalala/ Ssekalala (m) *[sseh-kah-lah-lah]* One that becomes angry (or irascible, or reluctant) [*Ganda*].

Sekalembe/ Ssekalembe (m) *[sseh-kah-lehm-beh]* Peacemaker; a respite of peace; that strolls (or walks leisurely, or walks slowly) [*Ganda*].

Sekalere/ Ssekalere (m) *[sseh-kah-leh-reh]* A small flute; small horn; string of a musical instrument; small strip; small layer; a shoelace; fringe; shred [*Ganda*].

Sekalo/ Ssekalo (m) *[sseh-kah-loh]* Finger millet [*Ganda*].

Sekalongo/ Ssekalongo (m) *[sseh-kah-lohn-goh]* (Father of) a twin who is small in physique [*Ganda*].

Sekaluvu/ Ssekaluvu (m) *[sseh-kah-luh-vuh]* (Little) gluttonous person [The *Ganda*].

Sekamaanya/ Ssekamaanya (m) *[sseh-kah-maah-ndjh-ah]* Difficult and self willed person; rogue; rascal [*Ganda*].

Sekamalira/ Ssekamalira (m) *[sseh-kah-mah-lih-rah]* One that makes sufficient for; that decides or resolves for; that finishes or completes for or on behalf of; that uses up (or consumes) on behalf of [*Ganda*].

Sekamata/ Ssekamata *[sseh-kah-mah-tah]* That involves behaving in a rude (or grouchy, or harsh) manner [*Ganda*].

Sekamatte/ Ssekamatte (m) *[sseh-kah-maht-teh]* That is behaved rudely to (or sternly to, or harshly to) [*Ganda*].

Sekamo/ Ssekamo (m) *[sseh-kah-moh]* That is highly skilled (or very proficient); that is of high expertise [*Ganda*].

Sekamuli/ Ssekamuli (m) *[sseh-kah-muh-lih]* Small flower [*Ganda*].

Sekamwa/ Ssekamwa (m) *[sseh-kah-mwah]* A talkative person; a rumor monger; loud mouth; mouth [*Ganda*].

Sekandagu (m) *[sseh-kahn-dah-guh]* Fortune teller; diviner; seer [*Ganda*].

Sekandi/ Ssekandi (m) *[sseh-kahn-dih]* Species of yam [*Ganda*].

Sekanninga/ Ssekanninga (m) *[sseh-kahn-nihn-gah]* That nails (or puts others on the spot) [*Ganda*].

Sekannyo/ Ssekannyo (m) *[sseh-kahn-ndjh-oh]* With a small tooth [*Ganda*].

Sekasagga/ Ssekasagga (m) *[sseh-kah-sahg-gah]* Beating of the bush (in hunting to drive out the pursued animals); a driving off; driving away/ or fanning away (e.g. flies); recruiting; a headband (or wreath) symbolizing victory; headband worn for reason of illness; that beats the bush; that drives away/ or fans away; that recruits [*Ganda*].

Sekasamba/ Ssekasamba (m) *[sseh-kah-sahm-bah]* Bracelet worn around the legs; necklace; metal collar; quarter (in soccer); small kick; that kicks (or stomps on, or stamps); that pedals (a bicycle); that puts the foot on (the car accelerator); small mass of floating vegetable matter that forms bogging masses in water; small plot of tilled land [*Ganda*].

Sekasanvu/ Ssekasanvu (m) *[sseh-kah-sahn-vuh]* Seven thousand; forced labor; small branch; small whip [*Ganda*].

Sekasi/ Ssekasi (m) *[sseh-kah-see]* Of (or with) a small land/ country [The

Ganda].

Sekasiko/ Ssekasiko (m) *[sseh-kah-sih-koh]* Of (or owning) a small bush (or small jungle, or small portion of uncultivated land) [*Ganda*].

Sekasula/ Ssekasula (m) *[sseh-kah-suh-lah]* One ·that spends the night; dweller; immigrant [*Ganda*].

Sekataba/ Ssekataba (m) *[sseh-kah-tah-bah]* That joins together (or unites, or reconciles) [*Ganda*].

Sekatawa/ Ssekatawa (m) *[sseh-kah-tah-wah]* That is preoccupied; one who bustles about, moving here and there; never ending [*Ganda*].

Sekatono/ Ssekatono (m) *[sseh-kah-toh-noh]* (A father of) one small in physical stature [*Ganda*].

Sekawu/ Ssekawu (m) *[sseh-kah-wuh]* A small cushion (or seat); a small carpet made of skins [*Ganda*].

Sekawunga/ Ssekawunga (m) *[sseh-kah-wuhn-gah]* (That is associated with) cornmeal (or flour meal); that nets/ catches (flying insects) [*Ganda*].

Sekawungu/ Ssekawungu (m) *[sseh-kah-wuhn-guh]* An eaglet; a young eagle [*Ganda*].

Sekayala/ Ssekayala (m) *[sseh-kah-yah-lah]* That is hungry (or starving); that of hunger/ or famine [*Ganda*].

Sekayiba/ Ssekayiba (m) *[sseh-kah-yih-bah]* A bird that resembles a dove [*Ganda*].

Sekayinga/ Ssekayinga (m) *[sseh-kah-yihn-gah]* Excellent; excessive; overwhelming [*Ganda*].

Sekayombya/ Ssekayombya (m) *[sseh-kah-yohm-bjah]* One that incites quarrels (or losing of tempers) [*Ganda*].

Sekayonga/ Ssekayonga (m) *[sseh-kah-yohn-gah]* The burnt out remains of food; sparks from a fire; fucus cloth [*Ganda*].

Sekazaana/ Ssekazaana (m) *[sseh-kah-zaah-nah]* A father of (or a favored master of) a maidservant (or of maidservants) [*Ganda*].

Sekema/ Ssekema (m) *[sseh-keh-mah]* That puts to test or tempts; temptation; tryings; one who whines (or groans, or grunts) [*Ganda*].

Sekennyula/ Ssekennyula (m) *[sseh-kehn-ndjh-uh-lah]* One that leaves or stops working on one's (or its) own accord; that draws oneself (or itself) out (of water) [*Ganda*].

Sekibaala/ Ssekibaala (m) *[sseh-tch-ih-baah-lah]* Termite hill [*Ganda*].

Sekibakke/ Ssekibakke (m) *[sseh-tch-ih-bahk-keh]* One that is of pleasant taste/ or pleasant smell/ or sweet odor [*Ganda*].

Sekibala/ Ssekibala (m) *[sseh-tch-ih-bah-lah]* Agricultural product (or produce); fruit; spot; stain; type; kind; species [*Ganda*].

Sekibanga/ Ssekibanga (m) *[sseh-tch-ih-bahn-gah]* Constructor; establisher; founder; seat of a paddler in a canoe [*Ganda*].

Sekibango/ Ssekibango (m) *[sseh-tch-ih-bahn-goh]* The shaft of a spear; that with a hump; that with a projecting part [*Ganda*].

Sekibembe/ Ssekibembe (m) *[sseh-tch-ih-behm-beh]* The crust (on burnt food); burnt portion adhering to the pan; (formation of) a crust or scab; a coagulation; a swarming; an abundance [*Ganda*].

Sekibo/ Ssekibo (m) *[sseh-tch-ih-boh]* Bug; rib of palm leaf [*Ganda*].

Sekibongo/ Ssekibongo (m) *[sseh-tch-ih-bohn-goh]* That spins and whirls around (or causes to spin) [*Ganda*].

Sekiboobo/ Ssekiboobo (m) *[sseh-tch-ih-boh-oh-boh]* Name-title of a chief (of *Kyaggwe*) and also in the past, the trade and diplomatic liaison partly entrusted to governing *Buganda*'s then tributary state of *Busoga* [*Ganda*].

Sekibumba/ Ssekibumba (m) *[sseh-tch-ih-buhm-bah]* The molder; the Creator; liver [*Ganda*].

Sekibuule/ Ssekibuule (m) *[sseh-tch-ih-buuh-leh]* That is thrashed (or beaten, or beaten hard, or thrown to the ground); (cattle) that is raided; that is proposed (or intended); that is associated with bachelorhood (or losing ones wife through separation or desertion); that is associated with a poor boy (or a poor kid) [*Ganda*].

Sekidde/ Ssekidde *[sseh-tch-ihd-deh]* Cloudy (or overcast) weather [*Ganda*].

Sekigudde/ Ssekigudde *[sseh-tch-ih-guhd-deh]* That has happened (or fallen, or occurred, or failed) [*Ganda*].

Sekiguude/ Ssekiguude (m) *[sseh-tch-ih-guuh-deh]* The gruel of crushed green beans; that insults grossly; that slanders maliciously [*Ganda*].

Sekijoba/ Ssekijoba (m) *[sseh-tch-ih-joh-bah]* That creates confusion or commotion; one who arranges for a great feast or banquet; one who gets soaked; one who gets messy such as with mud or liquids; the crest of the crested crane bird; the tuft of hair on a shaven head [*Ganda*].

Sekikongo/ Ssekikongo (m) *[sseh-tch-ih-kohn-goh]* A species of hard yam [*Ganda*].

Sekikwa/ Ssekikwa (m) *[sseh-tch-ih-kwah]* Having (some) bad luck [*Ganda*].

Sekimbega/ Ssekimbega (m) *[sseh-tch-ihm-beh-gah]* The spy; the detective [*Ganda*].

Sekimette/ Ssekimette *[sseh-tch-ih-meht-teh]* That is smeared on excessively (such as with cosmetics or creams); that is plastered on [*Ganda*].

Sekimpi/ Ssekimpi (m) *[sseh-tch-ihm-pih]* That is short [*Ganda*].

Sekimwaanyi/ Ssekimwaanyi (m) *[sseh-tch-ih-mwaah-ndjh-ih]* The coffee berry [*Ganda*].

Sekinnemye/ Ssekinnemye *[sseh-tch-ihn-neh-mjeh]* "It has been too much for me"; "I have failed (in my efforts) to do it" [*Ganda*].

Sekinonko (m) *[sseh-kih-noh-ohn-koh]* A piece of dried earth [*Ganda*].

Sekintu/ Ssekintu (m) *[sseh-tch-ihn-tuh]* That is associated with *Kintu* the legendary first king of and founder of the kingdom of *Buganda*; thing; matter; affair [*Ganda*].

Sekinyomo (m) *[sseh-tch-ih-ndjh-oh-moh]* A species of large black ant [The *Ganda*].

Sekinyomo-Ekitwaalenswa (m) *[sseh-tch-ih-ndjh-oh-moh-eh-tch-ih-twaah-lehn-swah]* "The large black ant that takes away the edible flying ants" [The *Ganda*].

Sekiranda/ Ssekiranda (m) *[sseh-tch-ih-rahn-dah]* One that flourishes (or creeps, or travels, or wanders around) [*Ganda*].

Sekirevu/ Ssekirevu (m) *[sseh-tch-ih-reh-vuh]* (One with) a prominent beard (or moustache) [*Ganda*].

Sekiriba/ Ssekiriba (m) *[sseh-tch-ih-rih-bah]* Garment; skin; hide [*Ganda*].

Sekirika/ Ssekirika (m) *[sseh-tch-ih-rih-kah]* That is at home [*Ganda*].

Sekirime/ Ssekirime (m) *[sseh-tch-ih-rih-meh]* A crop; that is cultivated [*Ganda*].

Sekiritta/ Ssekiritta (m) *[sseh-tch-ih-riht-tah]* That will kill (or murder, or destroy, or ruin, or abolish, or cancel) [*Ganda*].

Sekiro/ Ssekiro (m) *[sseh-tch-ih-roh]* The night [*Ganda*].

Sekiryango/ Ssekiryango (m) *[sseh-tch-ih-rjahn-goh]* Door way [*Ganda*].

Sekiryowa (m) *[sseh-tch-ih-rjoh-oh-wah]* One who does a favor (or benefits) for; a child sent to the king or a distinguished chief to perform voluntary services; obligation; favor; benefit [*Ganda*].

Sekisaka/ Ssekisaka (m) *[sseh-tch-ih-sah-kah]* Thicket; bush; one that forages (for food); the mode of foraging for food; the mode of digging up information [*Ganda*].

Sekisambu/ Ssekisambu (m) *[sseh-tch-ih-sahm-buh]* Patch of overgrown weeds; area under stubble [*Ganda*].

Sekisero/ Ssekisero (m) *[sseh-tch-ih-seh-roh]* A large basket that is plaited [*Ganda*].

Sekisibo/ Ssekisibo (m) *[sseh-tch-ih-sih-boh]* Sheep (or goat) pen; an enclosure for cattle; chicken coop [*Ganda*].

Sekisiwe/ Ssekisiwe (m) *[sseh-tch-ih-sih-weh]* That is seasoned [*Ganda*].

Sekisonge/ Ssekisonge (m) *[sseh-tch-ih-sohn-geh]* That is pierced [*Ganda*].

Sekisozi/ Ssekisozi (m) *[sseh-tch-ih-soh-zih]* Hill [*Ganda*].

Sekiti/ Ssekiti (m) *[sseh-tch-ih-tih]* Deteriorated (or dried up) tree; a wooden handle; coward [*Ganda*].

Sekitimba/ Ssekitimba (m) *[sseh-tch-ih-tihm-bah]* Net trap utilized in hunting large animals; a curtain [*Ganda*].

Sekitondo/ Ssekitondo (m) *[sseh-tch-ih-tohn-doh]* That is touchy (or easily offended); a drop; a spot; a blotch [*Ganda*].

Sekitooleko/ Ssekitooleko (m) *[seh-tch-ih-toh-oh-leh-koh]* That from which a part (or portion) has been removed (or taken off) [*Ganda*].

Sekitto/ Ssekitto (m) *[sseh-tch-iht-toh]* (Weather of) coldness (or dampness) [*Ganda*].

Sekituba (m) *[sseh-tch-ih-tuh-bah]* A species of tree from which barkcloth is extracted; that is associated with a subdivision of a clan; that is associated with a rank of chiefship [*Ganda*].

Sekitulege/ Ssekitulege (m) *[sseh-tch-ih-tuh-leh-geh]* Zebra [*Ganda*].

Sekituula/ Ssekituula (m) *[sseh-tch-ih-tuuh-lah]* One that sits (or remains); one who resides [*Ganda*].

Sekiwala/ Ssekiwala (m) *[sseh-tch-ih-wah-lah]* Tanner; one who scrapes (such as hides); rake; one who pulls/ or drags along [*Ganda*].

Sekiwunga/ Ssekiwunga (m) *[sseh-tch-ih-wuhn-gah]* That nets/ catches (such as flying insects) [*Ganda*].

Sekiwuunya/ Ssekiwuunya (m) *[sseh-tch-ih-wuuh-ndjh-ah]* That causes to make indistinct sounds (or to moan, or to groan) [*Ganda*].

Sekiya/ Ssekiya (m) *[sseh-tch-ih-yah]* A type of basket for trapping fish; that becomes tired (or weary, or exhausted) [*Ganda*].

Sekiyima/ Ssekiyima/ Ssekiima (m) *[sseh-tch-ih-yih-mah]* In the mannerism of the *Hima* people [*Ganda*].

Sekizimu/ Ssekizimu (m) *[sseh-tch-ih-zih-muh]* The whirlwind; dust devil [*Ganda*].

Sekiziyivu (m) *[sseh-tch-ih-zih-yih-vuh]* Dark; crowded; that impedes [The *Ganda*].

Sekkaza (m) *[ssehk-kah-zah]* One who makes or causes to dry; that makes firm; one who ascertains or knows well [*Ganda*].

Sekkennyula (m) *[ssehk-kehn-ndjh-uh-lah]* One who devours [*Ganda*].

Sekkoba/ Ssekkoba (m) *[ssehk-koh-bah]* (One with) a large belt [*Ganda*].

Sekkolo (m) *[ssehk-koh-loh]* Large stump of a banana tree [*Ganda*].

Sekkonge/ Ssekkonge (m) *[ssehk-kohn-geh]* A large stump of a tree; an obstacle; a stumbling block [*Ganda*].

Sekkono/ Ssekkono (m) *[ssehk-koh-noh]* Large arm [*Ganda*].

Sekkuubwa (m) *[ssehk-kuuh-bwaah]* A prominent elder [*Ganda*].

Sekkuuma (m) *[ssehk-kuuh-mah]* That watches over (or maintains, or protects) [*Ganda*].

Sekoba/ Ssekoba (m) *[sseh-koh-bah]* A species of hardwood tree; put together or combined; obtained by joint action [*Ganda*].

Sekolo/ Ssekolo (m) *[sseh-koh-loh]* A large ceremony; epiglottis; the stump of banana trees; uprooted; weeded out [*Ganda*].

Sekolya/ Ssekolya (m) *[sseh-koh-ljah]* Stalker; that creeps up to in an indirect way (or in a roundabout fashion) [*Ganda*].

Sekubata/ Ssekubata (m) *[sseh-kuh-bah-tah]* "Releasing them"; "freeing them"; "letting go of them" [*Ganda*].

Sekubatta/ Ssekubatta (m) *[sseh-kuh-baht-tah]* "Killing (or murdering) them"; "destroying (or ruining) them" [*Ganda*].

Sekubumba/ Ssekubumba (m) *[sseh-kuh-buhm-bah]* That forms or molds out of clay; that makes pottery (or pots); one who sculpts [*Ganda*].

Sekubunga/ Ssekubunga (m) *[sseh-kuh-buhn-gah]* That rambles (or wanders around aimlessly) [*Ganda*].

Sekulima/ Ssekulima (m) *[sseh-kuh-lih-mah]* Cultivating; digging; farming [*Ganda*].

Sekuwanda/ Ssekuwanda (m) *[sseh-kuh-wahn-dah]* That spits [*Ganda*].

Sekweyama/ Ssekweyama (m) *[sseh-kweh-yah-mah]* That takes an oath; one who vows [*Ganda*].

Sekyabira/ Ssekyabira (m) *[sseh-tch-ah-bih-rah]* That is warmed up; (food) that is warmed over [*Ganda*].

Sekyanzi (m) *[sseh-tch-ahn-zih]* The container used to capture the milking from cows [*Ganda*].

Sekyayi/ Ssekyayi (m) *[sseh-tch-aah-yih]* Dried plantain fiber; tea *[Ganda]*.

Sekyegobolo/ Ssekyegobolo (m) *[sseh-tch-eh-goh-boh-loh]* A profit; a gain; the bolt (of a gun or rifle) that is drawn *[Ganda]*.

Sekyeri/ Ssekyeri (m) *[sseh-tch-eh-eh-rih]* That from out there *[Ganda]*.

Sekyeru/ Ssekyeru (m) *[sseh-tch-eh-eh-ruh]* White; light skinned; clear (space); open (area) *[Ganda]*.

Sekyewa/ Ssekyewa (m) *[sseh-tch-eh-eh-wah]* Volunteer; that gives oneself to; that gives to oneself; that dedicates oneself to; that devotes oneself to; that exposes oneself to; that surrenders oneself; that sacrifices oneself to; that is proud (or pompous,or showy) *[Ganda]*.

Sekyola/ Ssekyola (m) *[sseh-tch-oh-oh-lah]* That carves/ makes patterns on (such as on pottery); that brings up (a child); that tends to/ cares for (such as an animal or a plant); a (large) groove (or nick, or carving, or cutting, or tribal marking) *[Ganda]*.

Sekyole/ Ssekyole (m) *[sseh-tch-oh-oh-leh]* Trail of the edible rat; that is carved/ or made patterns on (e.g. on pottery); that is brought up; that is tended to/ cared for (e.g. animal or plant); that is caused to have a groove (or a nick, or a carve, or cut, or a tribal marking) *[Ganda]*.

Sekyonda/ Ssekyonda (m) *[sseh-tch-ohn-dah]* Plaiting; a twining; a twisting *[Ganda]*.

Sekyoya/ Ssekyoya (m) *[sseh-tch-oh-oh-yah]* Feather; a solitary hair (on the body) *[Ganda]*.

Sekyoyo/ Ssekyoyo (m) *[sseh-tch-oh-oh-yoh]* Name-title of a deputizing chief (of *Kyaddondo*); desire (or hankering, or craving) *[Ganda]*.

Selukuma/ Sselukuma (m) *[sseh-luh-kuh-mah]* That makes a fire (or blows on a fire to keep it going); that heaps up (or piles together, or gathers together); that becomes concentrated (or localized) *[Ganda]*.

Selukuuma/ Sselukuuma (m) *[sseh-luh-kuuh-mah]* That watches (or watches over, or guards, or protects, or maintains, or keeps) *[Ganda]*.

Selwango/ Sselwango (m) *[sseh-lwahn-goh]* Of (or relating to) the leopard *[Ganda]*.

Semabumba (m) *[sseh-mah-buuhm-bah]* (Owner) of a moulding clay enterprise *[Ganda]*.

Semafumo (m) *[sseh-mah-fuh-moh]* The master spearman; the spear maker; spears *[Ganda]*.

Semaganda/ Ssemaganda (m) *[sseh-mah-gahn-dah]* Of the peculiarities of the *Ganda* ethnics *[Ganda]*.

Semaganye/ Ssemaganye (m) *[sseh-mah-gah-ndjh-eh]* That was allowed (or permitted, or given approval of, or authorized) *[Ganda]*.

Semagoma/ Ssemagoma (m) *[sseh-mah-goh-mah]* Drums *[Ganda]*.

Semagonge/ Ssemagonge (m) *[sseh-mah-gohn-geh]* That of the otters; that are twisted (or deformed, or disfigured, or crippled); that are wrecked (or ruined) *[Ganda]*.

Semagoye/ Ssemagoye (m) *[sseh-mah-goh-yeh]* That are mixed (or mixed up, or stirred together, or mashed up, or crushed) *[Ganda]*.

Semagulu/ Ssemagulu (m) *[sseh-mah-guh-luh]* (One with a peculiarity of) the legs [*Ganda*].

Semagumba/ Ssemagumba (m) *[sseh-mah-guhm-bah]* Large bones; large gatherings [*Ganda*].

Semajamba/ Ssemajamba (m) *[sseh-mah-jahm-bah]* In poor condition; bad; evil; dangerous [*Ganda*].

Semajwala/ Ssemajwala (m) *[sseh-mah-jwah-lah]/ **Semajwale/ Ssemajwale*** (m) *[sseh-mah-jwaah-leh]* Adornings of oneself; riggings of oneself; dressing of oneself up in something ill-favored [*Ganda*].

Semakaaya/ Ssemakaaya (m) *[sseh-mah-kaah-yah]* That cause to become bitter (or unpleasant to the taste); that cause to quarrel (or to get enraged); that cause to be bitter towards; that cause (a situation) to become serious/ or bad [*Ganda*].

Semakadde/ Ssemakadde (m) *[sseh-mah-kahd-deh]* Those that are worn out (or outdated, or old) [*Ganda*].

Semakalu/ Ssemakalu (m) *[sseh-mah-kah-luh]* That are dry (or stiff, or hard); (tracts) that are arid; (voices) that are clear (or distinct) [*Ganda*].

Semakookiro/ Ssemakookiro (m) *[sseh-mah-koh-oh-kih-roh]* Expansions; enlargements; building in addition to; additions to; amendments (such as of laws) [*Ganda*].

Semakubire/ Ssemakubire (m) *[sseh-mah-kuh-bih-reh]* That were struck (or knocked) in/ at/ for; that were beaten in/ at/ for [*Ganda*].

Semakula/ Ssemakula (m) *[sseh-mah-kuh-lah]* One that presents food to the king; a handsomely built (or gorgeous looking) man; that is magnificent (or wondrous); "(good) growth" [*Ganda*].

Semalago/ Ssemalago (m) *[sseh-mah-lah-goh]* With a large throat (or neck); with a husky, deep voice [*Ganda*].

Semalume/ Ssemalume (m) *[sseh-mah-luh-meh]* That of male animals; that of food devoid of sauce or relish [*Ganda*].

Semaluulu/ Ssemaluulu (m) *[sseh-mah-luuh-luh]* Utterings of warning sounds; attracting of attention by making sounds; sounds to warn or to attract attention that are produced by patting the mouth repeatedly with the palm of the hand; pearls [*Ganda*].

Semanda/ Ssemanda (m) *[sseh-mahn-dah]* Charcoal; name-title of the king [*Ganda*].

Semannya/ Ssemannya (m) *[sseh-mahn-ndjh-ah]* Reputes; names [*Ganda*].

Semannyalwajja/ Ssemannyalwajja (f/m) *[sseh-mahn-ndjh-ah-lwahj-jah]* "When the personage of names (or reputations) comes (or arrives)" [The *Ganda*].

Semanobe/ Ssemanobe (m) *[sseh-mah-noh-beh]* One divorced (or separated from) several times [*Ganda*].

Semasaazi/ Ssemasaazi (m) *[sseh-mah-saah-zih]* That are in the manner of the joker (or the jester); jokes; those of one whose word cannot be taken seriously [*Ganda*].

Sematengo/ Ssematengo (m) *[sseh-mah-tehn-goh]* Tremblings; acts of shivering; chilling (such as from a fever or cold); that of the colocynth berries [*Ganda*].

Sematiko/ Ssematiko (m) *[sseh-mah-tih-koh]* Mushrooms [*Ganda*].

Sematimba/ Ssematimba (m) *[sseh-mah-tihm-bah]* Decorations; exhibitions; showings off; that of the python [*Ganda*].

Semattire/ Ssemattire (m) *[sseh-maht-tih-reh]* Satisfied [*Ganda*].

Sematu/ Ssematu (m) *[sseh-mah-tuh]* With large ears [*Ganda*].

Semavugo (m) *[sseh-mah-vuh-goh]* (Loudly) talkative one; noise [*Ganda*].

Semayanja/ Ssemayanja (m) *[sseh-mah-yahn-jah]* That is associated with lakes; sailor; one whose mother made a sacrifice or offering to a deity in River *Mayanja*; that which spreads out [*Ganda*].

Semayengo/ Ssemayengo (m) *[sseh-mah-yehn-goh]* The water waves [The *Ganda*].

Semayenje/ Ssemayenje (m) *[sseh-mah-yehn-jeh]* Large cricket [*Ganda*].

Semayizzi/ Ssemayizzi (m) *[sseh-mah-yihz-zih]* That are associated with a hunter/ or a hunt [*Ganda*].

Semayugi (m) *[sseh-mah-yuh-jih]* (Owner) of/ or that associated with hunting bells [*Ganda*].

Semazzi/ Ssemazzi (m) *[sseh-mahz-zih]* Water [*Ganda*].

Sembajja/ Ssembajja (m) *[ssehm-bahj-jah]* One who engages in carpentry work [*Ganda*].

Sembala/ Ssembala (m) *[ssehm-bah-lah]* One good at (or one who engages in) counting (or reckoning) [*Ganda*].

Sembatya/ Ssembatya (m) *[sseh-mbah-tjah]* "I am scared (or frightened) of them"; "I fear (or honor, or respect) them" [*Ganda*].

Sembeeguya/ Ssembeeguya (m) *[ssehm-beh-eh-guh-yah]* "I stoop to being obsequiously dependent" [*Ganda*].

Sembera/ Ssembera (m) *[ssehm-beh-rah]* One who comes close (or approaches) [*Ganda*].

Semberege/ Ssemberege (m) *[ssehm-beh-reh-geh]* A very intelligent and daring person; small and reddish colored pig [*Ganda*].

Sembeza/ Ssembeza (f) *[ssehm-beh-zah]* To welcome; to bring near (or forward); to approach; to entertain (guests) with food/ drink.

Sembirimwa/ Ssembirimwa (m) *[ssehm-bih-rih-mwah]* "I am (thoroughly) backbitten (or slandered behind my back) through the volume of words" [*Ganda*].

Sembiro/ Ssembiro (m) *[ssehm-bih-roh]* That is associated with speed (or swiftness, or quickness); that is speedy (or fast) [*Ganda*].

Sembogga/ Ssembogga (m) *[ssehm-bohg-gah]* Of alluring look [*Ganda*].

Sembogo/ Ssembogo (m) *[sseh-mboh-goh]* Buffalo [*Ganda*].

Sembuuliro/ Ssembuuliro (m) *[sseh-mbuuh-lih-roh]* One indoctrinated (or preached to); indoctrination; preaching [*Ganda*].

Sembuusi/ Ssembuusi (m) *[ssehm-buuh-sih]* Good jumper (or flier, or astronaut); that causes to be doubtful (or to suspect, or to vacillate); that suspects (or has doubts about); one who flits (or flutters) about [*Ganda*].

Sembuuze/ Ssembuuze (m) *[ssehm-buuh-zeh]* "Let me ask (or inquire)"; "let me visit"; "let me greet"; "that I may ask (or inquire)"; "that I may visit"; "that I may greet" *[Ganda]*.

Sembuya/ Ssembuya (m) *[sseh-mbuh-yah]* The stormy wind; state of confusion; chaos; "I display ignorance (or naivete, or silliness)" *[Ganda]*.

Sembuzi/ Ssembuzi (m) *[sseh-mbuh-zih]* Goat *[Ganda]*.

Sembwa/ Ssembwa (m) *[ssehm-bwah]* Dog; species of small fly *[Ganda]*.

Semeere/ Ssemeere (m) *[sseh-meh-eh-reh]* Great stretch of water *[Ganda]*.

Semende/ Ssemmende (m) *[ssehm-mehn-deh]* Pigmoid (or colored) field mouse; kind of banana used for making beer *[Ganda]*.

Semerya/ Ssemerya (m) *[sseh-meh-eh-rjah]* That involve pretending to eat *[Ganda]*.

Semiganda/ Ssemiganda (m) *[sseh-mih-gahn-dah]* Bundles; bunches; turmoils *[Ganda]*.

Semitala (m) *[sseh-mih-tah-lah]* Land between two streams (or swamps); village; newly acquired land *[Ganda]*.

Semitego/ Ssemitego (m) *[sseh-mih-teh-goh]* Traps; bows; pitfalls; snares *[Ganda]*.

Semmambo/ Ssemmambo (m) *[ssehm-mahm-boh]* Wooden pegs for stretching animal hides; tent pegs *[Ganda]*.

Semmambya (m) *[ssehm-mahm-bjah]* (Associated with) dawning *[Ganda]*.

Semmanda/ Ssemmanda (m) *[ssehm-mahn-dah]* With large chest *[Ganda]*.

Semmandwa/ Ssemmandwa (m) *[ssehm-mahn-dwah]* The spirit medium; oracle; the human mouthpiece (or representative) of a deity; a deity affiliated witchdoctor *[Ganda]*.

Semmengo (m) *[ssehm-mehn-goh]* Lower millstones; grind stones; scales for weighing sacks (or bags of produce) e.g. of sugar and coffee *[Ganda]*.

Semmembwa (m) *[ssehm-mehm-bwah]* That has been turned into a burnt food crust *[Ganda]*.

Semmindi/ Ssemmindi (m) *[ssehm-mihn-dih]* (Smoking) pipe *[Ganda]*.

Semmombwe (m) *[ssehm-mohm-bweh]* That is striped *[Ganda]*.

Semmondo (m) *[ssehm-mohn-doh]* Serval cat *[Ganda]*.

Semmuli (m) *[ssehm-muh-lih]* Large reed *[Ganda]*.

Sempa (m) *[ssehm-pah]* Giver; "I give"; "give me" *[Ganda]*.

Sempabuka/ Ssempabuka (m) *[ssehm-pah-buh-kah]* Separation; a separation of oneself; a dispersal; a state of being scattered; an adjournment; a disbandment; "I separate myself" *[Ganda]*.

Sempagala/ Ssempagala (m) *[ssehm-pah-gah-lah]* "I sharpen (or grind)"; "I upbraid (or scold)"; "I improve"; the mode of sharpening (or grinding) [The *Ganda]*.

Sempagama/ Ssempagama (m) *[ssehm-pah-gah-mah]* A situation of being stuck *[Ganda]*.

Sempagi/ Ssempagi (m) *[sseh-mpah-jih]* Pillar; post; pole *[Ganda]*.

Sempago/ Ssempago (m) *[sseh-mpah-goh]* A narrow passage; a gorge [The *Ganda]*.

Sempala/ Ssempala (m) *[ssehm-pah-lah]* An antelope; poor man; poor fellow [*Ganda*].

Sempangi/ Ssempangi (m) *[ssehm-pahn-jih]* The master cultivator (of plots of land) [*Ganda*].

Sempasa/ Sempasa (m) *[ssehm-pah-sah]* A master axman; one who shatters with a lot of force; ax [*Ganda*].

Sempeebwa/ Sempeebwa (m) *[ssehm-peh-eh-bwah]* "I am given" [*Ganda*].

Sempeke/ Ssempeke (m) *[ssehm-peh-keh]* Grain; seed [*Ganda*].

Sempewo/ Ssempewo (m) *[ssehm-peh-woh]* Air; wind; breeze [*Ganda*].

Sempiira/ Ssempiira (m) *[ssehm-piih-rah]* A large fire deliberately set for a constructive purpose such as clearing a section of land; a disastrous fire; forest fire [*Ganda*].

Sempijja/ Ssempijja (m) *[ssehm-pihj-jah]* Stone anvils [*Ganda*].

Sempiri/ Ssempiri (m) *[ssehm-pih-rih]* Species of venomous snake [*Ganda*].

Sempungu/ Ssempungu (m) *[ssehm-puhn-guh]* Eagle; opening [*Ganda*].

Sempyangu/ Ssempyangu (m) *[ssehm-pjahn-guh]* That involve conceit/ or deceit [*Ganda*].

Semuddu/ Ssemuddu (m) *[sseh-muhd-duh]* Servant; a member of the cultivator social class as opposed to the aristocratic cattle keeping class; captive; a favorite of (or keeper of) many captives [*Ganda*].

Semugabi/ Ssemugabi (m) *[sseh-muh-gah-bih]* Very generous or liberal person; chief distributor [*Ganda*].

Semugala/ Ssemugala (m) *[sseh-muh-gah-lah]* Large framework structure built around an anthill to help in the catching and collecting of edible flying ants (*nswa*) [*Ganda*].

Semuganyi/ Ssemuganyi (m) *[sseh-muh-gah-ndjh-ih]* That causes to allow (or permit, or give approval to, or authorize) [*Ganda*].

Semugenyi/ Ssemugenyi (m) *[sseh-muh-geh-nyih]* Stranger; a visitor; a guest [*Ganda*].

Semugenze/ Ssemugenze (m) *[sseh-muh-gehn-zeh]* (Of those that) have gone [*Ganda*].

Semugenzi/ Ssemugenzi (m) *[sseh-muh-gehn-zih]* The departed; a traveler [*Ganda*].

Semugera/ Ssemugera (m) *[sseh-muh-geh-rah]* That distributes (or apportions) [*Ganda*].

Semugga/ Ssemugga (m) *[sseh-muhg-gah]* A river; large stream; a well [The *Ganda*].

Semuggala/ Ssemuggala (m) *[sseh-muhg-gah-lah]* That closes (the entrances) [*Ganda*].

Semuggya/ Ssemuggya (m) *[sseh-muhj-jah]* Newcomer; a recruit; one who has a newly acquired wife (or concubine) [*Ganda*].

Semugogo/ Ssemugogo (m) *[sseh-muh-goh-goh]* The stem (or stalk) of a plantain tree [*Ganda*].

Semugoma/ Ssemugoma (m) *[sseh-muh-goh-mah]* One that stampedes (or rampages) around; a drummer [*Ganda*].

Semugombe/ Ssemugombe (m) *[sseh-muh-gohm-beh]* Of the other world; that of hell; that is caused to be awkward (or clumsy); that is caused to bungle; that is caused to be big and ugly [*Ganda*].

Semugonda/ Ssemugonda (m) *[sseh-muh-gohn-dah]* One who is yielding (or soft, or obedient) [*Ganda*].

Semugongo/ Ssemugongo (m) *[sseh-muh-gohn-goh]* The back (of the body); ridge; keel of a canoe [*Ganda*].

Semugooma/ Ssemugooma (m) *[sseh-muh-goh-oh-mah]* That bends; that is bent (or warped, or wrecked, or damaged, or crooked) [*Ganda*].

Semugumbe/ Ssemugumbe (m) *[sseh-muh-guhm-beh]* Caused to gather together as a group; caused to assemble/ or congregate; caused to be barren (or sterile, or incapable of giving birth) [*Ganda*].

Semugunde/ Ssemugunde (m) *[sseh-muh-guhn-deh]* That is hurled down; that is thrown violently; that is stabbed; that is rocked heavily; that is dashed down [*Ganda*].

Semukaaya/ Ssemukaaya (m) *[sseh-muh-kaah-yah]* That causes to become bitter (or unpleasant to the taste); that causes to quarrel (or to get enraged); that causes to be bitter towards; that causes (a situation) to become serious (or bad) [*Ganda*].

Semukadde/ Ssemukadde (m) *[sseh-muh-kahd-deh]* An elder; a parent; old person; elder of the church; minister [*Ganda*].

Semukasa/ Ssemukasa (m) *[sseh-muh-kah-sah]* One born with two umbilical cords [*Ganda*].

Semukaya/ Ssemukaya (m) *[sseh-muh-kah-yah]* That is (or becomes) weary (or tired, or exhausted); that beats (or thrashes) [*Ganda*].

Semukeete/ Ssemukeete (m) *[sseh-muh-keh-eh-teh]* That is caused to have a heartburn; that is caused to have a sickening feeling (from eating food); that is caused to be harsh; that is bothered (or disturbed, or troubled) [*Ganda*].

Semukete/ Ssemukete (m) *[sseh-muh-keh-teh]* Apron; one who (such as a carpenter) wears an apron; one cut off (or cut down) [*Ganda*].

Semukkuto/ Ssemukkuto (m) *[sseh-muhk-kuh-toh]* A species of insect resembling a cricket, and which emits a stinging secretion; that of satiety; that of feelings of satisfaction after eating; of satisfaction [*Ganda*].

Semukkwiiri/ Ssemukkwiiri (m) *[sseh-muhk-kwiih-rih]* That tackles/ trips (such as in soccer) [*Ganda*].

Semukoteka/ Ssemukooteka (m) *[sseh-muh-koh-oh-teh-kah]* Hanging down; one who hangs down; one whose head hangs down [*Ganda*].

Semukulungwa/ Ssemukulungwa (m) *[sseh-muh-kuh-luhn-gwah]* That is molded (or kneaded, or circled around, or made round); that is rolled (or rubbed along) [*Ganda*].

Semukuutu/ Ssemukuutu (m) *[sseh-muh-kuuh-tuh]* Rogue; long knife [The *Ganda*].

Semukuye/ Ssemukuye (m) *[sseh-muh-kuh-yeh]* That crumples (or messes up) things [*Ganda*].

Semukwaya/ Ssemukwaya (m) *[sseh-muh-kwaah-yah]* One that makes rustling noises (through the vegetation); one who moves so quickly [*Ganda*].

Semulangwa/ Ssemulangwa (m) *[sseh-muh-laahn-gwah]* The talked about one (or one worth talking about); one who is announced (or advertised, or prophesied, or given notice of) [*Ganda*].

Semulema/ Ssemulema (m) *[sseh-muh-leh-mah]* That is lame [*Ganda*].

Semuligo/ Ssemuligo (m) *[sseh-muh-lih-goh]* The filthy (or squalid) one [*Ganda*].

Semumira/ Ssemumira (m) *[sseh-muh-mih-rah]* That swallows [*Ganda*].

Semunanira (m) *[sseh-muh-naah-nih-rah]* One that is brusque and persistent [*Ganda*].

Semunja/ Ssemunja (m) *[sseh-muhn-jah]* That moves aside (or veers, or swerves, or deviates) [*Ganda*].

Semunywa (m) *[seh-muh-ndjh-wah]* That is victorious; tendon in the lower rear part of the foot; close friend; that drinks (or absorbs) [*Ganda*].

Semusamba/ Ssemusamba (m) *[sseh-muh-sahm-bah]* Kicker; one who kicks [*Ganda*].

Semuso/ Ssemuso (m) *[sseh-muh-soh]* Knife [*Ganda*].

Semusoga/ Ssemusoga (m) *[sseh-muh-soh-gah]* Native of (or one descended from inhabitants of, or one associated with) the region of *Busoga* [*Ganda*, *Soga*].

Semutende/ Ssemutende (m) *[sseh-muh-tehn-deh]* That is praised (or commended, or spoken well of); that is described (or told about) [*Ganda*].

Semutezi (m) *[sseh-muh-teh-zih]* The animal trapper [*Ganda*].

Semutono/ Ssemutono (m) *[sseh-muh-toh-noh]* That is small in physical stature [*Ganda*].

Semutumba/ Ssemutumba (m) *[sseh-muh-tuhm-bah]* Bundle (of cloth); porter's load; burden [*Ganda*].

Semuwabula/ Ssemuwabula (m) *[sseh-muh-wah-buh-lah]* That informs (or announces to, or warns, or alerts) [*Ganda*].

Semuwanda/ Ssemuwanda (m) *[sseh-muh-waahn-dah]* Of the road [*Ganda*].

Semuwemba/ Ssemuwemba (m) *[sseh-muh-wehm-bah]* (Reddish-brown colored) sorghum or millet (for making beer); a spreadout [*Ganda*].

Semuwubi/ Ssemuwubi (m) *[sseh-muh-wuh-bih]* That causes to overlook (or to miss); that causes to (unintentionally) slip by; that causes to lose color; that causes to change beyond recognition [*Ganda*].

Semuwunda/ Ssemuwunda (m) *[sseh-muh-wuhn-dah]* Spike/ goad (e.g. the one at the end of a pole and used for killing lungfish) [*Ganda*].

Semuwuubi/ Ssemuwuubi (m) *[sseh-muh-wuuh-bih]* That causes to wave (or to swing about); that causes to be bothered; that causes to keep on the go; that causes to move about [*Ganda*].

Semuwuulu/ Ssemuwuulu (m) *[sseh-muh-wuuh-luh]* A bachelor; a widower; man separated from his wife [*Ganda*].

Semuyaba/ Ssemuyaba (m) *[sseh-muh-yah-bah]* One that is weak (or gravely sick); period of funeral rites or mourning; ruined [*Ganda*].

Semuyindi/ Ssemuyindi (m) *[sseh-muh-yihn-dih]* One of (or one associated with) East Indian descent [*Ganda*].

Semuzibu/ Ssemuzibu (m) *[sseh-muh-zih-buh]* A difficult one [*Ganda*].

Semuzinyi/ Ssemuzinyi (m) *[sseh-muh-zih-ndjh-ih]* Dancer [*Ganda*].

Semwanga/ Ssemwanga (m) *[sseh-mwahn-gah]* An opening [*Ganda*].

Semwango/ Ssemwango (m) *[sseh-mwahn-goh]* The frame of a door (or window) [*Ganda*].

Semwaya/ Ssemwaya (m) *[ssehm-wah-yah]* Plunderer; a marauder; a forager for food [*Ganda*].

Semwezi/ Ssemwezi (m) *[ssehm-weh-eh-zih]* The moon; moonlight [*Ganda*].

Semwogerere (m) *[sseh-mwoh-geh-reh-reh]* That is spoken for (or represented) [*Ganda*].

Semyalo/ Ssemyalo (m) *[sseh-mjaah-loh]* Harbors; countrysides; villages; abundance [*Ganda*].

Sendaga/ Ssendaga (m) *[ssehn-dah-gah]* "I show (or indicate, or point out)"; "I indicate my intention to depart (or to arrive)"; "I announce my arrival" [*Ganda*].

Sendagala/ Ssendagala (m) *[ssehn-dah-gah-lah]* The banana leaves; plantain leaves [*Ganda*].

Sendagire/ Ssendagire (m) *[ssehn-dah-gih-reh]* That is commissioned (or instructed, or commanded, or directed) [*Ganda*].

Sendago/ Ssendago (m) *[ssehn-dah-goh]* Songs; one that sings; (associated with) the throats [*Ganda*].

Sendawula/ Ssendawula (m) *[ssehn-dah-wuh-lah]* Agitator; that is associated with *Ndawula* a deity whose shrine was on *Mubende* Hill [*Ganda*].

Sendebwa (m) *[ssehn-deh-bwah]* The act of being leveled; the act of being pushed back [*Ganda*].

Sendege/ Ssendege (m) *[ssehn-deh-geh]* Small bell-like ornaments [*Ganda*].

Sendigya/ Ssendigya (m) *[ssehn-dih-jah]* "I will come forth (or forward)" [*Ganda*].

Senikaddiwa/ Ssendikaddiwa (m) *[ssehn-dih-kahd-dih-wah]* "I will grow old" [*Ganda*].

Sendikwanawa/ Ssendikwanawa (m) *[sehn-dih-kwah-nah-wah]* "Where shall I make friends?" [*Ganda*].

Sendiwala/ Ssendiwala (m) *[sseh-ehn-dih-wah-lah]* "I am far away" [The *Ganda*].

Sendiwannyo/ Ssendiwannyo (m) *[ssehn-dih-wahn-ndjh-oh]* "I am one with excessive abundance" [*Ganda*].

Sendowooza/ Ssendowooza (m) *[sseh-ehn-doh-woh-oh-zah]* "I think"; way of thinking; point of view; idea; concept [*Ganda*].

Sendyose/ Ssendyoose (m) *[ssehn-djoh-oh-seh]* "(In retrospect) it was appropriate (or beneficial, or befitting, or advantageous) that I did it (or that it occurred)" [*Ganda*].

Sendyowa/ Ssendyowa (m) *[sseh-ehn-djoh-oh-wah]* "I have a duty (or obligation) to"; "I do favors to" [*Ganda*].

Senfuka/ Ssenfuka (m) *[ssehn-fuh-kah]* Half throw in wrestling [*Ganda*].

Senfuma/ Ssenfuma (m) *[ssehn-fuh-mah]* That recounts or tells (a legend, or tradition, or tale); "I am of benefit to" *[Ganda]*.

Senfuuwa/ Ssenfuuwa (m) *[ssehn-fuuh-wah]* That plays a wind instrument such as a flute; mode of blowing on (a wind instrument) *[Ganda]*.

Sengaaga (m) *[ssehn-gaah-gah]* A copper wire bracelet *[Ganda]*.

Senggendo/ Ssenggendo (m) *[sseh-ndgh-ndgh-ehn-doh]* Journeys *[Ganda]*.

Sengiri/ Ssengiri (m) *[ssehn-jih-rih]* Wart hog; wild boar *[Ganda]*.

Sengo/ Ssengo (m) *[ssehn-goh]* Leopard *[Ganda]*.

Sengoba/ Ssengooba (m) *[ssehn-goh-oh-bah]* That steers (such as a vehicle, a boat, or a canoe); the beater (on a hunting expedition); that pursues (or chases, or follows after, or drives away, or dismisses); that defeats (such as an opponent in a game) *[Ganda]*.

Sengonzi (m) *[ssehn-gohn-zih]* That 'softens up' (or flatters); that makes soft (or softens); that makes obedient *[Ganda]*.

Sengoye/ Ssengoye (m) *[ssehn-goh-yeh]* Mashed up; crushed up; stirred together; hunting nets; garments; fabrics; clothing *[Ganda]*.

Senjala/ Ssenjala (m) *[ssehn-jah-lah]* Hunger; famine; a way of spreading out; a species of tiny insect found on stagnant water in plantain gardens; nails; talons; claws *[Ganda]*.

Senjobe/ Ssenjobe (m) *[ssehn-joh-beh]* The marsh antelope *[Ganda]*.

Senjovu/ Ssenjovu (m) *[sseh-ehn-joh-vuh]* Elephant *[Ganda]*.

Senkaaba/ Ssenkaaba (m) *[ssehn-kaah-baah]* "I cry (or weep, or mourn)"; mode of crying (or weeping, or mourning) *[Ganda]*.

Senkaali/ Ssenkaali (m) *[sseh-ehn-kaah-lih]* That is fierce (or stern); vehemence; strictness *[Ganda]*.

Senkaayi/ Ssenkaayi (m) *[ssehn-kaah-yih]* That causes to become (or is) bitter (or unpleasant to the taste); that causes to quarrel (or to get enraged); that causes to be (or is) bitter towards; that causes (a situation) to become serious (or bad) *[Ganda]*.

Senkandwa/ Ssenkandwa (m) *[ssehn-kahn-dwah]* A species of tree which bears white edible berries *[Ganda]*.

Senkanze/ Ssenkanze (m) *[ssehn-kahn-zeh]* "I have frightened"; "I have threatened" *[Ganda]*.

Senkatuka/ Ssenkatuka (m) *[sehn-kah-tuh-kah]* That walks fast *[Ganda]*.

Senkatuuka/ Ssenkatuuka (m) *[ssehn-kah-tuuh-kah]* That goes sour (or bad) *[Ganda]*.

Senke/ Ssenke (m) *[ssehn-keh]* A species of grass employed for roof thatching and for squeezing out banana juice for alcohol brewing *[Ganda]*.

Senkeezi/ Ssenkeezi (m) *[ssehn-keh-eh-zih]* That gets up early; acts of getting up early *[Ganda]*.

Senkenya (m) *[ssehn-keh-ndjh-ah]* Consuming; using up; eating into; eating away at; engulfing *[Ganda]*.

Senkima/ Ssenkima (m) *[ssehn-tch-ih-mah]* Monkey; monkeys *[Ganda]*.

Senkimba/ Ssenkimba (m) *[ssehn-tch-ihm-bah]* That has a look of disgust; that views with disgust (or scorn); that looks at threateningly; that is rude or insolent towards [*Ganda*].

Senkindu/ Ssenkindu (m) *[ssehn-kihn-duh]* Wild date palms [*Ganda*].

Senkole (m) *[ssehn-koh-leh]* That is of the territory of *Ankole*; that is made; that is done [*Ganda*].

Senkomago/ Ssenkomago (m) *[ssehn-koh-mah-goh]* Beating of barkcloth in processing it; that associated with beatings (or strikings, with blows) [The *Ganda*].

Senkongo/ Ssenkongo (m) *[ssehn-kohn-goh]* Ceaseless; species of hard yam [*Ganda*].

Senkonyo/ Ssenkonyo (m) *[ssehn-koh-ndjh-oh]* Short stick with a knob at the end [*Ganda*].

Senkooto/ Ssenkooto (m) *[ssehn-koh-oh-toh]* The geographical (or environmental) boundaries; coasts [*Ganda*].

Senkoto/ Ssenkoto (m) *[ssehn-koh-toh]* (With the peculiarity of a large) back of the neck [*Ganda*].

Senkubuga/ Ssenkubuga (m) *[ssehn-kuh-buh-gah]* That are urged on; that are hurried (or rushed); that are pestered (or annoyed); that are tossed about (in an illness); that are caused to be very sick [*Ganda*].

Senkubuge/ Ssenkubuge (m) *[ssehn-kuh-buh-geh]* Not thoroughly cooked; partly in a raw state; that are urged on; that are hurried (or rushed); that are pestered (or annoyed, or bugged); that are tossed about (in an illness); that are caused to be very sick [*Ganda*].

Senkugwa/ Ssenkugwa (m) *[ssehn-kuh-gwah]* Roars; growls; bellows; "I fall on (or upon) you"; "I fail you"; "I backbite (or slander) you"; "I hit on you"; "I catch on you" [*Ganda*].

Senkumba/ Ssenkumba (m) *[ssehn-kuhm-bah]* Barrenness (of the soil); infertility; "I march (or march off, or go away)"; "I swagger"; "I strut around" [*Ganda*].

Senkungu/ Ssenkungu (m) *[sseh-ehn-kuhn-guh]* Pride; behaving as important [*Ganda*].

Senkusu/ Ssenkusu (m) *[sseh-ehn-kuh-suh]* Parrot; parrots [*Ganda*].

Senkuta/ Ssenkuta (m) *[sseh-ehn-kuh-tah]* Skins; rinds; peels [*Ganda*].

Sennabulya (m) *[ssehn-nah-buh-ljah]* "I have not eaten (or consumed)"; "I have not taken up high office" [*Ganda*].

Sennambwa/ Ssennambwa (m) *[ssehn-nahm-bwah]* With a dog (or dogs) [*Ganda*].

Senninde/ Ssenninde (m) *[ssehn-nihn-deh]* That is waited for (or is awaited) [*Ganda*].

Sennoga/ Ssennoga (m) *[ssehn-noh-gah]* That picks (fruit from trees); one that in wrestling, hurls to the ground; small ball of mashed plantain which is dipped in relish before it is eaten [*Ganda*].

Sennono (m) *[ssehn-noh-noh]* Tradition (or heritage) of significance [The *Ganda*].

Sennungi (m) *[ssehn-nuhn-jih]* That is desirable (or right, or good, or handsome) [*Ganda*].

Sennyanja/ Ssennyanja (m) *[ssehn-ndjh-aahn-jah]* Large lake; large body of water [*Ganda*].

Sennyiga (m) *[ssehn-ndjh-ih-gah]* A cold fever [*Ganda*].

Sennyimba/ Ssennyimba (m) *[ssehn-ndjh-ihm-bah]* Singer; one with a manner or method of singing; songs [*Ganda*].

Sennyomo/ Ssennyomo (m) *[ssehn-ndjh-oh-moh]* A species of large black ant [*Ganda*].

Senzeni (f) *[sehn-zeh-nih]* "What have we done?": a name such as given to a newborn by its parents who are pointing out to neighbors that just because the family is well off should not merit the neighbors' jealousy and ill-feeling towards them [*Zulu*] (Turner 1992: 55).

Sepsi (f) *[tsehp-sih]* A nickname-abbreviation for *Nonceba*: "Mercy" [The *Xhosa*] (Neethling 1994: 92).

Shayimpimpi (m) *[tsh-ah-yihm-pihm-pih]* "Kill the spy" [The *Zulu*] (Herbert 1997: 11).

Shilingi (f/m) *[tsh-ih-lihn-gih]* Shilling (as adapted from the European word) : a name such given by the father to one who is the product of a difficult and costly pregnancy and birth [*Chaga*] (Raum 1967: 297).

Sibakhombisile (f/m) *[sih-bah-kohm-bih-sih-leh]* "We (i.e. the parents) have shown them (i.e. that there was not truth in the rumors)": a name such as given to one born to a mother that had taken an unexpectedly long period to give birth, and during which period she was rumored to be barren [*Zulu*] (Koopman 1987: 152).

Sibongile (f) *[sih-bohn-gih-leh]* "We are grateful (i.e. to God for this child)" [*Zulu*] (Herbert 1997: 8; Koopman 1987: 149).

Siboniwe (f/m) *[sih-boh-nih-weh]* "We have been seen" [*Xhosa*] (Neethling 1985: 90).

Sibusiso (m) *[sih-buh-sih-soh]* "Blessing" [*Zulu*] (Herbert 1997: 8; Koopman 1987: 151, 154, 155).

Sikhuluma (m) *[sih-kuh-luh-mah]* "The one who does not speak" [*Xhosa*] (Neethling 1985: 90).

Simba (m) *[sihm-bah]* Lion [*Chaga* and several other ethnics of eastern, central, and southern Africa] (Raum 1967: 340).

Simomo (f) *[sih-moh-moh]* A nickname-abbreviation for *Nomonde*: "Patience" [*Xhosa*] (Neethling 1994: 92).

Sindisiwe (f/m) *[sihn-dih-sih-weh]* "Recovered": a name such given to one who is the product of a difficult pregnancy or birth [*Zulu*] (Koopman 1987: 150).

Sindiswa (f) *[sihn-dih-swah]* "The one who escaped" [*Xhosa*] (Neethling 1994: 92).

Siphesihle (f) *[sih-peh-sih-leh]* "Beautiful gift" [The *Zulu*] (Koopman 1987: 151).

Siphiwe (m) *[sih-pih-weh]* "(The child) has been given to us" [*Xhosa*] (Thipa 1987: 109).

Sipho (m) *[sih-poh]* "Gift (from God)" [*Zulu*] (Koopman 1987: 148).

Sipho (m) *[sih-poh]* "Gift" [The *Xhosa, Zulu*] (Herbert 1997: 8; Thipa 1987: 109).

Siphokazi (f) *[sih-poh-kah-zih]* The mother associated with a gift (or the greatest gift) [*Xhosa*] (Thipa 1987: 109).

Sirry (f) *[sihr-ree]* A nickname-abbreviation for *Nomasirayeli*: "Israel" [The *Xhosa*] (Neethling 1994: 92).

Sithembile (m) *[sih-tehm-bih-leh]* "We have trusted" [The *Xhosa*] (Neethling 1994: 92).

Sithembiso (m) *[sih-sth-ehm-bih-soh]* "Promise": a name such as given by a mother to reflect the promise that the father of this child had given her upon becoming pregnant following a long relationship--the father later absconded to *Johannesburg*, abandoning mother and child, as he broke the promise of a marriage and a home [*Zulu*] (Turner 1992: 47).

Sithembiso (m) *[sih-sth-ehm-bih-soh]* Promise [*Zulu*] (Herbert 1997: 15).

Sivumelwano (m) *[sih-vuh-meh-lwah-noh]* "Agreement": a name such as given to one born in the month of the first meeting of a political body (Congress for a democratic South Africa--CODESA) [*Zulu*] (Herbert 1997: 11).

Sivuyile (m) *[sih-vuh-yih-leh]* "We are joyful" [*Xhosa*] (Thipa 1987: 111).

Siyabulela (m) *[sih-yah-buh-leh-lah]* "We are grateful" [*Xhosa*] (Thipa 1987 : 110).

Sizani (f/m) *[sih-zah-nih]* "Come and help!": a name such given to one who is the product of a difficult pregnancy or birth [*Zulu*] (Koopman 1987: 150, 151).

Sizwe (m) *[sih-zweh]* "Nation": a name such as given to a last born by its father to indicate that this child makes their nation (i.e. family) complete [The *Nguni, Sotho, Zulu*] (Herbert 1995: 2; Herbert 1990: 8).

Smonds (f) *[smoh-nds]* A nickname-abbreviation for *Nomonde*: "Patience" [*Xhosa*] (Neethling 1994: 92).

Solly (m) *[sohl-lee]* A nickname-abbreviation for *Solomzi*: "The eye of the home" [*Xhosa*] (Neethling 1994: 92).

Solomzi (m) *[soh-lohm-zih]* "The eye of the home" [*Xhosa*] (Neethling 1994: 92; Thipa 1987: 114).

Somagoloza (m) *[soh-mah-goh-loh-zah]* One who sits solitary, waiting for something; a boy who lives alone at a homestead [*Xhosa*] (Neethling 1985: 89).

Somazembe (m) *[soh-mah-zehm-beh]* "Father of the axes: the name can imply one who is cruel [*Xhosa*] (Neethling 1985: 89).

Songa (m) *[soh-ngah]* A name given to the older of twins [*Rega*].

Sono (m) *[soh-noh]* A nickname-abbreviation for *Sonosakhe*: "His sin" [The *Xhosa*] (Neethling 1994: 92).

Sonosakhe (m) *[soh-noh-sah-keh]* "His sin" [*Xhosa*] (Neethling 1994: 92).

Sooka (m) *[soh-oh-kah]* "Come first"; "be the first one to"; "do first"; this name is sometimes associated with the proverb "a situation where drinking water is limited results in discrimination, the herdsmen saying, 'Bring the nursing (or mothering) cows that they may drink first'" implying that precedence is given to elders, that those who possess little are meticulous when it comes to choosing heirs, and that it is favorites who are given things that are in short supply [*Ganda*].

Sposh (f) *[spoh-tsh]* A nickname-abbreviation for *Nosipho*: "Gift" [*Xhosa*] (Neethling 1994: 92).

Steh (m) *[steh]* A nickname-abbreviation for *Sithembile*: "We have trusted" [*Xhosa*] (Neethling 1994: 92).

Sukoji (f) *[suh-koh-oh-jih]* A name commonly given to a first born daughter who has one older male sibling [*Bari*] (Whitehead 1947: 45).

Sumuti (f) *[suh-muh-tih]* Fish: a name denoting misfortune that is commonly given to one who lost more than one older sibling (usually sister) to death [*Bari*] (Whitehead 1947: 45).

-T-

Tahonganyetso (f/m) *[tah-hoh-gah-ndjeh-tsoh]* "The unexpected": a name given by a mother to imply that she was not expecting to have a child at this stage [*Tswana*] (Herbert 1995: 3).

Tamli (m) *[tahm-lee]* A nickname-abbreviation for *Mlindi*: "The one who waits" [*Xhosa*] (Neethling 1994: 92).

Tankiso (m) *[tahn-kih-soh]* Gratitude: a name such as given to a newborn by its mother to indicate that she is so thankful to God that she did not miscarry, thankful that the pregnancy achieved fruition [*Sotho*] (Herbert 1990: 9).

Tayari (f/m) *[tah-yah-rih]* "Ready" (from the *Kiswahili* language) [The *Fipa*] (Willis 1982: 229).

Tebogo (m) *[teh-boh-goh]* Gratitude: a name such as given to a newborn by its mother to indicate that it is indeed the gift of a baby boy that she wished for, and that the family is so thankful to God for the baby [*Tswana*] (Herbert 1997: 8; Herbert 1995: 3; Herbert 1990: 9).

Teboho (m) *[teh-boh-hoh]* Gratitude [*Sotho*] (Thipa 1987: 110).

Tenda/ Ttenda (f) *[ttehn-dah]* Speak well of; praise; commend; glorify; glorification; honor"; this name is sometimes associated with the proverb "the funeral rites of one who was good are praisingly talked about endlessly (or cannot pass without being praised)" [*Ganda*].

Thabang (m) *[tah-bah-ndgh]* "Be joyful" [*Sotho*] (Thipa 1987: 111).

Thabo (m) *[tah-boh]* Joy [*Sotho*] (Thipa 1987: 111).

Thakathangani (f) *[tah-kah-tahn-gah-nih]* "With what do I bewitch?": a name such as given to a newborn by its parent who is implying denying the accusation that he or she is practicing witchcraft [*Zulu*] (Turner 1992: 54).

Thandeka (m) *[tahn-deh-kah]* "The lovable one" [*Xhosa*] (Neethling 1994: 92).

Thandekile (f) *[tahn-deh-kih-leh]* "The lovable one" [The *Zulu*] (Koopman 1987: 151).

Thandi (f) *[tahn-dih]* A nickname-abbreviation for *Noluthando* i.e. "Love" and *Nomthandazo* i.e. "Prayer" [*Xhosa*] (Neethling 1994: 92).

Thandies (f) *[tahn-deez]* A nickname-abbreviation for *Nomthandazo*: "Prayer" [*Xhosa*] (Neethling 1994: 92).

Thandisizwe (m) *[sth-ah-ndih-sih-zweh]* "Lover of the nation" [The *Xhosa*] (Wainwright 1986: 297).

Thandiwe (f) *[tahn-dih-weh]* "The loved one" [*Zulu*] (Koopman 1987: 151).

Thandos (f) *[tahn-dohs]* A nickname-abbreviation for *Noluthando*: "Love" [*Xhosa*] (Neethling 1994: 92).

Thanduxolo (m) *[sth-ah-nduh-xsoh-loh]* Lover of peace [The *Xhosa*] (Wainwright 1986: 295).

Thanduyise (m) *[tahn-duh-yih-seh]* "Love thy father" [The *Zulu*] (Koopman 1987: 149).

Thandy (m) *[tahn-dee]* A nickname-abbreviation for *Thandeka*: "The loveable one" [*Xhosa*] (Neethling 1994: 92).

Thapelo (m) *[tah-peh-loh]* Prayer: a name such as given to a newborn by its mother to indicate that, during the pregnancy, she fondly went to church every Sunday for the purposes of physical and spiritual healing [*Tswana*] (Herbert 1997: 8; Herbert 1995: 3; Herbert 1990: 9).

Thapelo (m) *[tah-peh-loh]* Prayer [*Sotho*] (Thipa 1987: 109, 110).

Themba (m) *[tehm-bah]* Hope [*Xhosa*, *Zulu*] (Herbert 1997: 8; Thipa 1987: 114).

Thembeka (m) *[tehm-beh-kah]* "Be faithful" [*Xhosa*] (Thipa 1987: 114).

Thembi (m) *[tehm-bih]* "Trust": a name such as given either to one born into a family that already has a disproportionately large number of female children, or to one born to a mother that took a relatively long time to conceive-- it is implied in the name that the parents trusted (God) that the child they longed for would eventually be born [*Zulu*] (Koopman 1987: 150).

Thembinkosi (m) *[tehm-bihn-koh-sih]* "Trust the Lord" [*Zulu*] (Koopman 1987: 149).

Thiau (f) *[sth-ih-yahw]* Arm rings: a name such as given to a girl wearing, or one who characteristically wears, arm rings [The *Nuer*] (Evans-Pritchard 1948: 169).

Thobeka (m) *[toh-beh-kah]* The obedient one; to be submissive [The *Xhosa*] (Neethling 1994: 92).

Thobi-Thobi (m) *[toh-bih-toh-bih]/* **Thobs** (m) *[toh-bs]* These are nicknames or abbreviations for *Thobeka*: "The obedient one"; to be submissive [*Xhosa*] (Neethling 1994: 92).

Thoja (m) *[toh-jah]* A nickname-abbreviation for *Thobeka*: "The obedient one"; to be submissive [*Xhosa*] (Neethling 1994: 92).

Thoko (f) *[toh-koh]* A pet form of the name *Thokozile*: "Having made happy (i.e. at the birth of this child)" [*Zulu*] (Koopman 1987: 155).

Thokoza (f) *[toh-koh-zah]* "Be happy (i.e. for the birth of this child)" [*Zulu*] (Koopman 1987: 150).

Thokozile (f) *[toh-koh-zih-leh]* "Having made happy (i.e. at the birth of this child)" [*Zulu*] (Koopman 1987: 150, 155).

Thokozile (f) *[toh-koh-zih-leh]* "Rejoiced" *[Zulu]* (Herbert 1997: 8).

Thozama (m) *[toh-zah-mah]* "Be humble/ meek" *[Xhosa]* (Thipa 1987: 114).

Thulani (m) *[tuh-lah-nih]* "Be ye quiet": a name such given to one born at a time of friction between either or both of parents and quarrelsome kinsfolk *[Zulu]* (Koopman 1987: 150).

Thulani (m) *[tuh-lah-nih]* "Hold your tongue": a name such as given to one born out of wedlock or infidelity *[Xhosa]* (Thipa 1987: 113).

Thulebona (f/m) *[tuh-leh-boh-nah]* "Quiet but aware": a name such as given to a newborn by its paternal grandmother who is reflecting that despite her son's reticence in not chastising his wife for the extramarital affair she engaged in, he is very much aware of the affair though he has not done anything about it *[Zulu]* (Turner 1992: 50).

Tia (m) *[tih-yah]* Name given to a third born *[Nuba]* (Seligman 1932: 386).

Tiop (m) *[tih-yohp]* Soil mixed with cattle manure and ashes: a name given to one whose previously born siblings died *[Nuer]* (Evans-Pritchard 1948: 167).

Tlala (m) *[tlah-lah]* Famine: name such as given to one born during a period of famine *[Sotho]* (Herbert 1990: 5).

Toar (f/m) *[toh-wahr]* Beer strainer *[Nuer]* (Evans-Pritchard 1948: 169).

Toar-Mathda (f) *[toh-wahr-mah-sth-dah]* "Beer strainer, my friend" *[Nuer]* (Evans-Pritchard 1948: 169).

Tobsie (m) *[tohb-sih]/* *Tosh* (m) *[toh-tsh]* Nicknames-abbreviations for *Thobeka*: "The obedient one"; to be submissive *[Xhosa]* (Neethling 1994: 92).

Tongun (m) *[toh-ngh-uhn]* A name commonly given to a first born amongst several (at least four) male siblings that have fortunately survived death *[Bari]* (Whitehead 1947: 45).

Tot (m) *[toh-oht]* A name given to the second born following the birth of his twin siblings *[Nuer]* (Evans-Pritchard 1948: 168); a name given to the third born following the birth of his twin siblings *[Nuer]* (Whitehead 1947: 46).

Toto (f) *[toh-toh]* A name given to a second born *[Nuba]* (Seligman 1932: 387).

Tshegofatso (f) *[tsh-eh-goh-fah-tsoh]* "Blessing": a name such as given to a newborn by its mother to indicate that the newborn is considered a blessing to the family *[Tswana]* (Herbert 1990: 9).

Tshepo (m) *[tsh-eh-poh]* "Hope": a name such as given to a newborn by its mother to indicate that her baby boy very much *[Sotho]* (Herbert 1990: 9).

Tshepo (m) *[tsh-eh-poh]* Hope *[Sotho]* (Thipa 1987: 114).

Tshiya (m) *[tsh-ih-yah]* Pillar *[Sotho]* (Thipa 1987: 114).

Tshoganyetso (f) *[tsh-oh-gah-ndjh-eh-tsoh]* "Unexpected": a name such as given to a newborn by its mother to indicate that she had not expected to have a child at that stage *[Tswana]* (Herbert 1990: 9).

Tshwene (f/m) *[tsh-weh-neh]* "Baboon": such is a derogatory-protection name usually given to one born following the deaths of several of the previously born siblings--such (normally temporary) names are intended to confuse the ancestral spirits through making them believe that the parents do not care for the newborn and therefore their taking it away (by dealing it a hand of death as happened to other children in the family) would not hurt or serve as punishment [*Sotho*] (Herbert 1990: 5, 6).

Tshweu (m) *[tsh-weh-yuh]* White [*Sotho*] (Herbert 1990: 10).

Tsie (m) *[tsih-yeh]* Locust: a name such as given to one born during a period of locust invasion [*Sotho*] (Herbert 1990: 5).

Tsietsi (m) *[tsih-yeh-tsih]* "Problem": a name such as given to one born out of wedlock or infidelity [*Sotho*] (Thipa 1987: 112).

Tubonje (m) *[tuh-bohn-dzeh]* "Understanding" [*Rega*].

Tunda (m) *[tuh-ndah]* A trap that catches ten animals [*Rega*].

Turyasingura (m) *[tuh-riah-tsih-nguh-rah]* "We shall succeed" [The *Kiga, Nyankore, Nyoro, Toro*].

Turyatamba (m) *[tuh-riah-tah-mbah]* "We shall heal" [The *Kiga, Nyankore, Nyoro, Toro*].

Turyatemba (m) *[tuh-riah-teh-mbah]* "We shall climb"; "we shall rise" [The *Kiga, Nyankore, Nyoro, Toro*].

Turyatunga (m) *[tuh-riah-tuh-ngah]* "We shall become rich" [The *Kiga, Nyankore, Nyoro, Toro*].

Turyomurugyendo (m) *[tuh-rjoh-muh-ruh-djeh-ndoh]* "We are involved in the journey" [*Kiga, Nyankore, Nyoro, Toro*].

Tusiime (f/m) *[tuh-siih-meh]* "Let us praise"; "may we praise" [The *Kiga, Nyankore, Nyoro, Toro*].

Tusingwiire (m) *[tuh-siih-nguih-reh]* "We have succeeded" [*Kiga, Nyankore, Nyoro, Toro*].

Tutu (f/m) *[tuh-tuh]* This is traditionally a female name, but can be given to a fourth born boy whose birth follows exclusively male siblings [The *Nuba*] (Seligman 1932: 386).

Tuwangye (m) *[tuh-wah-njeh]* "He is not mine" [*Kiga, Nyankore, Nyoro, Toro*].

Tweheyo (m) *[tueh-heh-yoh]* "Let us put in all our efforts" [*Kiga, Nyankore, Nyoro, Toro*].

Twesiime (f/m) *[tueh-siih-meh]* "We rejoice"; "we feel happy" [The *Kiga, Nyankore, Nyoro, Toro*].

Tweteise (f/m) *[tueh-tehy-seh]* "Let us repent" [*Kiga, Nyankore*].

Tweyanze (f/m) *[tueh-yah-nzeh]* "Let us be thankful" [The *Kiga, Nyankore, Nyoro, Toro*].

Twine (f/m) *[tuih-neh]* "We have"; "we possess" [*Kiga, Nyankore, Nyoro, Toro*].

Twinoburyo (f/m) *[tuih-noh-buh-rioh]* "We are active"; "we are hardworking" [*Kiga, Nyankore, Nyoro, Toro*].

Twinomujuni (f/m) *[tuih-noh-muh-juh-nih/ tuih-noh-muh-zuh-nih]* "We have the Savior"; "we are with the Savior" [*Kiga, Nyankore, Nyoro, Toro*].

Twongyeirwe (f/m) *[tuoh-njehy-rueh]* "More has been given to us" [*Kiga, Nyankore, Nyoro, Toro*].

Ubonga (m) *[uh-boh-ndgah]* A name given to a third born [*Anuak*] (Whitehead 1947: 46).

Uhuru (m) *[oo-huh-ruh]* Freedom: a name associated with political independence [The *Pare*, *Swahili* and several other ethnics of eastern, central, and southern Africa] (Herbert 1997: 10; Omari 1970: 66).

Ujulo (m) *[uh-juh-loh]* A name given to a second born [*Anuak*] (Whitehead 1947: 46).

Ulang (m) *[uh-lah-ndgh]* The name of a species of bird: a name commonly given to a first born of male twins, the second born named *Lado* [The *Bari*] (Whitehead 1947: 45).

Umot (m) *[uh-moht]* A name given to a first born [*Anuak*] (Whitehead 1947: 46).

Umwipi (m) *[uh-mwih-pih]* "Shorty" [*Fipa*] (Willis 1982: 229, 230).

Unathi (m) *[uh-nah-tih]* "You (i.e. the Lord) are with us"; "he (i.e. the Lord) is with us" [*Xhosa*] (Thipa 1987: 109, 111).

-V-

Valisisa (f/m) *[vah-lih-sih-sah]* "Close it tightly": a name such as given to a twelfth born by it's paternal grandmother who is urging the child's mother to get sterilized since she already has many children and the money available is not sufficient to feed all of them [*Zulu*] (Turner 1992: 53).

Vela (m) *[veh-lah]* Nickname-abbreviation for *Velaphi*: "Where do you come from?" [*Xhosa*] (Neethling 1994: 92).

Velaphi (m) *[veh-lah-pih]* "Where do you come from?": a name such as given to one born out of wedlock or infidelity, or one born to a mother that has taken an unexpectedly long time to have a child [The *Xhosa*] (Thipa 1987: 108, 112).

Velaphi (m) *[veh-lah-pih]* "Where do you come from?" [*Xhosa*] (Neethling 1994: 92).

Velephi (m) *[veh-leh-pih]* "Where do you come from?": a name such as given to a newborn whose father is expressing suspicion as to whether he is the parent [*Zulu*] (Turner 1992: 49).

Vido (m) *[vih-doh]/ Vista* (m) *[vihs-tah]* These are nicknames-abbreviations for *Vuyani*: "Be happy" [*Xhosa*] (Neethling 1994: 92).

Vikamatshe (f/m) *[vih-kah-mah-tsh-eh]* "Warding off stones": a name such given to one born at a time of a family quarrel [The *Zulu*] (Koopman 1987: 150).

Vusi (m) *[vuh-sih]* Nickname-abbreviation for *Vusumzi*: "Awaken the home" [*Xhosa*] (Neethling 1994: 92).

Vusi (m) *[vuh-sih]* A pet form of the name *Vusumuzi*: "Wake up the family" [*Zulu*] (Koopman 1987: 155).

Vusumuzi (m) *[vuh-suh-muh-zih]* "Wake up the family": a name such as given to the first born male child i.e. the one that awakens the family [*Zulu*] (Koopman 1987: 149, 155).

Vusumzi (m) *[vuh-suhm-zih]* "Awaken the home" *[Xhosa]* (Neethling 1994: 92).

Vusumzi (m) *[vuh-suhm-zih]* "Revive the home" *[Xhosa]* (Thipa 1987: 114, 115).

Vuvu (f) *[vuh-voo]* A nickname-abbreviation for *Nomvuyo* i.e. "Happiness" and *Nomvuzo* i.e. "Reward" *[Xhosa]* (Neethling 1994: 92).

Vuyani (m) *[vuh-yah-nih]* "Be happy" *[Xhosa]* (Neethling 1994: 92).

Vuyani (m) *[vuh-yah-nih]* "Be joyful" *[Xhosa]* (Thipa 1987: 111).

Vuyelwa (f) *[vuh-yeh-lwah]* "The one who gladdens" *[Xhosa]* (Neethling 1994: 92).

Vuyi (f) *[vuh-yih]* A nickname-abbreviation for *Vuyelwa*: "The one who gladdens" *[Xhosa]* (Neethling 1994: 92).

Vuyo (m) *[vuh-yoh]* Joy *[Xhosa]* (Thipa 1987: 111).

-W-

Waakalipa (f) *[waah-kah-lih-pah]* "The Fierce One" *[Fipa]* (Willis 1982: 229).

Waansakiloole (f/m) *[waahn-sah-kih-loh-oh-leh]* A satirical name such as given by the family midwife to a newborn whose mother is of attractive appearance, but is otherwise idle and of little use *[Fipa]* (Willis 1982: 230).

Wabenga (m) *[wah-behn-gah]* To get off from *[Rega]*.

Wabiwa (f) *[wah-bih-wah]* A name given to a child born with the umbilical cord tied around it *[Rega]*.

Wabulakombe (m) *[wah-buh-lah-kohm-beh]* "As God says" *[Rega]*.

Wakenge (m) *[wah-kehn-geh]* A name given to a twin born at a time of twin ceremonial activity in the neighborhood *[Rega]*.

Wakilongo (m) *[wah-kih-loh-ngoh]* "Family member" *[Rega]*.

Wakubenga (f) *[wah-kuh-beh-ngah]* "The one that is despised" *[Rega]*.

Wakusomba (f) *[wah-koo-soh-mbah]* "The one that despises you" *[Rega]*.

Walumona (m) *[wah-luh-moh-nah]* Name given to the sole child that survives death *[Rega]*.

Wamagali (f/m) *[wah-mah-gah-lih]* The one associated with bicycles *[Kiga, Nyankore, Nyoro, Toro]*.

Wamagezi (f/m) *[wah-mah-geh-zih]* "He/ she is intelligent" *[Nyoro, Toro]*.

Wamagyezi (f/m) *[wah-mah-jeh-zih]* "He/ she is intelligent" *[The Kiga, Nyankore]*.

Wandimoyi (f) *[wahn-diih-moh-yih]* "One belly" *[Rega]*.

Wani (m) *[wah-nih]*/ ***Wanike*** (m) *[wah-nih-keh]* A name commonly given to a third born amongst several (at least four) male siblings that have fortunately survived death *[Bari]* (Whitehead 1947: 45).

Waso (m) *[wah-soh]* "Never trust people" *[Rega]*.

Watuna (m) *[wah-tuh-nah]* A bastard: one whose father is irresponsible [The *Rega*].

Watuwindwake (f/m) *[waah-tuh-wihn-dwah-keh]* A satirical name such as given by the family midwife to a newborn whose parents are so occupied with other things to the detriment of their children whom they neglect as a result [*Fipa*] (Willis 1982: 230).

Wec (m) *[wehk]* Cattle camp: a name given to one born in a cow camp [The *Nuer*] (Evans-Pritchard 1948: 167).

Weeraga (m) *[weh-eh-rah-gah]* "Where it goes"; this name is commonly associated with the proverb "where a gun points is where it kills (or conquers)" which is more so related to the past whereby the spear based local military technology was no match for the gun power of the colonialists, and the slave and ivory raiders [*Ganda*].

Welongo (m) *[weh-loh-ngoh]* "A family member (is the one that treats you in the proper way)" [*Rega*].

Wembabazi (f/m) *[weh-mbah-bah-zih]* "The merciful one" [*Kiga, Nyankore, Nyoro, Toro*].

Wethu (f) *[weh-too]* A nickname-abbreviation for *Nomawethu*: "One of us" [*Xhosa*] (Neethling 1994: 92).

Wetumba (m) *[weh-tuh-mbah]* One who is boastful athough he does not have much [*Rega*].

Wezo (f) *[weh-zoh]* A nickname-abbreviation for *Nomawezo*: "Crossing" [*Xhosa*] (Neethling 1994: 92).

Wia (m) *[wih-yah]* Cry of warning: a name given to one whose previously born siblings died [*Nuer*] (Evans-Pritchard 1948: 167).

Wilondja (m) *[wih-lohn-dzah]* An only son, whose begotten children following marrying, are consequently considered his younger brothers and sisters [*Rega*].

Witumbila (m) *[wih-tuhm-bih-lah]* One who praises himself [*Rega*].

Wityan (f) *[wih-tjahn]* A cow name [*Nuer*] (Evans-Pritchard 1948: 170).

Wobusobozi (f/m) *[woh-buh-soh-zih]* "The one with authority/ power" [*Kiga, Nyankore, Nyoro, Toro*].

-Y-

Yabawe (f/m) *[yah-bah-weh]* "He/ she is the one"; "it is him/ her" [The *Kiga, Nyankore, Nyoro, Toro*].

Yamwendelelwa (m) *[yah-mweh-ndeh-leh-lwah]* "The one you always talk about" [*Rega*].

Yar (m) *[yahr]* Sulky [*Nuer*] (Evans-Pritchard 1948: 169).

Yekize (f/m) *[yeh-kih-zeh]* "Heal yourself" [*Kiga, Nyankore, Nyoro, Toro*].

Yerinda (f/m) *[yeh-rih-ndah]* "You be careful"; "protect yourself" [The *Kiga, Nyankore, Nyoro, Toro*].

Yesiime (f/m) *[yeh-siih-meh]* "Rejoice"; "be happy" [*Kiga, Nyankore, Nyoro, Toro*].

Yetware (f/m) *[yeh-tuah-reh]* "Take your time" [The *Kiga, Nyankore, Nyoro, Toro*].

Yigga (m) *[yihg-gah]* "Hunt"; this name is sometimes associated with the proverb "an elderly person will (or can) go on a hunt, but when asked to go to war he will refuse" which mirrors the commonplace lame excuse--since the man is confident of his hunting speed, he should not bring up the excuse of being too advanced in years to participate in war [*Ganda*].

Yoleka (f/m) *[yoh-leh-kah]* "Show (something)" [*Kiga, Nyankore, Nyoro, Toro*].

Yoliswa (f) *[yoh-lih-swah]* To delight [*Xhosa*] (Neethling 1994: 92, 1985: 90).

Yorora (f/m) *[yoh-roh-rah]* "Bring up"; "nurture" [*Kiga, Nyankore, Nyoro, Toro*].

-Z-

Zaagyenda (m) *[zaah-jeh-ndah]* "They (i.e. the hardships, or problems) have gone"; "I wish they (i.e. the hardships, or problems) would go away" [*Kiga, Nyankore, Nyoro, Toro*].

Zaahura (f/m) *[zaah-huh-rah]* "Rescue"; "they (i.e. the hardships, or problems) keep (you)" [*Kiga, Nyankore, Nyoro, Toro*].

Zaakumumpa (f/m) *[zaah-kuhmuh-mpah]* "If only they (i.e. the hardships, or problems) could cause him/ her to be mine" [*Kiga, Nyankore, Nyoro, Toro*].

Zaalibwenda (f/m) *[zaah-lih-bueh-ndah]* "If they like it"; "however they want it" [*Kiga, Nyankore, Nyoro, Toro*].

Zaalibwije (f/m) *[zaah-lih-buih-zeh]* "Let them (i.e. the hardships, or problems) come" [*Kiga, Nyankore, Nyoro, Toro*].

Zaatwoshaho (f/m) *[zaah-tuoh-tsh-ah-hoh]* "They (i.e. the hardships, or problems) have persisted on us" [*Kiga, Nyankore, Nyoro, Toro*].

Zalibagire (f/m) *[zaah-lih-bah-gih-reh]* "Let them (i.e. the hardships, or problems) afflict as they want" [*Kiga, Nyankore, Nyoro, Toro*].

Zanazo (f/m) *[zah-nah-zoh]* "Come with him/ her": a name such as given to a newborn by the mother's mother-in-law who is airing the suspicion that the child is not her son's offspring since it was born only seven months after the marriage, and therefore the mother had likely come into the marriage after the conception of this child [*Zulu*] (Turner 1992: 49).

Zandile (m) *[zahn-dih-leh]* "They (i.e. the children) have increased": a name such as given to one born into a family that already has many children [The *Zulu*] (Koopman 1987: 149).

Zanele (m) *[zah-neh-leh]* "They are enough" [*Xhosa*] (Neethling 1994: 92).

Zangire (f/m) *[zah-ngih-reh]* "They have refused" [*Kiga, Nyankore, Nyoro, Toro*].

Zani (m) *[zah-nih]/ Zaza* (m) *[zah-zah]* Nicknames-abbreviations for *Zanele*: "They are enough" [*Xhosa*] (Neethling 1994: 92).

Zarikubanza (m) *[zah-rih-kuh-bah-nzah]* "It is better that they (i.e. the hardships, or problems) afflict you earlier (than later in life)" [*Kiga, Nyankore, Nyoro, Toro*].

Zibize-Theku (m) *[zih-bih-zeh-sth-eh-kuh]* "The evil of Durban": a name such as given by a rural based mother to reflect that she was told by one of the women in the community at the time of the birth of this child that her husband who is a migrant worker in Durban had another spouse living with him in town [*Zulu*] (Turner 1992: 47-48).

Zibuyile (f) *[zih-buh-yih-leh]* "They (i.e. the cattle) have returned": a name such given to a newborn by the father to metaphorically imply that (upon getting married) she serves as compensation for the bride dowry that the father gave over to his wife's family [*Zulu*] (Koopman 1987: 151); or a name given to one born into a family in which the male far outnumber the female children [*Zulu*] (Herbert 1997: 6).

Ziinamaani (m) *[ziih-nah-maah-nih]* "They (i.e. the hardships, or problems) are of such tremendous power/ strength" [*Kiga, Nyankore, Nyoro, Toro*].

Zikaburomuliisa (m) *[zih-kah-buh-roh-oh-muh-liih-sah]* "They (i.e. the cattle kraals) still lack a herder to look after them" [*Kiga, Nyankore, Nyoro, Toro*].

Zikampikaho (m) *[zih-kah-mpih-kah-hoh]* "They (i.e. the hardships, or problems) have got to me" [*Kiga, Nyankore, Nyoro, Toro*].

Zikamukuba (m) *[zih-kah-muh-kuh-bah]* "They (i.e. the hardships, or problems) have crumpled him/ her" [*Kiga, Nyankore, Nyoro, Toro*].

Zikandonda (m) *[zih-kah-ndoh-ndah]* "They (i.e. the hardships, or problems) still hunt me out" [*Kiga, Nyankore, Nyoro, Toro*].

Zinhle (f) *[zihn-leh]* "They (i.e. daughters) are beautiful": a name such as given to a newborn by its father who is expressing pride in himself as a new father, or in his child [*Zulu*] (Koopman 1987: 152).

Zinkuratiire (m) *[zih-nkuh-rah-tiih-reh]* "They (i.e. the hardships, or problems) are following me" [*Kiga, Nyankore, Nyoro, Toro*].

Zinukile (f/m) *[zih-nuh-kih-leh]* "Suspected himself of witchcraft": a name such as given to a newborn by its paternal grandmother after her son quarreled with her neighbor and demanded to know whether he had not been invited to a gathering of neighbors because he was suspected of witchcraft; thereafter, the whole family viewed him with close suspicion, giving rise to this name of his child born soon after the quarrel [*Zulu*] (Turner 1992: 54).

Ziphezinhle (f) *[zih-peh-zihn-leh]* "Beautiful gifts" [*Zulu*] (Koopman 1987: 151).

Ziqede (m) *[zih-keh-deh]* "Cease them (i.e. the intrusions)": a name such as given to a first born by its paternal relatives and is directed to the child's mother who habitually joins in conversations and offers her advice and opinion on family matters without being invited to do so--the name is to draw her attention to the fact that her excessive intrusion into family matters is not welcome [*Zulu*] (Turner 1992: 51).

Ziribarwomu (m) *[zih-rih-bah-ruoh-muh]* "They (i.e. the hardships, or problems) will (eventually) be counted by one (person)" [The *Kiga, Nyankore, Nyoro, Toro*].

Ziryaharugo (m) *[zih-riah-hah-ruh-goh]* "They (i.e. the hardships, or problems) are by the cattle fence (waiting)" [*Kiga, Nyankore, Nyoro, Toro*].

Zithulele (m) *[zih-tuh-leh-leh]* "Keep oneself quiet": a name such as given to a newborn by its mother who is expressing that she will keep composed about the issue that involved a dispute with her in-laws leading to her being ordered back to her parent's home; since upon return she failed to carry with her a domestic animal as customary compensation for her insulting behavior, because her family could not afford the animal, she became shunned [*Zulu*] (Turner 1992: 50).

Zola (f) *[zoh-lah]* A nickname-abbreviation for *Nokuzola*: "The calm and meek one" [*Xhosa*] (Neethling 1994: 92).

Zolani (m) *[zoh-lah-nih]* "Be calm" [*Xhosa*] (Neethling 1994: 92).

Zoleka (m) *[zoh-leh-kah]* To be calm [*Xhosa*] (Neethling 1994: 92).

Zolie (f) *[zoh-lee]* A nickname-abbreviation for *Zoliswa*: "To make calm"/ "one who calms" [*Xhosa*] (Neethling 1994: 92).

Zoliswa (f) *[zoh-lih-swah]* One who calms; to make calm [The *Xhosa*] (Neethling 1994: 92).

Zondeka (f/m) *[zoh-ndeh-kah]* "If only they (i.e. the hardships, or problems) would leave me alone" [*Kiga, Nyankore, Nyoro, Toro*].

Zoona (f/m) *[zoh-oh-nah]* "All of them" [*Kiga, Nyankore, Nyoro, Toro*].

Zoororwa (f/m) *[zoh-oh-roh-ruah]* "They are brought up" [*Kiga, Nyankore, Nyoro, Toro*].

Zozo (f/m) *[zoh-zoh]* A nickname-abbreviation for *Nokuzola* i.e. "The calm and meek one," *Zolani* i.e. "Be calm," *Zoleka* i.e. "To be calm," and *Zoliswa* i.e. "To make calm"/ "one who calms" [*Xhosa*] (Neethling 1994: 92).

Zukie (f) *[zuh-kee]* A nickname-abbreviation for *Zukiswa*: "The one to be praised" [*Xhosa*] (Neethling 1994: 92).

Zukiswa (f) *[zuh-kih-swah]* "The one to be praised" [The *Xhosa*] (Neethling 1994: 92).

Zulu (m) *[zuh-luh]* "Sky": the name of the first ancestor of the *Zulu* ethnics [*Zulu*] (Koopman 1987: 156).

Zuzwa (m) *[zuh-zwah]* "The gained one": a name such as given to a boy who remarkably gained his health back, following having been an alarmingly sickly child during his first few years of life [*Zulu*] (Koopman 1987: 154, 155).

Zwakushiwo (f/m) *[zwah-kuh-tsh-ih-woh]* "The rumor": a name such as given to a first born by the father who heard shocking rumors that his wife had attempted to leave him shortly before their marriage, just after he had fulfilled the bride dowry obligations; or a name given to a newborn by a grandmother to whom it was rumored that her then grandchild-to-be was conceived out of infidelity [*Zulu*] (Turner 1992: 47).

Zwayi (m) *[zwah-yih]* A nickname-abbreviation for *Mzwandile*: "The home has expanded" [*Xhosa*] (Neethling 1994: 92).

Zwelenduna (m) *[zweh-lehn-duh-nah]* "The headman's country": a name such as given to a newborn by its father who is sarcarstically reminding a village headman (*nduna*) that has an inflated opinion of his importance, that the land he is laying claim to does not indeed belong to him but to a local chief [*Zulu*] (Turner 1992: 55).

Zwelikabani (m) *[zweh-lih-kah-bah-nih]* "Whose land is this?": a name such as given to a newborn by its father who is the oldest of four sons of a chief, and he is chastising his younger brothers for going against custom by contesting the right of their older brother to receive a larger share of the inheritance, even threatening to kill him if he does not share the inheritance with them--the child was born during the dispute between the brothers [The *Zulu*] (Turner 1992: 52).

References

Asante, Molefi K. *The Book of African Names*. Trenton, NJ.: Africa World, 1991.

Chuks-Orji, O. *Names from Africa*. Chicago, IL: Johnson, 1972.

Crane, L. *African Names: People and Places*. Urbana, IL: University of Illinois, 1982.

Daeleman, Jan. "Proper Names used with 'Twins' and Children Succeeding Them in Sub-Saharan Languages." *Onoma* 21, (1977): 189-195.

Doke, Clement M. *The Lambas of Northern Rhodesia: A Study of Their Customs and Beliefs*. London, England: George G. Harrap and Company, 1931.

Evans-Pritchard, E.E. "Nuer Modes of Address." *Uganda Journal* 12, no. 2 (1948): 166-171.

Hemans, T.J. "A Note on Amandebele Names." *NADA* 9, no. 5 (1968): 74.

Herbert, Robert K. "The Politics of Personal Naming in South Africa." *Names* 45, no. 1 (March 1997): 3-17.

_____."The Sociolinguistics of Personal Names: Two South African Case Studies." *South African Journal of African Languages* 15, no. 1 (1995): 1-8.

Herbert, Robert K. and Senna Bogatsu "Changes in Northern Sotho and Tswana Naming Patterns." *Nomina Africana* 4, no. 2 (1990): 1-20.

Hollis, A.C. *The Nandi: Their Language and Folk-lore*. Oxford, England: Clarendon, 1969.

Jackson, S.K. "The Names of the Vashona." *NADA* 34 (1957): 116-122.

Kagwa, Apolo. *Ekitabo kye Mpisa za Baganda*. London, England: Macmillan, 1952.

_____. *The Customs of the Baganda*. New York: Columbia, 1934.

Kimenyi, Alexandre. *Kinyarwanda and Kirundi Names: A Semiolinguistic Analysis of Bantu Onomastics*. Lewiston, NY: Edwin Mellen, 1989.

Koopman, Adrian. "Zulu Names and other Modes of Address." *Nomina Africana* 1, no. 1 (1987): 136-164.

Lawson, Edwin D. *More Names and Naming: An Annotated Bibliography*. Westport, CT: Greenwood, 1995.

_____. *Personal Names and Naming: An Annotated Bibliography*. Westport, CT: Greenwood, 1987.

Madubuike, I. *A Handbook of African Names*. Colorado Springs, CO: Three Continents, 1994.

McKinzie, H. and I. Tindimwebwa. *Names from East Africa*. Nairobi, Kenya: McKinzie, 1980.

Mohome, Paulus M. "Naming in Sesotho: Its Sociocultural and Linguistic Basis." *Names* 20 (1972): 171-185.

Murphy, John D. *Luganda-English Dictionary*. Washington, DC: Consortium, 1972.

Musere, J. and C.J. Odhiambo. *African Ethnics and Personal Names*. Los Angeles, CA: Ariko Publications, 1999.

Musere, Jonathan. *African Proverbs and Proverbial Names*. Los Angeles,

CA: Ariko Publications, 1999.

Musere, Jonathan. *Traditional African Names.* Lanham, MD: Scarecrow Press, 1999.

_____. "Proverbial Names of the Baganda." *Names* 46, no. 1 (March 1998): 73-79.

_____. "Proverbial Names in Buganda." *Onoma* 33 (1997): 89-97.

Neethling, S.J. "Xhosa Nicknames." *South African Journal of African Languages* 14, no. 2 (1994): 88-92.

Neethling, S.J. "Naming in Xhosa Folk-tales: A Literary Device." *South African Journal of African Languages* 5, no. 3 (1985): 88-90.

Nsimbi, Michael B. *Luganda Names, Clans, and Totems.* Pasadena, CA: Munger Africana, 1980.

_____. *Amannya Amaganda n'Ennono zaago.* Kampala, Uganda: East African Literature Bureau, 1956.

Omari, C.K. "Personal Names in Socio-cultural Context." *Kiswahili* 40, no. 2 (September 1970): 65-71.

Pongweni, Alec J. *What is in a Name?: A Study of Shona Nomenclature.* Gweru, Zimbabwe: Mambo, 1983.

Raum, O.F. *Chaga Childhood.* London, England: Oxford, 1967.

Roscoe, John. *The Baganda: A Study of Their Native Customs and Beliefs.* London, England: Macmillan, 1911.

Sanyika, Bekitemba. *Know and Claim Your African Name.* Dayton, OH: Rucker, 1975.

Seligman, C.G. and Brenda Z. Seligman. *Pagan Tribes of the Nilotic Sudan.* London, England: George Routledge and Sons, 1932.

Ssaalongo, Y.S. and Y. Semugoma. *Ndi-Mugezi: Kitabo kya Ngero za Luganda.* London, England: Macmillan, 1952.

Stewart, Julia. *1001 African Names.* New York, NY: Citadel, 1996.

_____. *African Names.* New York, NY: Citadel, 1993.

Suzman, Susan M. "Names as Pointers: Zulu Personal Naming Practices." *Language in Society* 23, no. 2 (1994): 253-272.

Tembo, Mwizenge S. *What does Your African Name Mean?: The Meanings of Indigenous Names among the Tonga of Southern Zambia.* Lusaka, Zambia: Institute for African Studies, 1989.

Thipa, H.M. "What Shall We Name Him?" *Nomina Africana* 1, no. 2 (1987): 107-117.

_____. "By Their Names You Shall Know Them." In *Names 1983*, ed. P.E. Raper. Pretoria, South Africa: HSRC, 1986.

Turner, Noleen S. "Zulu Names as Echoes of Censure, Discontent and Disapproval within the Domestic Environment." *Nomina Africana* 6, no. 2 (1992): 42-56.

Wainwright, A.T. "Bird Names and Xhosa Poetry." In *Names 1983*, ed. P.E. Raper. Pretoria, South Africa: HSRC, 1986.

Wako, Daniel M. *The Western Abaluyia and Their Proverbs.* Nairobi, Kenya: Kenya Literature Bureau, 1985.

Walser, Ferdinand. *Luganda Proverbs.* Berlin, Germany: Reimer, 1982.

Whitehead, G.O. "Personal Names among the Bari." *Man* 42 (March 1947): 45-46.

Willis, Roy. "On a Mental Sausage Machine and other Nominal Problems." In *Semantic Anthropology,* ed. David Parkin. London, England: Academic Press, 1982.

Zawawi, S.M. *What is in a Name? = Unaitwaje? : A Swahili Book of African Names.* Trenton, NJ: Africa World, 1993.